Don't Wave Goodbye

Don't Wave Goodbye

*The Children's Flight from Nazi Persecution
to American Freedom*

EDITED BY PHILIP K. JASON AND IRIS POSNER

Westport, Connecticut
London

Library of Congress Cataloging-in-Publication Data

Don't wave goodbye : the children's flight from Nazi persecution to American freedom
/ edited by Philip K. Jason and Iris Posner.
   p. cm.
   ISBN 0–275–98229–7 (alk. paper)
     1. Refugees, Jewish—United States.   2. Refugees, Jewish—United States—Biography.
3. Refugee children—United States.   4. Refugee children—United States—Biography.
5. World War, 1939–1945—Jews—Rescue.   I. Jason, Philip K., 1941–   II. Posner, Iris.
HV640.5.J4.D66   2004
940.53'1835'0830973—dc22   2003064763

British Library Cataloguing in Publication Data is available.

Library of Congress Catalog Card Number: 2003064763
ISBN: 0–275–98229–7

First published in 2004

Praeger Publishers, 88 Post Road West, Westport, CT 06881
An imprint of Greenwood Publishing Group, Inc.
www.praeger.com

Printed in the United States of America

The paper used in this book complies with the
Permanent Paper Standard issued by the National
Information Standards Organization (Z39.48–1984).

10 9 8 7 6 5 4 3 2 1

Copyright Acknowledgments

The editors and publisher gratefully acknowledge permission for use of the following
material:

From *Bill Graham Presents* by Bill Graham and Robert Greenfield (© 1992 by The Estate of
Bill Graham). Used by permission of Doubleday, a division of Random House, Inc. For
United Kingdom rights to the same, © 1992 by Bill Graham and Robert Greenfield, reprinted
by permission of the William Morris Agency, Inc. on behalf of the authors.

From *Hearing a Different Drummer* by Benjamin Hirsch (© 2000 by Benjamin Hirsch). Used
by permission of the author and the publisher, Mercer University Press.

Chapter 9 from *Motherland* by Fern Schumer Chapman (© 2000 by Fern Schumer Chapman).
Used by permission of the author and Viking Penguin, a division of Penguin Group (USA).

From "A Child Must Be Sheltered" by Henny Wenkart, which first appeared in the *Jewish
Women's Literary Annual*, Vol. 3, 1998. Used by permission of the author.

From "Kaufmann Letters" by Gabrielle Kaufmann Koppell. Used by permission of G. Oliver
Koppell and the Leo Baeck Institute, New York. Thanks to Arthur Kern for translating these
letters.

From Interview with Gabrielle Kaufmann Koppell at the Bronx Institute, April 28, 1982. Used by permission of G. Oliver Koppell and the Lehman College Library, The City University of New York.

From "Autobiography of Jack Steinberger" (© 1988 by The Nobel Foundation). Used by permission of Jack Steinberger and The Nobel Foundation.

Letter to Eleanor Roosevelt by Morris C. Troper dated July 7, 1941; and information from the program for "Dinner of the United States Committee for the Care of European Children," dated September 19, 1941. Used by permission of the American Jewish Joint Distribution Committee Archives. Letter to Eduard M. M. Warburg from Albert Einstein, dated June 25, 1941. Used with permission of l'Oeuvre de Secours aux Enfants, Paris (OSE) and the American Jewish Joint Distribution Committee Archives.

Excerpts from previously unpublished or privately published diaries, memoirs, presentations, and letters by the following contributors:

Kurt Admon, Judith Tydor Baumel, Martin Birn, Henry Birnbrey, Joel Goldwein (for the writings of his father, Manfred Goldwein, and for translations of those writings), Arnold Isaak, Charles Juliusburg, Walter Kron, Thea Kahn Lindauer, Michel Margosis, Camilla Tidor Maas (and her cowriter, Sarah Cudzillo), Phyllis Finkel Mattson, Ruth Safrin Finkelstein, Richard Schifter, Ruth Schlamme Schnitzer (translated by Anita Rothschild and Susan Steiner), Henry Schuster, Lea Wasserman Schwarz, Manfred Steinfeld, Trudy Kirchhausen Turkel, Rose Marie Phillips Wagman (for her own work as well as the diary of her mother, Ilse Hamburger Phillips, translated by Margot Strauss Garon), and W. Howard Wriggins.

Brief quotations used in the front matter: Linda Stern, who quotes the words of Mina and Paul Beller in her narrative, "They Wouldn't Let Us Wave: A Mother's Story"and used by permission of One Thousand Children®, Inc. Werner Michel, from his keynote address to the Descendants of the Shoah Conference in Chicago, June 30, 2002. Robert Braun, quoted in Erwin Tepper's unpublished paper on children who came to the United States under the auspices of the Brith Sholom Lodge (this paper was delivered at the One Thousand Children gathering in Chicago on June 30, 2002).

Photographs and illustrations from the following organizations and periodicals: American Jewish Joint Distribution Committee, American Psychological Association, *Atlanta Buckhead*, *Aufbau*, Bill Graham Archives, *Bronx Home News*, Corbis-Bettmann Archive, *The Dumas Clarion*, JewishEncyclopedia.com, Landesentschaedigungsbehoerde, Ninety-Second Street YM-YWHA, One Thousand Children®, Inc., U.S. Holocaust Museum and Memorial, U.S. Senate Historical Office, and U.S. House of Representatives; and from the following individuals: Kurt Admon, Judith Tydor Baumel, Paul and Mina Beller, Martin Birn, Peter Blau, Ilan Braun, Robert Braun, Fern Schumer Chapman, Michael Dubrow, Alan Entin, Ruth Safrin Finkelstein, Harry Fischbach, Joel Goldwein, Benjamin Hirsch, Warren Hirsch, Charles Juliusberg, Walter Kron, Jack Lewin, Thea Kahn Lindauer, Camilla Tidor Maas, Lotte Goldschmidt Magnus, Gudrun Maierhof, Michel Margosis, Phyllis Finkel Mattson, Werner Michel, Helga Weiss Milberg, Erich Rosenfeld, LeAnne Shaw, Richard Schifter, Ruth Schlamme Schnitzer, Henry Schuster, Moses Sequerra, Jack Steinberger, Manfred Steinfeld, Faye Lazega Stern, Abraham Szyller, Trudy Kirchhausen Turkel, Paul Tuz, Rose Marie Phillips Wagman, Henny Wenkart, and Werner Zimmt.

Paul Beller's parents, Leo and Mina, Vienna, 1928. Their son, Paul, would later be one of the fifty children, including Kurt Admon, Henny Wenkart, Robert Braun, and Erwin Tepper, rescued by the Brith Sholom Lodge of Philadelphia in 1939. Archives of One Thousand Children®, Inc.

Werner Michel arrived in the United States with eight other children in December 1936, at age 12. During his career in the military he was awarded the Legion of Merit, the Bronze Star, and awards for service in Europe in WWII, as well as the Korean and Vietnam Wars. He retired from the Army as a Colonel in 1974 and was later named Assistant Secretary of Defense for Counter Intelligence. Archives of One Thousand Children®, Inc.

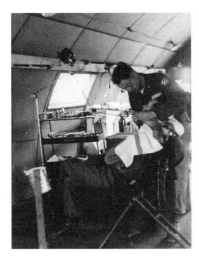

Dr. Robert Braun, D.D.S., one of the fifty "Brith Sholom children," practicing dentistry, U.S. Army, 1954, Korea. Many of the OTC boys were either drafted or volunteered for service in the armed forces in WWII and/or Korea. Several had distinguished careers in the military. Archives of One Thousand Children®, Inc.

There was the day, in Vienna, in the fall of 1939, when her husband Leo gave in to despair. "Let's go up on the fifth floor and jump down, both together," he said to her. Who could blame him? The family business had been confiscated, their friends had betrayed them, all efforts at escape had been shut down, and now they were on the run from Nazi storm troopers.

But there was a reason Mina couldn't commit suicide. "He would not have a mother and father," was all she said. Those eight words turned Leo around too, and gave them both the will to continue their struggle for another day.

The "he" that gave purpose to the Bellers' suffering was Paul, their only child, whom they had sent to America a few months before, not knowing if they would ever see him again.

"We had to stand straight when we were watching the train. The Nazis told us we couldn't wave. It was to punish us more."
—Linda Stern,
"They Wouldn't Let Us Wave: A Mother's Story"

Parents, leave your children in your hometown. Put them on a train so that the departure will be as unobtrusive as possible.
—Werner Michel
(Colonel, U.S. Army, Retired, and former Inspector General for Intelligence, Department of Defense and Assistant to the Secretary of Defense for Intelligence Oversight)

There was a requirement that we not wave goodbye out of the window when departing because Jews were not allowed to give the Hitler salute and waving might be mistaken for one.
—Robert Braun

*On behalf of the "One Thousand Children," this book
is dedicated to the memory of*

*the parents who let them go,
the families who took them in,
the individuals and organizations that made their rescue
and resettlement possible,
and
the one and a half million children who found no refuge
and perished in the Holocaust.*

CONTENTS

Preface   xiii

Acknowledgments   xv

Introduction *by Judith Tydor Baumel*   1

Chapter 1   In Short   19
Henry Schuster/Trudy Kirchhausen Turkel/Jack Steinberger

Chapter 2   Trepidations   31
Manfred Steinfeld/Kurt Admon/Martin Birn/Henny Wenkart

Chapter 3   Paths of Escape   75
*Ruth Safrin Finkelstein/Lea Wasserman Schwarz/Camilla Tidor Maas
and Sarah Cudzillo/Michel Margosis/Richard Schifter/Henny Wenkart/
Morris C. Troper/Albert Einstein/W. Howard Wriggins*

Chapter 4   Coming to America   123
*Manfred Goldwein/Ilse Hamburger Phillips/Ruth Schlamme Schnitzer/
Lea Wasserman Schwarz/Walter Kron*

Chapter 5   Transitions   153
*Henry Birnbrey/Charles Juliusburg/Martin Birn/Bill Graham and
Robert Greenfield/Gabrielle Kaufmann Koppell/Thea Kahn Lindauer*

Chapter 6   Becoming an American   197
*Phyllis Finkel Mattson/Ruth Schlamme Schnitzer/Bill Graham
and Robert Greenfield/Arnold Isaak*

Chapter 7   Full Circle   233
Charles Juliusburg/Arnold Isaak/Benjamin Hirsch/Fern Schumer Chapman/
Rose Marie Phillips Wagman/Phyllis Finkel Mattson

Afterword *by Richard Schifter*   265

Final Thoughts   273

PREFACE

Resistance to Hitler's plan for the destruction of the Jewish people took numerous forms. Many, unable to escape the long night that became known as the Holocaust, desperately sought to save their children by sending them away. Refuge was found for a very small portion of these children in a few countries, among them the United States. However, the history of these rescues by private individuals and organizations in America is virtually unknown. Who were these children and what became of them? Why don't Americans, historians, and even the rescued children themselves know of the effort that was made to save unaccompanied children by placing them with relatives and other foster families across America? Why isn't this small but significant success in the face of powerful countervailing forces represented in the permanent exhibitions of Holocaust museums; the curriculums of educators; and in books, films, and public ceremonies? Why were only a little more than one thousand unaccompanied children rescued from Nazi persecution by America between 1934 and 1945?

Established in 2000, One Thousand Children®, Inc. (OTC), a nonprofit research and education organization, began to seek answers to these questions in order to bring this important part of America's response to the Holocaust out of the shadows. *Don't Wave Goodbye* is one significant outcome of that search. Using contemporary and retrospective first-person accounts of OTC children, family members, and rescuers, we are able to give voice to those persons and to share their accounts of struggle, sacrifice, and courage that have been mostly hidden for close to sixty years.

The reader should keep in mind that while this collection of accounts does contain the work of a few professional writers and historians, only a small number of the writings were undertaken with the intention of publication. Most of the accounts were written by ordinary people who lived through extraordinary times and felt compelled to leave a record of their experiences. Often, the reader will encounter the translated German or faltering schoolchild English of young people keeping diaries or writing home. On other occasions, we have the opportunity to share insights and memories written for parents, children, and grandchildren.

Our editorial practice has been to intrude minimally on letters and diaries written by children for whom English had only just become a functional language. For these texts, for those of foreign-born adults writing in unpolished English, and for many writings that have been translated from German, we have often normalized punctuation, capitalization, and spelling, but on many occasions we have left nonstandard usage unchanged in order to reflect the speaker's situation and voice. That is, we have respected the reader's comfort while trying to maintain the authentic flavor of these writings. In some instances, precise meanings (including the intentions behind obvious errors) are unrecoverable. That is the truth of informal writing not meant for publication.

Though several of our writers attempt historical narrative, most are not trained historians. However, even if a number of these documents don't meet the test of professional accuracy and interpretation of the past, they nonetheless convey a personal version of historical reality that is the basis of their individual and communal understanding of each writer's world. Our editorial policy has been to respect these personal truths and to interfere as little as possible.

ACKNOWLEDGMENTS

On behalf of the One Thousand Children® (OTC), their families and rescuers, we would like to thank all the contributors who were willing to recall and share their memories of pain and loss as well as triumph, and light those recesses of our history that contain important lessons for our country and all Americans. We are also indebted to the many OTC children, OTC second and third generations, and friends of OTC, whose financial support has allowed the continued search for the OTC children and rescuers and the collecting and archiving of their stories.

Our deepest thanks also go to two intrepid souls who went before us, lighting the path we followed to find the OTC children whose words made this book possible: Professor Judith Tydor Baumel and Alan Schorr, the author and publisher respectively of *Unfulfilled Promise* (1990), the only scholarly work ever published about the history of the rescue and resettlement of the OTC children. Without their scholarship and personal commitment to seeking the truth about this terrible era of our world's history, this book would not exist. Dr. Baumel's generous, patient, and expert assistance to One Thousand Children, Inc. as its historical advisor proved invaluable.

Other people and organizations who so generously provided OTC assistance that enabled us to identify and locate OTC children and rescuers include Fama Mor at the Simon Wiesenthal Center; Martin Goldman, Michael Haley Goldman, and Megan Lewis at the U.S. Holocaust Memorial Museum; Michael Engel at the Shoah Foundation; Linda Klein at the American Red Cross Tracing Service; OTC tracing volunteer Adriana Sandler; Morris Ardoin and Valery Bazarov at the

Hebrew Immigrant Aid Society; Gunnar Berg at the YIVO Institute for Jewish Research; Misha Mitsel, Sherry Hyman, and Shelley Helfand at the American Jewish Joint Distribution Committee; Lynn Slome at the American Jewish Historical Society, Anita Kassof and Chana Kotzin at the Jewish Museum of Maryland; Herb Rosenbleeth at the National Museum of American Jewish Military History; Karen Franklin and Frank Mecklenberg at the Leo Baeck Institute; Jack Sutters at the American Friends Service Committee; Shulamith Berger at Yeshiva University; Ina Remus at The Jacob Rader Marcus Center of the American Jewish Archives; the reference staff of the Hebrew Union College–Jewish Institute of Religion; Ken Waltzer and Julie Avery at Michigan State University; Frances O'Donnell at the Andover-Harvard Theological Library; Jerome Verlin and Selma Goldberg at Brith Sholom; Roberta Elliot at Hadassah; Leah Rabinovits and Elaine Schnall at the Conference on Jewish Material Claims against Germany; Steve Adler at Mishpocha; Steven Siegel at the Ninety-Second Street YM-YWHA; Jennifer Schulman at B'nai B'rith International; Kurt Goldberger at the Kindertransport Association of America; OTC children Arthur Kern, Henry Schuster, Henry Frankel, Robert Braun, Louis Maier, and Walter Reed; Janet Munch at Lehman College Library; Denise Moorehead at the Unitarian Universalist Service Committee; Lauren Waits at the ChoicePoint Foundation; Michael Zolno of the Chicago 2002 Decendants of the Shoah gathering, researchers Gudrun Maierhof, Ghandra DiFiglia, Laura Gumpert, and Ilan Braun; Gerald Holton and Gerhard Sonnert at Harvard University; genealogist Maggie Linz; Susan King and JewishGen.org; and the many members of the press who carried the story of the One Thousand Children across America and Europe and to Israel.

We are also enormously grateful to Roxana Huhulea at the New York Circle of Translators and members Carmen Berelson, Susan Steiner, Gisella Brett, Gregory Mehrten, and Susan Glasser, who generously donated their professional services to OTC.

A very special thanks is due to David Birenbaum and Jeff Magenau at Fried, Frank, Harris, Shriver & Jacobson; John Malloy and Eric Tobias at the Washington Area Lawyers for the Arts; and Adam Chase and Briana Thibeau at Dow, Lohnes & Albertson for generously providing OTC the legal counsel necessary to bring a book like *Don't Wave Goodbye* to the public. Among the tiny group of volunteers who give OTC life is founding Board member Tony DeJesus, whose generosity and support has never wavered and who is one of the people to whom OTC owes its very existence.

We are most deeply grateful to Lenore Moskowitz, OTC cofounder, for the generous gift of her personal resources, unwavering belief in

OTC's mission and this book, and faith that despite the odds we would succeed.

Finally, we want express our heartfelt thanks to Heather Staines, our acquisitions editor at Praeger, who championed this book and ultimately made its publication possible.

INTRODUCTION*

The world we live in can be a terrible place. It does not take a historian to note that the history of humanity is usually not characterized by attributes such as kindness, benevolence, tolerance, and humility. Yet many among the One Thousand Children are alive today just because of those attributes, and due to the efforts of individuals and organizational activists—both Jewish and Gentile—who may not have chosen these terms as their motto, but nevertheless lived by them. These people took part in one of the lesser known yet significant rescue efforts of the Holocaust period: the rescue of approximately one thousand unaccompanied refugee children from Nazism to the United States during the Hitler era.

Let me start with my "calling card." I am not just a historian researching an interesting topic. I did not decide to study the rescue and resettlement of Jewish children—Jewish by Nazi definition, which includes what rescue organizations termed "non-Aryan Christians"—in the United States during the Holocaust as a purely historical topic of academic interest. I was raised as the youngest child in a family with two older siblings who had been rescued through this operation during the 1940s. Born almost a decade and a half after the war's end, I grew up knowing that—unlike millions of Jewish children who lost their lives under the Nazis—my brother and sister survived due to a four-country, transcontinental odyssey, and—as it has so well been

*Keynote Address for the "2002 Reunion of One Thousand Children" held as part of *A Gathering of Descendants of the Shoah and Their Families,* June 30–July 2, 2002, Palmer House Hilton Hotel, Chicago.

termed by others—"the kindness of strangers." When I chose history as a profession, I knew that one of my first historical studies would be of the circumstances surrounding their rescue, in order to better understand not only where they came from and how they got here, but who they are today.

I would like to go back more than half a century to describe how a group of dedicated individuals, and later organizations, rose to the threat of Nazism, faced American immigration laws and child-settlement bureaucratic limitations, and took upon themselves the challenge of saving hundreds of children from discrimination and possible death.

THE BEGINNING OF THE CHILD REFUGEE SCHEME

Our story begins in the spring of 1933, only weeks after Hitler came to power, when the particularly touching plight of Jewish children in Nazi Germany moved several American Jewish organizations to suggest various means of assistance. In the middle of that year, the Executive Committee of the American Jewish Congress, a Zionist-oriented organization connected with the World Jewish Congress, adopted a resolution expressing the hope that some forty thousand German-Jewish children would be cared for by private families throughout the world. A considerable number of these children were expected to reach the United States. Why not adult refugees? Well, children were preferred over adult refugees for a number of reasons. First, they would not compete with labor during the economic depression that had gone on since the beginning of the decade. Second, American immigration regulations already stipulated that the secretary of labor would accept bonds for unaccompanied children, something that would allow them to enter with relatively little bureaucratic difficulty. Third, as opposed to adult refugees who might arouse antipathy from various populations, children would arouse more sympathy than any other group.

Throughout the end of 1933 and early 1934, a subcommittee of representatives from the American Jewish Committee, the American Jewish Congress, and B'nai B'rith worked on a program that would bring 250 German-Jewish children to the United States. Only children born in Germany would be considered in order to enable them to enter under the German quota. Eighteen percent of the children would be of Eastern European parentage. The organizers hoped that one thousand children could eventually be brought out of Germany and resettled in the United States. Originally they set the age limit at fourteen, as the fourteen- to sixteen-year-old age group was the most difficult to place, but the committee soon determined that sixteen would be the upper age limit. Ideas generate bureaucracy, and this case was no exception. In order to create the necessary machinery for such an undertaking, an organization known as [the] German-Jewish Children's Aid was formed to be in charge of posting bonds for the refugee children, preventing their becoming public charges, arranging their transfer to the United States, and caring for them after arrival.

One of the prominent figures involved in German-Jewish Children's Aid was Cecilia Razovsky. Razovsky had been born in St. Louis to an immigrant family and was active for many years in refugee transfer and resettlement organizations where she used both her knowledge of immigration rules and procedures and her personal acquaintance with those responsible for administrating the laws. Now she began using these abilities in order to further the work of German-Jewish Children's Aid, convincing American government officials of the need to assist the scheme and not hinder it with administrational stumbling blocks. Luckily for many of the former refugee children and their families, in most cases she was successful.

On Friday, November 9, 1934, after fifteen months of planning, the first small group of German-Jewish refugee children arrived in New York, accompanied by Dr. Gabrielle Kaufmann. Immediately upon arrival the children were sent to Jewish foster families primarily in and around New York City, a resettlement policy that would be changed as time went on and the organizations responsible for the

Cecilia Razovsky, Executive Director of German-Jewish Children's Aid, Inc. (later known as European-Jewish Children's Aid, Inc.), which was a focal point for the planning and execution of the rescues and resettlement of the One Thousand Children in the United States. Courtesy of the American Jewish Joint Distribution Committee Photo Archives.

children feared creating a refugee enclave in New York and its surroundings.

Due to Razovsky's efforts, and those of other German-Jewish
Children's Aid activists, these boys were supposed to have been the
first of 250 unaccompanied refugee children that the American government would permit into the country. But now the organization was
faced with the ironic situation of having permission to bring children
to the United States but lacking sufficient foster homes in which to
resettle them and the money to cover their resettlement.

By American law, children could only be placed in foster homes of
their own religion, and these homes had to be able to offer a certain
minimum standard that included giving a child his or her own toothbrush and facecloth, a separate bed for each child, and no more than
two children in a room. Let's remember that these were the years of
the Great Depression, when your average American family was going
through great financial strain. Traditional and Orthodox Jewish families, often quite attuned to the need for benevolent activities such as
fostering, usually had a smaller income than the average Jewish family. They often had large families, lived in crowded quarters, and as
thus, were not eligible for the foster family scheme. Just to give you
an example, a Jewish family in New York heard of the program and
greatly desired to help refugee children. Turning to the refugee organizations involved in the program, they were inspected by the Child
Welfare Bureau. The family already had five children of their own: the
four boys slept in one bedroom, the girl slept on a folding cot in the
living room. Even though they could offer a warm family atmosphere,
they were turned down by the child welfare services, which claimed
that they couldn't offer a refugee child the minimum conditions that
the children's bureau demanded—two children to a room.

Thus, German-Jewish Children's Aid found itself facing opposition
on several fronts: Jewish social workers in Germany were still not attuned to a project that would separate children from their families and
were protesting the scheme; each refugee child cost German-Jewish
Children's Aid $500 a year that was paid to his or her foster family;
and to top everything off, even with the meager number of children
signed up for the project, there were not enough foster families to go
around. Those few wonderful families that had taken refugee children
had heard of the program through word of mouth, organizational affiliation, and the rare pulpit appeals in synagogues. No large-scale
public appeals were being made for fear of giving the project too much
publicity, which could cause a great rise in the anti-Semitism that already existed in the United States.

As a result, by March 1, 1938, [the] German-Jewish Children's Aid had only 351 children under its auspices, including a number of non-Aryan children from Germany, and its directors were contemplating terminating the scheme. Just to recall, non-Aryan children were Christian children born to families in which a parent or grandparent had either been Jewish and converted to Christianity or had remained Jewish but married a Christian. In either case, according to the Nazi racial laws, the children of such a union were not Aryans and therefore subject to discrimination and potential persecution.

The events of the spring, summer, and autumn of 1938—the Anschluss, or in other words, the Nazi invasion of Austria; the Evian refugee conference; the Munich agreement and the Nazi takeover of the Sudetenland in Czechoslovakia; the deportation of thousands of Polish Jews from Germany; and finally, Kristallnacht, the pogrom of November 9–10, 1938—were turning points for Central European Jewry and with it, for the refugee organizations dealing with its plight. It was obvious to the refugee organizations that their work was not coming to an end but just beginning; at the end of 1938 there began a series of legislative battles in the American Congress regarding German refugees in general and refugee children in particular. The most notable one was the proposal of Robert Wagner and Edith Nourse Rogers in early 1939 to permit twenty thousand refugee children from Germany into the United States over and above the existing quota. The idea was to create a framework that would circumvent the American quota system of the time, which permitted only about 150,000

Senator Robert Wagner, who with Representative Edith Rogers introduced the Wagner-Rogers Bill in Congress in 1939. The bill would have allowed the entry of 20,000 German Jewish children into the United States. After joint House and Senate hearings for much of 1939, the bill died in Congress. U.S. Senate Historical Office.

Representative Edith Nourse Rogers, who with Senator Robert Wagner introduced the Wagner-Rogers Bill in Congress in 1939. U.S. House of Represenatives.

immigrants a year to enter the country, some 26,000 of whom could come from Germany. But as a result of pressures from isolationist groups who tried to stranglehold the bill, after committee hearings during the first half of the year, the final bill gave preference to child immigrants from Germany over adult immigrants, but all within the existing quota. In order to not discriminate against refugee adults who might be in more danger than children, Wagner and Rogers ultimately withdrew the congressional bill, in the hope that the isolationists would also withdraw their bills to limit immigration even more.

THE WAVES OF REFUGEE CHILDREN

Let's turn now to the various waves of refugee children who began reaching the United States during the Holocaust. From early 1939 onward, efforts of German-Jewish Children's Aid to bring refugee children to the United States entered high gear. When war broke out in Europe, in September 1939, the major transportation routes through Western Europe were closed to children trying to leave Greater Germany. Most children had come by boat via Southampton, England. However, there were still children from Germany who managed to leave even after that date, traveling via Italy and later through occupied France, and on to Portugal, or via Holland and Sweden. A few children even came to the United States via Siberia and Japan, landing in San Francisco.

In 1939, another small group of children came to the United States from Belgium and the Netherlands. Most were unaccompanied children from Germany and Austria who had been sent there until they could be joined by their parents and were cared for privately by Jewish refugee committees. Soon after reaching Western Europe, these organizations tried to send children to the United States. Additional children from these countries escaped to England and were brought to America with the next group of refugee children, those coming from Great Britain.

In 1940, a new group of children who were fleeing the Blitz reached the United States, including some refugee children who had reached Britain from Central Europe in 1939. Most of the British children were not Jewish, not considered non-Aryan, and not included in "refugee child issue," as it was known. Unlike the refugee children from Germany, these British children were welcomed publicly by various groups with open arms, and were transferred through and cared for by an organization known as the United States Committee for the Care of European Children, which would later play a part in the rescue of Jewish and non-Aryan Christian refugee children.

In 1941, larger groups of refugee children began reaching the United States, this time from another location—France. Almost all of these children were actually refugees from Central Europe who had found shelter in children's homes in France. Most of these orphanages were connected with an organization known as Oeuvre de Secours aux Enfants (OSE), to which I will return. The last group of children reaching the United States were from Spain and Portugal, again, mostly refugees from Germany, Austria, Czechoslovakia, and France, who had found protection there, at times with their families. These were the children arriving in the United States between 1943 and 1945.

THE ORGANIZATIONS AND ACTIVISTS

As the situation worsened in Europe, the number and scope of organizations dealing with refugee children in the United States broadened. Despite inevitable tensions and disagreements among the multiple organizatons working to rescue unaccompanied children and resettle them in the U.S., they managed to create a network of cooperation that made it possible to plan, finance, and carry out rescues and resettlements for twelve years across three continents. There were large-scale refugee organizations offering special services to refugee children such as the National Coordinating Committee and the National Refugee Service; as well as child refugee organizations such as German-Jewish Children's Aid and Oeuvre de Secours aux Enfants (OSE), a Franconization of the original Russian initials, as the organization had been established in St. Petersburg in 1912 as a health and child care organization. At the time of the revolution, OSE moved to Germany and after the Nazi rise to power it was transferred to France, establishing a small branch in the United States.

Faye Lazega Stern, her younger sister, and 14-month-old brother (bottom right), believed to be the youngest OTC child brought to the United States, are among this group of children in Lisbon, Portugal, who arrived in the United States in 1943. Also included are Joel and Samuel Sequerra, representatives of the American Jewish Joint Distribution Committee in Spain who were responsible for arranging the rescue of hundreds of children escaping through Spain and Portugal. Photo from collection of Moses Sequerra. Archives of One Thousand Children®, Inc.

First meeting since arriving in the United States in 1943 of shipmates Abraham Szyller, Peter Blau, Faye Lazega Stern, Paul Tuz, and Harry Fischbach at the first National Reunion of the One Thousand Children, Chicago, 2002. Archives of One Thousand Children®, Inc.

There were also small-scale refugee organizations offering special services to refugee children in the United States, such as the United Fund and Self Help; funding organizations such as the National Council of Jewish Women, the Hebrew Immigrant Aid Society (HIAS), and the American Jewish Joint Distribution Committee (often referred to as "the Joint"); special care bodies such as the American Friends Service Committee (AFSC); and government organizations such as the United States Children's Bureau and the President's Advisory Committee on Political Refugees. Another important group was the United States Committee for the Care of European Children, originally established to bring British children to North America during the Blitz, but later dealing with several groups of primarily Jewish refugee children from France who were brought to the United States between 1941 and 1943 with the assistance of the OSE and the Quaker movement (AFSC). There were also small Jewish organizations, such as the Brith Sholom Lodge in Philadelphia, whose activists Gilbert and Eleanore Kraus traveled to Europe at great personal risk in 1939 and rescued fifty children threatened by Nazi persecution.

Not only did the number of American organizations dealing with refugee children grow; their European counterparts also grew in number, particularly Jewish social welfare and refugee organizations that dealt with choosing the children, preparing their documentation, and making their travel arrangements. Among the noted activists in Germany, for example, were Kate Rosenheim, director of the Children's Emigration Department of the Central Organization of Jews in Germany, and her dedicated staff workers such as Herta Souhami and Norbert Wollheim. The organization coordinated with Jewish organizations worldwide to find emigration opportunities for children at risk.

These people, young and old, who spent day and night trying to ease the transfer of refugee children fleeing Nazism, had their American

Kate Rosenheim, Director of the Children's Emigration Department of the Central Organization of German Jews in Berlin, which sought and coordinated rescue of German Jewish children from 1933 to 1941. Rosenheim worked with organizations around the world and is credited with saving thousands of children, including over 600 of the One Thousand Children who came to the United States. Office of Restitutions, Republic of Germany.

counterparts. Among the American activists who deserve special mention with regard to the fate of the OTC children are Cecilia Razovsky, whom I already mentioned and who was also the assistant to the executive director of the National Refugee Service (NRS), and Lotte Marcuse of the German-Jewish Children's Aid. Until 1937, Marcuse had also been a worker in the NRS; however, in March 1937 she became placement director of German-Jewish Children's Aid. Marcuse had received a diploma in social work from the Prussian Ministry of the Interior in recognition of her services in aiding military families. After coming to the United States in 1921 she gained experience in the field of children's social services, and following her move to German-Jewish Children's Aid she became active in all activities concerning the transfer and resettlement of Jewish refugee children. Marcuse had her difficult side, and had a strong bias against Orthodoxy. The price was paid by observant or traditional children who were not always placed in observant homes, even when those were available. However, without her assistance, dozens if not hundreds of children would have had a harder bureaucratic struggle in their transatlantic odyssey. Another important activist was Dr. Ernest Papanek, a political refugee from Vienna who became an OSE educator in France, later moving to the United States where he tried to assist in the resettlement of several hundred children brought to America from OSE homes in France. Papanek, the more easygoing educator, and Marcuse, the more rigid bureaucrat, clashed over the question of the children's upbringing. The refugee children became objects of organizational struggle over issues such as whether to keep them together during resettlement to make them feel more at home, or distance them from each other, forcing them to mix rapidly with American children. Luckily, few if any of the children were aware of these struggles at the time.

THE PROCESS

And what of the refugee children and their foster families? The bureaucratic processing sequence was different depending on whether the children arrived from Germany, France, or Spain and Portugal. Children from Germany were usually selected through the office in Berlin, went through preliminary physical examinations, and German-Jewish Children's Aid (which in the middle of the war was renamed "European-Jewish Children's Aid") was informed in order to make travel arrangements. The bureaucratic details that involved the American Department of Labor, the Department of State, photographs, birth certificates, affidavits, and other documents, usually in triplicate, are illustrated in the following story.

When I was a student, studying about American immigration laws, my teacher tried to illustrate how much documentation was necessary for a person to enter the United States from Europe in the 1930s. He held out to the class what looked like one very long sheet of paper, with many lines of small print that were to be filled in. Then he stood up on the desk at the front of the room (and he was not short), held the document in his hand high above his head, and let what turned out to be an accordion sheaf of paper open up, until the last page reached the floor. Showing us this incredibly long document, he stated laconically, "This is what people requesting a visa to the United States had to fill out—in triplicate."

Following the German takeover of Austria and Czechoslovakia, similar emigration procedures were followed in Vienna and Prague.

After receiving permission to immigrate, families of refugee children were informed of the travel arrangements, the amount of luggage they were permitted to take, and permissible items. Although these escapees were always asked to keep luggage to a minimum, it was a rare parent who didn't take the opportunity to try and save a few valuable items, such as family photo albums. Not knowing what the children would be given in the United States, there were families in Germany that sold all their possessions and sent children with steamer trunks full of clothing in sizes that would keep them until age twenty-one! As a result, there are stories such as that of the uncle who meets his ten-year-old niece at the pier, saying, "I thought you were a poor refugee and here you come with three suitcases!" However, I have never come across a story of children taking valuable possessions to the United States that beats the one I heard from Norbert Wollheim, whom I mentioned earlier, regarding a transport of children he accompanied to England. One of the very small boys on the transport was carrying a priceless Stradivarius violin, and going through British customs the officers stopped the group, thinking this was a clear-cut case of using refugees to smuggle goods. Knowing that the entire group would be sent back to Germany, Wollheim protested, and having absolutely no idea if the boy could even play, he stated vehemently, "[O]f course this is the boy's violin, he is a child prodigy." Suddenly, with the blood pounding in his head, he noticed that all the British were standing at attention and realized that he was hearing music. It turned out that before giving the boy the violin to take out of Germany, his father had taught the child to play one song, just in case. The song was "God Save the King," and it ended up saving the lives of more than a hundred children on that particular transport.

The other groups of refugee children followed a different procedure. Children in France were chosen from OSE homes by activists of the American Friends Service Committee, and brought out through Spain and Portugal. After France was cut off following the German invasion of late 1942, Spanish Loyalist children, French and German-Jewish refugee children in Spain and Portugal, and non-Aryan Christian children of the same background reached the United States by boat via Lisbon. The story of the first group going through Portugal taught refugee activists a lesson for further groups. Before putting the children on the boat for America, in an attempt to compensate for years of deprivation, the good-hearted activists fed them unlimited amounts of chocolate and candies. Like most normal children would do, they gorged themselves and spent the first two days of the journey sick to their stomachs. Learning from the mistake, refugee activists decided to dole out the sweets very sparingly while the children got on board in order to avoid this problem.

After the first years during which children went directly to foster parents, most groups of refugee children reaching the United States went through a few days of reception care. During this time, children who had gone through "refugee shock"—the trauma of flight through several countries—could recover from their ordeal before having to meet their foster family and begin acclimating to life in America.

Throughout this reception period, the children underwent medical examinations, had time to relax and orient themselves, and were allocated to children's agencies throughout the United States. They were temporarily placed in and around New York City in institutions such as the Clara De Hirsch Home, the Gould Foundation, the Seaman's Church Institute, the Academy, the Hebrew Orphans Asylum, and the Pleasantville College School. While the earlier groups were first taken on excursions around New York, the experience of later groups made it preferable to bring them directly to the reception center. This was particularly true with regard to the groups arriving after the outbreak of war whose members were much more traumatized than those in the earlier groups. For example, a group from Austria arriving in April 1940 was taken to see *Pinocchio* and a gangster film, but only two of the children could appreciate them. Some of the children arrived undernourished, needing immediate medical care. This was particularly true of the children arriving from France, and later from Spain and Portugal, who had gone through difficult wartime experiences.

Children coming from OSE homes in France showed the greatest signs of wartime trauma. Some hoarded food for the first few days until it was explained to them that there was enough food for them in the reception shelter. Some of the older boys who had spent time in camps were rowdy, and there were even cases of stealing, a survival technique they had learned in occupied Europe.

Then there was the problem of language. Most of the children spoke German, a few knew French, and the workers dealing with them spoke in German and Yiddish until the children began to pick up American expressions, which some already had at the reception center. These were the languages that some of the foster families initially used with the refugee children that came to live with them. There were also cases of mix-up until they learned the language. One girl thought the word "juice" was really "Jews" and that it was a special drink for refugees only.

This brings us to the area of foster families and resettlement. Foster families in the United States who agreed to take refugee children stated that they would care for them until they reached the age of twenty-one, see that they were educated, and guarantee they would not become charges of the state. Most of the children were assigned social workers from local social service agencies to oversee their resettlement process. Difficulties sometimes arose when relatives offered to care for refugee children. Although often given preferential consideration, these homes were subject to investigation and supervision by the accredited child-care agencies. They did not always meet the necessary standard, and, in addition, the responsibilities and expenses of caring for refugee children were not always made clear to the relatives. As a result, there were families who once faced with the reality, requested that their young relative be removed from their home and given to another foster family. In some cases, this caused resentment among the children who felt abandoned by their flesh and blood. In other cases, where there had been a lack of chemistry from the onset between the young refugees and their relatives, both breathed a sigh of relief at parting.

Among the foster families who had no blood relation to the refugees, the majority were decent, genuinely wishing to offer a home to a refugee child. However, there were those whose motives were not always pure. Some wanted children to act as companions to their own children, and there were even a few who wanted the children to act as servants and maids for the family. These families were, of course, checked out and rejected by the child welfare organizations.

The situation was very different from that of the refugee children who had found homes in Britain, larger numbers of whom were almost "pressed into service" as companions and maids. This outcome was due to the fact that the British system did not involve the in-depth investigations by child welfare organizations that the American system required. It was also a factor that stemmed from the different nature of the rescue operation in Britain and the much larger numbers of children who found refuge there. If the American organization sponsoring the conference is called OTC for "One Thousand Children®," the corresponding British organization could be called TTC, standing for "Ten Thousand Children." The British government, worried that they would be pressed into opening the doors of Palestine—to which they held the mandate—to hundreds of thousands of refugees from Greater Germany, made the magnanimous gesture of allowing in almost ten thousand refugee children during the nine months before the outbreak of the war. Although the United States took in almost three times the total number of refugees that the British did during the 1930s and 1940s, there were very few such "gestures" and the refugees—both child and adult—all entered under the existing sacrosanct immigration quotas.

Most of the refugee children in the United States were ultimately placed in large cities, with approximately 27 percent in the greater New York area. Other cities where refugee children were resettled included Chicago, Philadelphia, St. Louis, Los Angeles, Cleveland, Detroit, Baltimore, Boston, Newark, Atlanta, Pittsburgh, Cincinnati, and Kansas City. Cities having between two and ten children included Albany, Bridgeport, Buffalo, Columbus, Dallas, New Orleans, Omaha, Portland, Rochester, Seattle, Dayton, Denver, Hartford, Indianapolis, Louisville, Milwaukee, Minneapolis, New Haven, and Washington, D.C. Wilmington, El Paso, Houston, Manchester, Nashville, Oklahoma City, Providence, San Antonio, Shreveport, Spokane, and Stockton had one refugee child each.

Once the children were settled, the local child-care agencies were responsible for them, along with their foster parents. Each child maintained contact with a social worker until his discharge at age twenty-one. Contact was usually on a monthly basis and these meetings were often used for purchasing clothes with money from the local child-care agency. There were refugee children for whom this was always a struggle; they wanted fashionable clothing, while their case worker was always steering them toward things that were practical and could be worn for years.

How did these children feel about the adventure that they were going through? Among the important issues that I want to mention are parents, foster parents, language, schooling, and future.

A large number of the children had left their parents in Europe, with communication after the outbreak of war becoming difficult, if not nonexistent. There were children who were angry with their parents for having sent them away. "My most vivid memories were a constant desire to be reunited with my family and occasionally I would be angry for having been sent here," stated a girl who reached the United States in 1939. With the outbreak of war, those children who had reached the United States before September 1939 were naturally frantic about their parents' fate. Those arriving during wartime had often already been cut off from their parents for weeks, months, and even years. This situation, however, did not lessen their fears regarding what was going on in Europe in general and regarding their parents' fate in particular.

Foster parents were another issue. Some of the children took very well to their new families, others less so. There were children who needed to be placed several times until the social services found an environment that was suitable for them. While the large majority of foster parents were people who out of the goodness of their hearts wanted to host a refugee child, there were still many cases of expectations in conflict with reality. When thousands of refugee children reached Britain within a period of a few months, the refugee agencies there learned that the easiest children to place were young girls with blond hair and light eyes, who were thought of as being more malleable, less demanding, and more likely to become "a member of the family." Older, dark-haired boys were the hardest to place, as they were considered the most foreign-looking and thought of as being troublemakers. In the United States, the division was not as harsh or clearcut; however, older children of both sexes were considered harder to place than younger ones and foster parents usually preferred girls to boys. These difficulties were illustrated by the number of boys who needed re-placing in foster homes throughout the prewar and war years.

Language was an important issue in the children's Americanization. Very few of them knew any English upon arrival. However, most of them picked up English quickly, depending, of course, upon the age they were when reaching the United States. According to most scholars of language, the cutoff date for accents is around age fifteen. If a child moves to a new country before the age of ten, he or she will usually speak without an accent. Between ten and fifteen, it depends how good an ear they have. After the age of fifteen, most children will retain some foreign inflection and at times, even a true foreign accent in their new language. This pattern seems to have held true for most of the refugee children who came to the United States.

Education was a concern of all those involved in the refugee child issue: the refugee organizations, the children, their parents, foster parents, social workers, and of course, educators. The release form that parents or guardians had signed in Europe entrusted German-Jewish Children's Aid with the education and training of their children. Due to their interrupted education and language difficulties, some refugee children were initially put back several grades or placed in a combined class for foreigners of all ages. Within a short period, however, most children were permitted to enter their regular grades. Two studies on the education of young refugees concluded that the children enjoyed learning and viewed school as a challenge, not a chore. Accustomed to the rigid European system of education, most refugee children adapted rapidly to the more flexible American system. Viewing education as a challenge, several refugee children received educational prizes or grants for exceptional scholarship. For example, a fifteen-year-old refugee girl in New York City won a citywide high school contest for her essay, "What It Means to Me to Be an American," and another refugee girl received first prize in a national contest for her essay entitled "Why National Unity Is Important to My Country."

The academic excellence in high school that many refugee children achieved could not be translated into professional training. Although many of the children had come from families with white-collar professional backgrounds, budgetary limitations of child welfare services often made it difficult to obtain higher education and training. After completing high school, children were expected to earn their keep. Nevertheless, family tradition, the desire for education, and the GI Bill were among the factors that enabled many refugee children to complete professional training later in life, often after their military service. Among former refugee children are found college professors, nurses, physicians, lawyers, businesspeople, insurance agents, writers, manufacturers, and restaurant owners.

All of those that I have had the privilege of meeting and interviewing are loyal Americans, aware of the wonderful qualities of the country that gave them a home and the unique society that absorbed them. It is probably for that reason that the Jewish refugee children who came to the United States did not exhibit two characteristics that I found in a study of those children who went to Great Britain. While a considerable number of the children who came to Britain ended up in Israel and an equally striking number ended up converting to Christianity, I found almost no parallels among the children who came to America. By placing children with families of their own religion, the American child-care agencies made sure that they would not be pressured through proselytizing by their foster families. Similarly, the unique nature of American society—originally a melting pot of immigrants—made almost all of the children feel comfortable enough to remain in the country that became their home. To my knowledge, these two qualities of the child refugee experience in the United States are unparalleled in any other country that gave sanctuary to children persecuted by the Nazis during the prewar and wartime period.

CONCLUSIONS

I cannot conclude without making an observation that belongs more to the realm of current events than to past history. After spending many years of my life studying the history of the refugee children's movement during the Holocaust, both in Great Britain and in the United States, I find myself pondering what would happen if a similar situation should arise today. True, there is no longer a quota system for immigrants to the United States, and there is the precedent of the Vietnamese orphans brought to America in an airlift after the collapse of Saigon. But what would happen if we were talking not about several hundred children or even a thousand, but of one hundred thousand children, which was approximately the number of persecuted Jewish and non-Aryan Christian children in Germany before the outbreak of the Second World War?

What would be the reaction of the American legislature if asked to pass emergency rescue bills to bring tens of thousands of children to the United States for an unspecified amount of time, just like the Wagner-Rogers Bill of 1939? And more specifically, what would happen if these children were Jewish? Would the American administration risk going against a worldwide growing tide of anti-Semitism in order to back such a step? Would American Jewish organizations be willing to pressure the government on this matter, take out full-page advertisements appealing for the large-scale rescue of Jewish children, and turn to Jews throughout the United States to open their homes to young unaccompanied refugees? And, if given cold, "logical" reasons why such a plan would be unfeasible, how long would these organizations continue to "buck the system" in order to generate enough publicity that would pressure the government into bringing these children to America? Would today's religious and nonsectarian welfare and service organizatons be willing to divert time, funds, and volunteer efforts from other deserving groups and causes in order to work cooperatively for the rescue of these threatened children?

Forget the government and private organizations for a minute. What of the American people? Would Americans open their arms to these hoards of children who would not know a word of English, have different customs, and—on top of everything else—not for a month, or a year, but for an unspecified amount of time? Would their charitable nature extend to doing much more than writing a check or making a

Judith Tydor Baumel, Ph.D.,
author of *Unfulfilled Promise: Rescue
and Resettlement of Jewish Refugee
Children in the United States,
1934–1945* (1990). Archives of
One Thousand Children®, Inc.

one-time gesture, to taking on a full-time responsibility that would probably upset their household ways and change every facet of their daily life? Would they be willing to shortchange their own children in order divide up their emotional and even financial resources among a group that included one more child, a refugee, a stranger? Would they be willing and able to cope with the traumas that such children would bring into a household, and be subject to pressure from some of those children to vouch for and save their parents who were still overseas?

When put this way, it sounds very different from the bland academic subtitle of my study of the OTC, "The Rescue and Resettlement of the Jewish Refugee Children in the United States, 1934–1945."

While I would hope that the American government and the American people would rise to such an hour, I pray that they will never again be put to the test.

Professor Judith Tydor Baumel
Chair, Interdisciplinary Graduate Program
in Contemporary Jewry, Bar-Ilan University,
Ramat-Gan, Israel

Chapter 1

IN SHORT

*T*hese narratives, while brief, show the arc and variety of experience among the One Thousand Children (OTC). They serve as a preamble to the more detailed writings distributed among the following chapters.

Henry Schuster's memoir underscores the accelerated panic following the "Night of Crystal" in November 1938. It was no longer possible to misread Hitler's intentions or to deny the sweeping, seemingly unstoppable influence and power of Nazi policies. He gives voice to the special place in OTC history of HIAS (Hebrew Immigrant Aid Society), OSE (Oeuvre de Secours aux Enfants), the American Jewish Joint Distribution Committee (often called "the Joint"), and the American Friends Service Committee. Finally, Schuster's conclusion, evoking the lingering questions of identity and survivor guilt, reveals one unhappy undercurrent of a story that is essentially optimistic.

Trudy Kirchhausen Turkel's narrative traces a series of escape paths: her own, that of her brother, and that of her parents—all miraculously reunited, though with their relationships handicapped by the dislocations. Her sister's path to Palestine reminds us of another desired destination of Jewish escapees from persecution. Turkel's swift and comfortable Americanization is less usual for those children who came at her age—ready to enter high school— than it was for children who came a few years younger.

Jack Steinberger was brought to the United States on one of the early transports. He, like many others, found the American Dream readily available to a new, hardworking, and aspiring immigrant. As a Nobel laureate, his level of achievement and degree of recognition are exceptional, and yet as a group, the One Thousand Children® turned out to be impressive achievers in their new land. Like Steinberger, these individuals continue to thank the many, many generous souls who made their American lives possible.

"KINDER TRANSPORT"

By Henry Schuster [2000]

My father died as a young man of forty-nine years old in 1935. I was nine years old, my oldest sister was fourteen, and Margot was thirteen. It was very difficult for my mother to care for us. Upon my sister Bertel's graduation from the 8th grade, she was accepted by a Jewish Finishing School. Margot and I remained in school for another year.

Bertel, now sixteen years old, found employment as a nanny for the Director of the Jewish Home for the Aged's two young sons. A Jewish dentist in the city of Offenbach hired Margot, only fifteen, as a nanny and maid. Mother got a job to care for an old Jewish woman as a live-in caretaker.

After my father died, I was shuffled from relative to relative until I was accepted into the Jewish orphanage in Frankfurt. The orphanage was next door to the old age home and I could visit my beloved sister every day.

The Liebermanns immigrated to Bolivia in 1938. They had met my mother and realized that she would be the most capable person to

Henry Schuster, three years old, with parents, Rosa and Abraham, Germany, 1929. Archives of One Thousand Children®, Inc.

assume the directorship of the home. My sister Margot joined Mother and Bertel at the old age home. Now I would see my entire family every day and Mother always had a goody for me. Life was beautiful now.

Even in times of danger, the United States vigilantly enforced its immigration policy. The German quota was twenty-five thousand a year. This included Jews and non-Jews, as well as Jewish children. The HIAS (Hebrew Immigrant Aid Society) was able to provide visas for a limited amount of children from Germany and Austria. During the 1930s, the United States State Department, under the leadership of Cordell Hull, used the excuse that the immigrants would flood the job market. This policy included children, but certainly they would not have taken any jobs from anyone.

On October 28, 1938, 17,000 Jews of Polish descent, many of whom had been living in Germany for decades, were arrested and relocated across the Polish border. The Polish government refused to admit them, so they were interned into a camp on the Polish frontier. Among those deportees was Zindel Grynspan, who was born in western Poland. In 1911, he moved to Hanover, Germany, and established a business. He married and started his family. Zindel's oldest son was living in Paris with his brother and attended school. However, the rest of the family was also deported. The Nazis confiscated all their belongings, including the house and business. When seventeen-year-old Herschel received the news about what happened to his family, he decided to get revenge. With pistol in hand, he arrived at the German Embassy in Paris to kill the German Ambassador. The Ambassador was not at the embassy. Herschel confronted the third ranking official, Secretary Ernst Von Rath, and shot him.

Hitler and his gang used this act as a conspiracy by the Jews of Germany and Austria against the government. It was absurd; however, the vicious propaganda Minister Goebels went on national radio and ordered his goons, the Brownshirts (S.A.) [*Sturmabteilung* or "Storm troopers"], to act immediately against Jews in any manner they wished.

November ninth became the infamous Kristallnacht. Many homes were looted; existing businesses were looted and destroyed. Thousands of windows were smashed, hence the name of "The Night of the Broken Glass." All Jewish men from the age of eighteen were arrested and incarcerated into the notorious concentration camps, Dachau and Buchenwald. All synagogues were destroyed and torched. All Holy Scriptures were strewn into the streets and desecrated.

Desperation now existed. It was time to flee Germany as fast as possible. If one had means to buy their freedom from the camps, the stipulation was to leave the country within several days. It was still possible. Many families, including mine, had no way to escape. Parents wanted to save their children and found ways for them to leave Germany and Austria.

Realizing the imminent danger for German and Austrian Jews, several European countries opened their borders for children. These children became known as the "Kinder Transports." England was the most gracious and accepted 10,000. France, Belgium, Holland, Denmark, and Switzerland also accepted some. Israel (then Palestine under the British mandate) was allowed to receive a small number. I assume this act of limitation was to please the Grand Mufti.

The French Rothschild family sponsored several hundred children to France. Yes, I was one of the lucky ones. Eleven of us left Frankfurt on March 8, 1939. For us children, it was exciting to now be free of constant harassment at the hands of the Nazis. Mother, Bertel, and Margot accompanied us to the train station. Years later I realized the sad look on my mother's face was from the realization that she might never see or touch me again. Now, as father and grandfather, I realize the pain of saying goodbye forever to your children.

We arrived in Paris late in the afternoon and were taken to the Rothschild Hospital. The Baroness greeted us. We then met the contingent of children that arrived from Berlin and Stettin. The next morning a large group arrived from Vienna. A few days later, the group was disbanded. Most went to a newly opened children's home operated by an organization known as the OSE (Oeuvre de Secours aux Enfants).

Three of us boys were sent to an Orthodox French Boys School. Two weeks after arriving at the school, my two so-called siblings and an adult supervisor accompanied me to the local synagogue in the Bois de Boulogne. Before I recited my portion of the Torah, the Rabbi spoke. At that time, I did not speak enough French to understand his remarks. I looked up to the balcony and saw and heard ladies crying. I became so distraught that I started to cry. After a few minutes, fully controlled, I performed my Torah reading.

Two weeks later, the school closed for Passover. The three of us were returned to the Rothschild Hospital. The Baroness came daily and picked us up for various exciting outings in Paris. She took us up the Eiffel Tower, riding a camel at the Paris Zoo, and many other delightful excursions. Instead of returning to Ecole Maimonides, we were reunited with our companions at the OSE home.

Sometime during the summer of 1939, approximately thirty children from the ship *St. Louis* joined us. As the German Army ap-

Boarding pass for
transit on the
SS *Mouzinho*, from
Lisbon to the
United States, 1941.
Archives of One
Thousand
Children®, Inc.

proached Paris, the home was disbanded and we escaped to Southern France.

In 1941, the United States relief organization called The American Jewish Joint Distribution Committee convinced the Roosevelt Administration to accept children from France. Eleanor Roosevelt was very instrumental in convincing the State department to issue visas. A non-Jewish organization was needed to make all the necessary arrangements. The American Quakers [American Friends Service Committee] took on this task. They persuaded the Petain Government to issue exit visas for two hundred refugee children to leave France.

I was on the first transport of one hundred children (in the French OSE initiative) to come to the United States via Spain and Portugal. We arrived at Staten Island in June of 1941. Those that had relatives were sent all over America to be with them. I was placed with distant relatives in Shreveport, Louisiana. Life in Shreveport had its good times and unhappy times. However, I realized that I was not wanted. On my eighteenth birthday I entered into the Army Air Corps.

For years, we children of the "Kinder Transports" asked ourselves, Why me? Why did thousands of others perish and we were saved? Who picked us? We still don't know.

FROM "BIOGRAPHY"

By Trudy Kirchhausen Turkel [2001]

I was born on January 13, 1924, in Heilbronn, Germany, the middle child of Julius and Else Michel Kirchhausen. My older sister, Irene, was two and a half years old and my younger brother, Martin, was to come eight and a half years after me.

Little did my parents expect that the coming years would bring us to the four corners of the world. My father was a self-employed textile merchant and manufacturer of work clothes dealing with small storekeepers in small towns. We lived comfortably in a modern apartment the entire time I grew up in Heilbronn. My father had served in the German Army during WWI for four years and was in the ski-troops and had been decorated as a soldier. I attended public schools until I was ten years old and then entered a private school known as Madchen Realschule. In 1932, when my brother was born, we were aware of the threat to Jewish people of Germany but never dreamed it would affect a war veteran's family. Every month after Hitler came to power, new and sweepingly devastating laws were passed and were enforced immediately.

By 1936 no Jewish child could attend public schools or even private schools. It became necessary for the Jewish communities to organize and staff Jewish schools in order to educate the children. That involved all the Rabbis, Cantors, Hebrew schoolteachers, and Jewish secular teachers who were then teaching all grades in every subject in very limited space. I was in the Judenschule, as it was called, from 1936 until

Trudy Kirchhausen Turkel at the first Yom HaShoah ceremony held in memory of the lost families and rescuers of the One Thousand Children. The ceremony was held at and conducted by the Moses Montefiore Anshe Emunah Hebrew Congregation, Liberty Jewish Center, Baltimore, Maryland, May 18, 2001. Archives of One Thousand Children®, Inc.

my emigration in October of 1938. These two years were extremely important in my education and development. They afforded me a chance to meet all kinds of children and also made playtime available, which otherwise did not exist. The teachers attempted to teach some English although the second language in south Germany was French rather than English. Zionism was the ideal inspiration of Jewish youths under these circumstances and everyone yearned to make *aliyah* to Palestine. My sister was able to get into a community near Cologne where they prepared youths for agricultural work in Palestine. She was able to spend two years there and to obtain an affidavit to immigrate to Palestine in March of 1938.

My father lost his business but started to work for the Jewish Self Help Agency in Stuttgart. He prepared the documents and transactions necessary for people who had visas to leave the country and he helped them pack their belongings, in some cases even accompanying them to the port of embarkation, thus helping them to expedite their departures. Through this work with the Agency he found out about the very secret and limited Kindertransport of Jewish children to the United States. He applied for me without telling me, and so one day in May of 1938 he came home and told me that I needed to get a children's passport just in case I would be one of the children selected to go to America. I was stunned and could not comprehend what he had said. I was fourteen years old and frustrated with my restricted existence as a Jewish child. There was no escaping the fact that few options existed for my family of four to leave the Third Reich as a family intact. I knew that there was no help to come from our relatives, who had just emigrated themselves, so I agreed that my father's decision was one way, if it worked, to increase the chances of the rest of the family's future.

From that day on I thought of nothing but the chance to go into a new world. I prepared myself for the separation from my family by developing a philosophy that has stood me in good stead from then until now. I decided that no matter what happened to me I could learn something from it, either how to be or not to be.

When I was summoned to appear before the U.S. Consul in Stuttgart on October 20, 1938, to be examined as to my worthiness and good health for entry into the United States, I went with little apprehension. My parents had received a battery of instructions of what, how, and when things would happen if I were granted a visa. All this material was thoroughly studied and complied with, and after my return from Stuttgart with visa in my hand, I had to get the necessary papers together to leave Heilbronn and Germany. I was scheduled to depart

from Hamburg on the SS *Hamburg* on October 27, 1938. After an emotional parting from my family and friends, I traveled to Hamburg with
my one suitcase and my tennis racket under my arm. I was met at the
station by a kind lady who took me to a Jewish hostel where I met the
other seven children who were to cross the ocean with me. We stayed
overnight and on October 28, 1938, we boarded the SS *Hamburg* along
with two young ladies who were to chaperon us on the sea voyage.

The experience aboard the ship was terrific. Such luxury and so
much freedom of movement I had not experienced for many years, and
I enjoyed every minute of it. I met a young American girl who was
returning with her parents from a visit with relatives in Germany. She
and I became fast friends and we became inseparable during the crossing. It was hard to say goodbye to her when we landed in New York.
The morning we sailed into the harbor of New York and saw the Statue
of Liberty, I cheered loud and clear and knew that I was going to this
new home free from fear and destruction.

When we disembarked we were greeted by the ladies of the Committee who took care of us and our belongings and took us to a hostel where
we were to spend the night. We were to see the city of New York guided
by these ladies, but an aunt of mine, disobeying the instructions, insisted
on taking me home to Brooklyn where I was greeted by all the relatives.
I spent the day there and was returned to the hostel by my aunt in the
evening. It took me a number of years before I saw the city of New York.
In the morning we said goodbye to each other and the ladies took each
of us to the various stations from where we were to reach our assigned
cities and new homes. It was clear that none of the eight children knew
each other before our common journey and we did not know where the
others were being sent. I did get the address from the only other girl
amongst us and I wrote to her a few times but we lost contact after a
time. I was to accompany a twelve-year-old boy to St. Louis, Missouri,
and take care of his needs on the trip.

Gunther Goldschmidt and I were taken to Grand Central Station
and escorted into a Pullman coach where the porter was told we were
traveling alone and that he should make sure we got off in St. Louis
all right. The trip was uneventful as we were confined to the compartment due to our lack of the English fluency. We ate bananas and
Hydrox ice cream, which was sold periodically by a vender who went
through the cars. In St. Louis, we were met by the head of a private
children's agency named Sommers Children's Bureau. Mrs. Esrog took
us to her office where the family that would take care of Gunther was
waiting to greet him and take him home. That was the last time I saw
or heard from Gunther. I went to Mrs. Esrog's home where I stayed
with her family for two weeks before she found a family for me.

That was the beginning of my three-and-a-half-year stay in St. Louis, Missouri. After a three-week orientation period, I started to attend Soldan High School. I was in my element and quickly learned English and became assimilated into American life. My foster parents were good people with two teenaged children of their own, and I became an adjunct member of the family and performed the household chores assigned to me after school and weekends. I stayed with this family the entire time I lived in St. Louis. The best time for me was during summer vacation. I was sent to a Habonim camp in New Buffalo, Michigan, for one month. It was a Zionist youth camp and I loved it. I became a counselor and so was no expense to the sponsor.

In July of 1941, my parents arrived in New York after a seven-week journey from Spain aboard a freighter. They settled in Brooklyn, with one of my mother's sisters. They obtained work and started saving in order to defray the expenses they had to pay the relatives for the tickets and for rent. I was delighted when they arrived and announced their arrival via an airmail postcard that I still have. Since I was in school in my senior year, I could not see them until the summer of 1942. I was able to speak to them on the telephone when the principal of my high school arranged a phone call from his office. What a joy there was on both ends of the wires.

I continued my studies in St. Louis and as a senior I was granted permission to work for a florist in University City. I attended school in the morning and left in the afternoon to work in the flower shop. I was scheduled to graduate from school in February 1942.

Two weeks before graduation I was singled out by a Jewish sorority, Sigma Delta Tau [SDT], to be the recipient of a four-year scholarship. It would pay for my room and board, tuition and books, travel money, and spending money. They offered this opportunity to one refugee girl in the United States and they had selected me. I was stunned, delighted, but also torn between loyalty to my parents. I knew I wanted to help them, live with them, and work, but realized the tremendous advantage this educational opportunity would give me. I left the decision to my parents and they gladly agreed to let me attend the University of Oklahoma, which had offered to sponsor me with room and board. The National Scholarship Chairman of the sorority came to give me all the details and also took me shopping to outfit me for my new adventure at an American university. I started living in Norman at the SDT house, where the girls were all very friendly and nice. This was in February 1942 and I was initiated into the sorority pledge class of 1942. It was a wonderful feeling to be so accepted by such a lovely group of girls. The war turned the University of Oklahoma into a Navy Air Base, and all fraternity and sorority houses were taken over. That meant a transfer for me. I was sent to the University of Nebraska. There I met my future husband and at the end of my junior year, I left Lincoln to join him in Chicago where he was employed by an insurance company. We were married in June 1944 in Chicago and lived there for four years.

My husband took a Government position shortly after we were married. He became a claims authorizer for the Social Security Administration. I found work in a war industry concern and worked in the office.

To complete my family history, I must mention here what tore our family apart in Europe. Our family was composed of five persons, my father and mother, my sister Irene, myself, and my little brother Martin, in 1938 six and a half years old. I indicated my sister left in March 1938 for Palestine. I immigrated to the United States in October 1938 with a Kindertransport, and my brother Martin was sent to England in March 1939 with the British Kindertransport. That left only my parents in Germany, making it more possible for them to be able to immigrate.

My brother was placed with a lovely family living in the country. They had four children of their own and Martin fitted in well. There he learned English quickly and was entered into school for the first time in his life. Later on, he was placed into a Jewish orphanage in order to keep up with his Jewish education. He spent the entire period of WWII in England. I was in touch with him and the foster parents, as I was also with my sister who was on a kibbutz in Palestine. And I could write to my parents in Germany informing them of the status of the other siblings. My parents came to the United States in July 1941, and as soon as the war was over in Europe in 1945, they requested to have their son sent to them by the British government. When Martin arrived in the U.S. in March of 1945, he was twelve and a half years old and spoke beautiful Oxford English but knew not a word of German. My husband and I took a bus from Chicago to help welcome him in New York.

We were all overjoyed to have been united again; the only problem was communication between my parents and my brother. There was hardly any and he was mostly on his own while living with them.

"AUTOBIOGRAPHY"

By Jack Steinberger [1988]

I was born in Bad Kissingen (Franconia) in 1921. At that time my father, Ludwig, was forty-five years old. He was one of twelve chil-

Jack Steinberger with foster father, ca. 1935. Jack, with colleagues Leon Lederer and Melvin Schwartz, discovered a new type of neutrino for which they were awarded the Nobel Prize in Physics in 1988. Their work included the creation of a basic research tool that made possible the study of one of the four fundamental forces in nature. Archives of One Thousand Children®, Inc.

dren of a rural "Viehhändler" (small-time cattle dealer). Since the age of eighteen he had been cantor and religious teacher for the little Jewish community, a job he still held when he emigrated in 1938. He had been a bachelor until he returned from four years of service in the German Army in the First World War. My mother was born in Nuremberg to a hop merchant, and was fifteen years the younger. Unusual for her time, she had the benefit of a college education and supplemented the meager income with English and French lessons, mostly to the tourists, which provided the economy of the spa. The childhood I shared with my two brothers was simple; Germany was living through the postwar depression.

Things took a dramatic turn when I was entering my teens. I remember Nazi election propaganda posters showing a hateful Jewish face with crooked nose, and the inscription "Die Juden sind unser Ungluck" ["The Jews are our Misfortune"], as well as torchlight parades of SA storm troops singing "Wenn's Juden Blut vom Messer fliesst, dann geht's noch mal so gut" ["When the blood of Jews flow from the knife, all is great"]. In 1933, the Nazis came to power and the more systematic persecution of the Jews followed quickly. Laws were enacted which excluded Jewish children from higher education in public schools. When, in 1934, the American Jewish charities offered to find homes for 300 German refugee children, my father applied for my older brother and myself. We were on the SS *Washington*, bound for New York, Christmas 1934.

I owe the deepest gratitude to Barnett Faroll, the owner of a grain brokerage house on the Chicago Board of Trade, who took me into his house, parented my high school education, and made it possible also for my parents and younger brother to come in 1938 and so to escape the Holocaust. New Trier Township High School, on the well-to-do Chicago North Shore, enjoyed a national reputation, and, with a swimming pool, athletic fields, cafeteria, as well as excellent teachers, offered horizons unimaginable to the young emigrant from a small German town.

[Young Jack's "unimaginable horizons" led him, in 1988, to the Nobel Prize in Physics.]

Chapter 2

TREPIDATIONS

*T*he narratives in this chapter trace an evolution from fairly comfortable Jewish living through the growing signs of threat to the Jewish community—a threat that first manifest itself in Germany and then throughout the domain of Nazi influence and conquest—and ending in unforeseen calamity. The sense of impending threat changes during the twelve-year period of the relocation enterprise (1934–45). In later years, particularly after November 1938, the sense of urgency intensifies.

Manfred Steinfeld's narrative indicates the incremental buildup of anxiety in a small town over a five-year period. Steinfeld's overview of local history, including his summary of the centuries of Jewish life in his region of Germany, helps to explain the resistance or reluctance to accept the ominous nature of the Nazi threat.

Kurt Admon's story, which involves the annexation of Austria, acknowledges a segment of Austrian (particularly Viennese) Jewry that wore its Jewish identity lightly and was hardly prepared to be marked as guilty of a lineage it only casually acknowledged. Admon traces the programmatic inflammation of what he considers an inherent, but usually subdued, anti-Semitism and the rapid acceleration of actions that separated—extracted—Jews from the communities of which they had been a part. He also describes the up-welling of violence against Jews and sets it within the larger context of political and economic conditions in Europe during the 1930s. His chilling portrait of Kristallnacht cannot be read without sharing its horror. At the same time, Admon's re-creation of the texture of daily life is remarkable in its selection of authentic, culturally resonant details.

Martin Birn's memoir relocates the tale of growing horror and panic to Stuttgart and other German communities. The reader can follow the steps of *recognition and response that led his parents to arrange for his relocation to the United States, just as Manfred Steinfeld's and Kurt Admon's parents had done for their sons.*

Henny Wenkart stresses the tendency among Jewish parents to protect their children from the harsh truths that they themselves were only reluctantly coming to face. She even suggests a sense of gamesmanship, an uplifting pleasure in outwitting the Nazis accompanied by a bravado that was consoling to the children, who were not fully aware of what was transpiring. Though this excerpt from her memoir stops short of recording the details, she too was maneuvered into a position that allowed rescue in advance of catastrophe.

In each of the narratives, we are compelled to experience the individual human dramas—the simple and stark reality of these communities, these neighbors, these hunted and haunted parents who created a future for their children out of an overwhelming living nightmare. It is hard to imagine, by the time each child is prepared for his or her parentless journey to an unknown destiny, that there was a time not very long before—a time that stretched back for generations—during which their families lived vibrant lives among small or larger numbers of Jews in an easy or only mildly uneasy accord with their Gentile neighbors.

"REFLECTIONS OF JOSBACH—LIFE IN THE 30s"

By Manfred Steinfeld [1969]

The date: January 30, 1933, the place: Josbach, a small town of 419 people in south central Germany. The Steinfeld family is anxiously awaiting the visit of Dr. Heinrich Hesse from Rauschenberg to treat Hanschen Steinfeld, the grandmother, who seems to be the matriarch of the family, and who has been ill for over a week. The doctor arrives around 4:30 p.m., as it has been snowing continuously for the day. He greets Mrs. Steinfeld and gives her some medication, and on the way out says, "Something wonderful has happened today. Adolf Hitler has been made the new Chancellor!" The remark is quickly passed over and the impact of that day will not be realized for many days to come. The Doctor then leaves to treat another patient in the town. Grandma Steinfeld recovers a few days later, and is soon well again.

The Steinfeld and Katten families are two of the Jewish families who have lived in the town for almost 200 years. Now there are a total of six Jewish families living in Josbach: two Steinfelds (my father's brother Solomon), three Kattens, one Fain. Their livelihood is earned in the typical small town fashion, which seems to be repeated in almost every town where there are from six, seven, eight, or nine Jewish families living. One dry goods store (operated by my mother),

Entrepreneur Manfred Steinfeld (right) receiving the Horatio Alger Award from the Horatio Alger Association of Distinguished Americans, 1981. Archives of One Thousand Children®, Inc.

another one will own a hardware store, a third will be a livestock trader. However, in Josbach there is one additional trade—and that is a confectionery store, and during the first part of the year it also becomes a Matzoh Bakery. The Matzoh Bakery was founded in the year 1851 and the son-in-law, by the name of Hans Fain, who married a Steinfeld, has taken over the business.

Each of the families in the town have either two or three children, and among the Steinfelds and Fains, there are a total of eight children: three in my family—including myself, my sister Irma, and my brother Herbert; two in Solomon Steinfeld's family—Trudie and Martin (my first cousins); three in the Fain family—Hermann, Hans, and Selma. In the Katten families there are five children—Albert and a younger daughter named Tillie, and three children in the other Katten family— Heinz, Martha, and Ilse.

The sixth family consists of a spinster, Metah Katten, who has a younger niece living with her.

The Jews in this town have made their livelihood in this fashion since the beginning of the nineteenth century, and when one visits the cemetery in the town of Halsdorf, four miles south of Josbach, which has served since the beginning of the twentieth century, one realizes how these families made their living over the past 200 years.

There is an ancient cemetery located in a town by the name Hatzbach (which even today has over fifty percent of the monuments still standing), and the earliest burial in this cemetery was about 1815.

The names of Steinfeld, Katten, Stern appear, and it is evident that these three families were really dominant among the Jews within a radius of approximately fifteen to twenty miles. It also appears that the surname of some of these families were taken prior to the granting of full rights by Napoleon in 1811, and the significance of the names of Steinfeld, Katten, or Stern cannot be explained today. However, we must assume that one name was taken because of a "stonefield" close to their home. One explanation of the name Katten is that it was derived from the German word "Chatten," the antecedent of the Hessians. Literally translated, the word means "heathens."

The Steinfelds lived in Josbach since about the mid-eighteenth century, and the Katten family, which was my mother's maiden name, originated from an adjacent town named Halsdorf. She was born in the town of Rauschenberg, which was only eight miles away from Josbach. The community of Rauschenberg dates back to the mid-fourteenth century, with a population today of about 3,000. It was the seat of a local Count, with a very substantial castle overlooking the town.

The Jews in this town, numbering about twenty families, in addition to the normal mercantile trade, had grocery stores, butcher shops, and other retail establishments.

We know that in the town of Rauschenberg there have been Jews of Spanish heritage since the beginning of the fifteenth century, as the name Marannoh appears in some of the ancient death and marriage registers.

The Jews in the province of Hesse date back to the eighth century, when the first Jews were settled in the town of Fulda, and subsequently in such well-known Jewish communities as Darmstadt, Frankfurt, Worms, Marburg, and Giessen. The towns of Marburg and Giessen had Jews living there as early as 1300.

It appears that Jews settled in these towns because they were given protective rights by the local governing magistrate. During the days of the feudal system, in the fifteenth or sixteenth centuries, administration of a locale was usually the responsibility of a Duke, Count, or Baron (Landesherren).

They granted the Jews protective custody for the payment of a fee, and gave the Jews limited citizenship. The size of the protective fee varied according to the settlement fee for Schutzjuden (Protected Jews). It is for this reason that in the province of Hesse, 492 small towns had Jews as residents.

Usually the local authorities that granted Jews limited citizenship and gave them protective custody allocated one, two, or three Jewish families to almost every single town. The records show that those towns having no Jewish population after World War I did have Jews living there at one time, during the seventeenth, eighteenth, or nineteenth centuries.

Life itself for Jews, and Germans, was very primitive by today's standards. Most towns were founded in the thirteenth, fourteenth, or fifteenth centuries, and the livelihood of the inhabitants came primarily from agriculture. It was basically a peasant type of living conditions, the land was plowed by a hand-pushed plow, pulled by oxen or cows, and only the well-to-do families had horses for this task.

There was no indoor plumbing in most of the towns, although our home was the only one in the town that had indoor plumbing and a flush toilet. The reason being that the town well was located adjacent to our home, and in the 1920s, my father had connected indoor plumbing and running water directly from the water pump.

Pogroms and persecution of the Jews took place periodically, especially during the Crusades, or after the Thirty-Year War, or after the Black Plague. However, it appears that after ten or twenty years after each pogrom, the Jews returned and settled again.

In 1933, there were in the province of Hesse 401 Jewish communities, which were registered and had synagogues. For instance, the town of Josbach had its own synagogue, but we were part of the Jewish community of Halsdorf, since we normally did not have the required ten men for a minyan [the quorum required for Jewish communal worship] and only conducted services when a Bar Mitzvah took place, or during the High Holidays. For during those days, a tenth man would come from an adjacent town.

The only business activities that took place in the town, not dominated by the six Jewish families, was the town tavern. It seems that either the first or last house of each town was the town tavern, and also offered overnight accommodations to the weary traveler.

Most travel in those days was conducted by either walking or riding a bicycle. Only one family in our town owned an automobile, and in most instances, the rest of the travel was conducted by the use of a horse and buggy, or again the bicycle.

The Germans of the town, in addition to being involved in agriculture, also had a town carpenter, painter, shoemaker, and tailor. This made up all the trades which were basically needed to fulfill the needs of the community.

Mail in our town was received from another town, approximately twenty miles away by the name of Treysa, by means of a postal bus, which delivered the mail each day, five days a week, and covered approximately twenty towns. The post office of the town was located in the center of our town, and this was a part-time job for one of the Germans who acted as Postmaster and also had a gasoline pump.

Since the Jews of the town controlled most of the mercantile trade, at least seventy percent of the mail was destined for them. It was always a happy occasion for the Jewish children to meet the Post Bus. At five o'clock each afternoon, when the bus came to town, we would run to pick up the mail for our parents. I can vividly recall the window where I picked up the mail, it was adjacent to the cow barn and manure pile. (You measured the wealth of a German farmer by the size of his manure pile. This indicated the amount of livestock he had, since animal manure and human waste were used for fertilizer in the fields. This was supplemented by chemical fertilizers.)

In the center of the town there was also a community Bake House, where the entire town baked bread and cake. Each Friday morning, this Bake House was reserved for the six Jewish families of the town, who would bake cakes for the Sabbath and make challah for the Sabbath. This was a tradition accepted by all of the town's residents.

Next to the Bake House, was the Town Bulletin Board, on which was posted the daily newspaper, and the townspeople would go there on Saturdays and Sundays to read the daily or weekly edition of the papers on display there.

Education in the town consisted of a two-room schoolhouse: grades one through four in one room and five through eight in another room. Since this was a peasant community, the intelligence of the Jews far exceeded those of the local Germans. The total number of students were approximately seventy, of which ten were Jews. There was just one teacher on duty and he had been there prior to World War I—a man in his late fifties or early sixties, by the name of Wolf. I can vividly recall the four spinster daughters who lived with him, since their home was directly across from ours.

Jewish education for the Jewish children of Josbach and Halsdorf was given by a teacher from the Jewish community of Gemuenden, who visited each of the towns on a weekly basis. Every Tuesday afternoon he would visit our town and we would receive our religious instructions. (Gemuenden had Jews living there as early as 1735, when the first Schutzjuden settled there. In 1735, there were already five families living in the town. The synagogue was built in 1823, and the school was founded in 1848.)

Our teacher's name was Dr. Spier and his father had already taught in this particular town since 1869, when he had twenty-nine students, and Herr Spier continued the education of the Jewish children in the community until 1938.

Our home faced the town church, which was on top of an ancient cemetery dating back to the fourteenth century. Our home consisted of three bedrooms, two on the lower floor and one on the upper floor, an attic, and an additional bed and living room on top of the store, where the dry goods and textiles were displayed. At one time, this had been two separate homes, but late in the nineteenth century they were combined into one home and the living room and bedroom over the store were only utilized when we had company.

My father had six brothers and sisters, and one brother married and remained in the town. The other brother had a successful business in a large town about 100 miles away, and the sisters were all married and had settled in various towns, all of which were in the province of Hesse.

In addition, each family had what was known as a "root cellar." At harvest time, enough vegetables would be put away for the winter in the root cellar. The vegetables consisted of potatoes, turnips, and a variety of other vegetables, which grew in abundance. Those vegetables unable to be kept in the cellar during the winter would be bottled in mason jars, and the pantries were fully stocked to last from one harvest to another.

Each home had a wood-burning stove, which was utilized for cooking, and also the flue would give off some heat for the upstairs rooms. Central heating was unknown in any of the towns, and in order to keep warm in the winter you utilized a heavy down comforter.

On January 30, 1933, when Hitler came to power, the day just passed as just another day. The Nazi party had not really made any significant inroads in the town itself. There was only one German who had joined the party in the late 1920s; his name was Heinrich Haupt. The Mayor of the town was Heinrich Henkel, and the administration of the town was simple, to say the least.

The police administration came under the jurisdiction of the town of Rauschenberg. When Hitler came to power, the Jews in our town plus the surrounding towns were really not concerned because they had unanimously agreed that the NSDAP (the initials of the Nazi Party) would not last long in power.

Only twenty-five percent of the population were members of the Party, and the Social Democrats coupled with the Christian Center Party still constituted the largest segment of the population.

Probably one of the reasons that the Jewish population of Hesse felt secure in their surroundings was due to their illusion of having served the Fatherland during World War I. The Jewish participation in World War I had amounted to approximately fifteen percent of the Jews living in Germany, while the participation of the Jews in the province of Hesse had amounted to nineteen percent. Of those who served from the province of Hesse, eleven to twelve percent were either killed or missing, and statistics indicate that approximately twelve percent of those who served were volunteers. The Jews who survived World War I were proud of having served, and this gave them the additional sense of false security that nothing would ever happen to them. Initially during the Nazi persecution, exemptions were made for World War I veterans, but this was eliminated in 1937.

I should also add at this point, that in addition to the businesses of the Jewish families, they each owned a substantial amount of land, which was either leased out to tenant farmers or worked by the families themselves. Also, each family had a nice-sized garden where all the vegetables that were required were grown. Also, they owned chickens, goats, and cows, utilized for their meat requirements.

It was customary that all of the Jewish families would meet at each other's homes Friday night after dinner, or on Saturday afternoon after lunch, and discuss current happenings. I can recall being at a Saturday afternoon study session and hearing that there was very little future for the Nazis. As I have previously said, only one citizen of the town had joined the Nazi Party in the late 1920s, and he had not been successful in recruiting any others in this particular town. However, in some of the surrounding towns, twenty-five to thirty percent of the population were members of the Nazi Party.

The Germans' love for uniforms probably induced many of the young people to join the S.A., which was the official party organization. They received their brown shirts with the swastika armband, and rather than know what the party stood for they joined because of the nice-looking uniform.

It was shortly after Hitler came to power that the first incident of any open anti-Semitism could be noticed in the town. The first Jewish boycott was called in May of 1933, and all of the Jewish stores were boycotted by the local population. It really did not affect business in our town, since most of the sales were really made by visiting the various customers in their homes.

The population still dressed in native costumes, and the women made all their own skirts and blouses according to the ethnic customs prevalent in the community.

They would purchase the textile goods and ribbons from our store, and we would normally deliver right to their homes. I can recall making these deliveries, by bicycle, to the various surrounding towns. However, with the first boycott, the Jewish families of our town became aware of what was happening and they became concerned, although there was no open discrimination against us.

The local newspaper on display on the town bulletin board was no longer a Frankfurt paper, but now was the official party organ, *The Voelkischer Beobachter*. One of the things that became apparent to the Jewish community was the constant traffic that went through the center of our town, which was part of the main highway between Frankfurt and Kassel. The automobile and military traffic increased, almost on a daily basis.

In 1934, after Hitler had been in power for one year, the local German community organized the Hitler Youth and for those under fourteen years of age, a group called the Jung Folk, or Young People, was organized. I remember distinctly being invited to the first meeting of this particular group, which was the age group of ten to fourteen, and asked to join. After the first meeting, however, I was made unwelcome and told, "No Jews allowed here." That was really the first incident of discrimination that took place against the Jewish youth in our town. There was one other incident, where several windows were broken in our home by a group of Nazi bicyclists when they passed through our town and sang the Horst Wessel Lied, or the Horst Wessel song, which became the official Nazi Party song.

In the election of 1935, there was only a choice to vote "yes" or "no," and the only candidate was Hitler. Each of the Jews in the town were forced to vote and they cast their ballot under the column marked "yes," since they did not want to be different from the rest of the town. I remember distinctly having my grandmother picked up by a horse-drawn wagon since she had become an invalid, and taken to the nearest polling place to cast her ballot.

At the Saturday afternoon Kaffe Klatch, we would hear about the persecution of the Jews in the larger towns where the boycott had become more effective. Store windows at Jewish merchants would be broken and Jews would be arrested and not heard from for four to six weeks after their arrests. None of these took place in Josbach. I remember only one incident where two SS men came to arrest my Grandmother, because she held the first mortgage on property in the next town, which was owned by these particular members of the SS. They came under the pretense of arresting her, but primarily to frighten her since they had not made any payments anyway.

I ran to get the Mayor of the town, who came immediately, and he ordered the SS men out of town, since they did not have proper warrants for her arrest. Incidentally, the only party member, to whom I have referred previously, had become Mayor. Many of the Jewish people of the town were among his friends, and every Saturday night he would join them in playing an old favorite German card game, called Skat.

In 1935, all the students were witnessing the first military maneuvers, which took place in the local vicinities, and no distinctions were made between the Jewish and German students. All the Jewish students participated in witnessing these activities.

About the same time, the anti-Semitic newspaper *Der Stuermer* took the place of the official party newspaper on weekends. And now hate propaganda against the Jews reached down towards the lowest level of the German communities. In addition, military instructions took place in the elementary school, and training with wooden guns started in the sixth grade. Shortly thereafter, my brother Herbert, who was participating in the military instructions, broke his arm with the wooden rifle. Subsequently, the Jewish students were barred from this activity. Anti-Semitism became more prevalent in all daily activities.

A new teacher preaching the official party line was transferred into our town about 1935, and the Nazi doctrine now was the dominant educational tool. In recreational activities, the Jewish students were really not excluded, but they were made fun of and generally pushed around. It became more and more apparent that the official anti-Semitism was reaching down to the local level, and was becoming more effective on a day-to-day basis.

In 1936, the first arrest of one of my relatives took place—an Uncle who lived in Rauschenberg was held in supposed protective custody for over six weeks. We had heard about the disappearance of those who opposed the Nazi philosophy and the disappearance of many Jewish men from other towns, but there was always the hope that Nazi regime would be toppled.

When Hindenburg died in 1935 and Hitler came to power as the supreme leader, the hope for the demise of the Nazi Party disappeared. The German population in the town itself still remained very friendly to the Jewish inhabitants, but as time passed they became afraid to deal with them on a business basis. Purchases from Jewish merchants continuously decreased. It was getting more difficult, on a daily basis, to earn a living. We had a live-in maid since 1926, and this stopped in 1934 since it was degrading for a German to work for a Jewish family.

Through contacts with Jews from surrounding towns we learned of violent attacks of anti-Semitism, consisting of arrests, disappearances, boycotts, breaking of windows, beating up of children, calling of obscene names, etc., and this became a daily occurrence. On a typical Saturday morning we would attend services in the next town,

Halsdorf, which was three miles away. We had to pass a locally operated flour mill, and as we passed by the mill, the owner would let all of his dogs loose and say "Go, get the Jews." After several incidents of this type of harassment, we bypassed his mill in order to prevent this type of situation.

In 1936, one of the Katten families decided to immigrate to the United States, since their son had left in the '20s, and all of the Jewish families became aware of the future we were facing. Subsequently, in late '37, the Fain family decided to emigrate to Argentina and my mother decided it was time to make preparations to leave also. She was concerned about the welfare of her three children, since she had been a widow since 1929. My father, Abraham, died of pneumonia when my sister Irma was six years old, my brother Herbert was three years old, and I was five years old.

In a town very close to Josbach, an agricultural kibbutz [a communal farm] had been started to train those who wanted to immigrate to Palestine. In 1937, I spent my vacation with one of my Aunts who lived in Speyer, one of the oldest Jewish communities, dating back to the eighth century. At that time, my mother was convinced it was imperative to leave Germany. She submitted my name to the HIAS [Hebrew Immigrant Aid Society], and also applied for an affidavit to her sister and brother, who were already living in the United States. I qualified and received my affidavit from HIAS, and left Germany in July of 1938. My mother took me to the railway station in Kirchhain, ten miles away, and I took an express train to Hamburg. I crossed the Atlantic on the SS *New York*, and landed in America on July 12, 1938.

My brother went to the kibbutz training station, and left for Palestine approximately five months later, in December of 1938. He went to a kibbutz near Pardess Channa, near Tel-Aviv.

In November of 1938, concurrent with Crystal Night [Kristallnacht], all Jewish property was confiscated and Jews were being eliminated from all types of commerce and business, and no contact with Germans was allowed.

My sister received her visa to go to England in the summer of 1939, but unfortunately the war started the week she was to leave and she was unable to get out of Germany. Our home was transferred by means of a forced sale to a German family, but my mother and sister were permitted to stay in the rooms over the store.

I corresponded with my mother until January of 1942, and received a letter at that time in which she mentioned the impending deportation of the Jews to Littmanstadt in Poland. The records show that she left Germany in the middle of 1942, and was deported to Latvia with many other German Jews.

From information that I was able to gather from one of my cousins, who survived several concentration camps (she had been separated from her mother and sister), both my mother and sister had survived the persecution and hardships of the Riga ghetto and Stutthof concentration camp until the beginning of 1945. Both perished at that time, when the Russians advanced eastwards causing the Germans to accelerate the mass extermination program and in their haste to flee westwards, killed thousands and thousands of camp inmates.

Those who perished in the Nazi camps were my mother, Paula, my sister, Irma, Hermann Katten and wife and daughter, and the spinster, Metha Katten. One of Hermann Katten's daughters survived in Berlin living with a German family.

My brother Herbert was killed by the British at Kibbutz Schluchot, near Pardess Channa on October 25, 1945, at age of eighteen. He was a member of the Irgun, an underground group fighting for the establishment of a Jewish homeland.

I returned to Josbach in May of 1945 as an American soldier, and noted that the town had not been damaged during the war. I returned subsequently in 1966, with Fern, Michael, Paul, and Jill, and again with Jill in 1976.

Small towns do not change, except that agriculture is automated today. Every family has a car, and each home has a television set. The population is approximately the same size as in 1938.

[On May 2, 1945, Manfred Steinfeld, who translated the surrender documents of the German forces east of the Elbe, and his 82nd American Airborne Division liberated the survivors of the concentration camp Wobbelin, four kilometers outside Ludwigslust, in northern Germany. The rescue effort was the final mission for Steinfeld and his fellow paratroopers, who also helped bury the dead, those not lucky enough to be liberated. Steinfeld's military service earned him a Bronze Star and Purple Heart. Years later, philanthropist Steinfeld undertook the rededication and reconstruction of the Wobbelin memorial.]

FROM "FRAGMENTS"

By Kurt Admon [1997]

"My Vienna(?)"

Nazi Germany occupied Vienna (and all of Austria) on March 13, 1938, but of course we felt it breathing on our necks long before, when reports of their assaults on German Jewry reached us.

"Brith Sholom child" Kurt Admon
with parents, 1932. Archives of
One Thousand Children®, Inc.

From 1934 on, the Fascist dictatorship of the Christian-Socialist Party under the leadership of Schuschnigg ruled Austria. This party preached Austrian independence, but it had no monopoly on Fascist ideology in Austria; side by side with it there was a large Nazi Party, which in addition to its Fascist platform aimed at unification with Germany. The question of independence versus unification was a serious and violent bone of contention between the two Fascist parties. In 1934, the Austrian Nazis tried to stage a Putsch [a secretly plotted attempt to overthrow the government]; they started the attempted takeover by murdering the then-Chancellor of Austria, Dolfuss, but failed to topple the government. The regime was wary of outlawing the Nazi Party, what with Big Brother watching every move from across the border. It solved the problem by forbidding all political activity other than that of the ruling party. The Social-Democratic (Socialist) Party rose up in revolt against the dictatorial decrees, but more on this later.

We lived in the 20th District, at 32 Treustrasse, a working-class district that also had a fair-sized Jewish population. Just a few blocks away, in Spaungasse, lived Willy and Pepi, Mama's younger brother and sister. Their apartment was in the back of their grocery store. Both apartment and store had belonged to their parents. As happened in those distant days of nearly a century ago, child death was a frequent occurrence; of the eight children who were born, only four survived:

Jetti, the eldest, later to become Arye's mother, then Berta, my mother, Willy, and Pepi, the youngest. The whole family, parents and four children, had migrated from Galicia to Vienna during World War I, settled down in that store-apartment complex, earned their livelihood and lived in that place from then on. Over the years, the two older daughters married and moved away, the parents died, but the place continued to be the family center. Jetti, with her husband Jusio, and son Poldi (short for Leopold, which became Arye in Hebrew), i.e., the Silberbach family, lived further away, in Karl Marx Hof.

The Karl Marx Hof housing complex deserves some attention. The Austrian Social-Democratic Party, under the leadership of (the Jew) Victor Adler, was known for its unusual mixture of Marxist ideology and constructive activities. Toward the end of the twenties, when the party controlled the Vienna Municipality, it started to promote workers' housing projects, and caused the Municipality to construct low-cost housing for the city's proletarian and low-income population. This activity of the Municipality continued, even after the Social-Democrats were removed from power; after World War II, the Vienna Municipality renewed its construction of municipal housing projects. The flagship of all these projects was the Karl Marx project, a huge structure built in one of the city's northern outskirts, still standing and functioning today. The original population in the project was mainly (only?) composed of "Comrades," among them our Silberbachs. During the battles of the 1934 Socialist uprising against the Christian-Socialist dictatorship, this housing project was one of the major centers of conflict. I remember my fear caused by the sound of cannon fire resounding in the city; after the uprising was crushed (ending in the utter defeat of the Social-Democrats), the damage in the housing project was repaired. Many Sundays thereafter, when we passed by the Karl Marx Hof on our way to picnic in the Wiener Wald, the Vienna Forests, we could identify these repairs by the color of their plaster, which distinguished them from the surrounding walls.

Mama's family came to Vienna from Galicia, during World War I. Papa came to Vienna after the War, when he was discharged from the Austrian Army, which he had joined in Galicia as a young volunteer. His oldest sister, Berta (same name as Mama), immigrated to the United States at that time, part of the tremendous wave of Jewish immigration which rolled into the U.S. before its gates were closed by very restrictive immigration laws. Twenty years later, Berta would play a pivotal role in the attempted rescue of her brother, my father, and the successful escape from extinction of his family. The only representative of the "old-time" Viennese Jews, considered more prestigious than the newer "Ostjuden," in our family circle was Jusio; despite his "veteran" status, he was alone, the only son of parents who had died before I became conscious of the world. On the other hand, I met many relatives from Mama's side of the family. A name I remember specially is that of Tante Kruh, an aunt of my grandparents' generation. Although all of these people, excepting Jusio, stemmed from Galicia, I never heard a word of Polish spoken among them; Yiddish was used only in the presence of Tante Kruh. The only other use of Yiddish was in singing old Yiddish melodies; from early childhood I recall the popular cradle song "Roshinkes un' Mandeln" ["Raisins and Almonds"], the sad melody "Oif'n Pripitchik," ["In the Fireplace"], the humorous "Oz der Rebbe lacht" ["When the Rabbi Laughs"], and others. Whenever I hear "Klezmer" music, old memories spring to life and with them nostalgia for the old melodies.

We were a secular family, but on Yom Kippur we fasted and went to a local synagogue; I, of course, tried to prove my manhood by joining the full fast even though (or because?) I was told that young children are not required to fast. On Pesach [Passover] we held a Seder [ritual meal] at home. My outstanding memory of that yearly ceremony is of the time I became very drowsy because of sipping too much wine, and finally was carried off to bed before the end of the Seder, losing my chance to look for, and find, the Afikoman. My acquaintance with rituals were so slight that I had no knowledge of the various blessings, broches in Yiddish, which are to be recited on various occasions over the day, neither of their content nor even of their existence. One summer, I chanced upon the existence of a blessing when washing hands; I was at a day camp, evidently operated by the Jewish Community Center, the Juedische Kultusgemeinde, when a fellow camper told me to "say a broche" when washing my hands. So, all that summer, every time I washed my hands I said "a broche," and only many years later did I become aware of his real intent.

Every year we participated in the celebration of Herzl Day. Herzl was buried in Vienna (his remains were transferred to Jerusalem only a few years after the establishment of the Jewish State which he had envisioned) and on his memorial day, the "Yahrzeit" [anniversary of someone's death], tens of thousands of Jews, especially the youth, went in festive procession, on foot carrying the Blue-White flag, on bicycles decorated with blue-white streamers, to pay a respectful visit to his grave. At the time, I had no idea of who this Herzl was, but the yearly event left its impression in my memory.

My parents sent me to an afternoon Jewish school. Their purpose was, no doubt, to introduce me to Jewish studies—Bible, Hebrew, etc.—but my main activity was to "play hooky" from class, running off to the nearby home of a "partner in crime." He had a large collection of tin soldiers (this was—not to forget—during the pre-plastic ages), with which we could conduct sweeping war maneuvers on the apartment floor. Hebrew—zero; prayers—I can't recall someone trying to teach me. A more positive educational-cultural effect from this connection to the Jewish school was my induction into the boys' choir of the associated synagogue. We had at least one public appearance, documented in a picture of the choir and its leader, all of us ensconced in talitot [prayer shawls]. A few years later, on Kristallnacht, I watched this synagogue go up in flames.

Willy, the young uncle of twenty-and-something, went off to the training farm of a Zionist youth movement. A few months later, he returned to us in Vienna and taught us Hebrew songs he had learnt there. The "Song of the Emek" is lodged in my brain ever since that night more than sixty years ago, when Willy dimmed the gas light in our living room (yes, yes, in the mid-nineteen-thirties, in a central district of a courtly capital of Central Europe, the electricity network had not yet reached the apartment houses), and began singing, in subdued voice "Numa emek erets tiferet anu l'chamishmeret" ["Sleep, O valley, glorious land, we are thy guardians"]. His Zionist affiliation played a key role, four to five years later, in saving his life, as well as the lives of his sister Jetti and her family.

In short, it would be difficult to claim that our lives were permeated by Jewish substance, neither religious nor secular. Nevertheless, I was aware, even as a very young child, of being a Jew, and felt this to be a source of pride. Once, when I was about five years old, I was given an embroidered shirt of the well-known Russian style. Some Austrian woman remarked, upon seeing me, "Oh what a cute little Russian boy." My reply was angry, "No, I'm not a Russian, I'm a Jew!"—loud and clear.

The Thirties were years of intense political struggles in Europe. The Capitalist-Liberal system was in the grip of deep crisis, economic crisis, moral crisis, and therefore also crisis of acceptance and dominion. Dissenters from the Left and from the Right challenged its legitimacy. These struggles penetrated our home with the thunder of cannon fire, sounds that brought with them worry for the well-being of relatives caught in the midst of civil war raging in our city. Then there was the Italian-Abyssinian War, and names like Addis Ababa and Haile Selassi I recall from early childhood, despite the fact that television hadn't even been invented, and without radio, since we didn't have electricity in our home yet. This would indicate a home with political consciousness; interesting, I have no recollection from that time of the anti-Fascist war in Spain. Only ten years later did this war assume the legendary dimensions it has for me. Jusio, we already know was a Socialist, identified by virtue of living in Karl Marx Hof. Another, later, sign of his political leanings was his connection in Israel (first Palestine) with ex-Viennese, such as Hanna Lamdan, in the left-wing "Achdut Avodah" Party. I have the distinct impression that Papa's politics were further left, if not an outright Communist, then at least a sympathizer. Pepi has said more than once that, "the apples (Dani and I) don't fall far from the tree." At home we had books published in the cheap Soviet editions that I recognized again in Israel in 1948–49. From home I remember especially a book of short stories by Gorki; some of the stories I read as a child, i.e., "Baker's Apprentice," and many pages were folded into paper airplanes.

Papa was a tailor; during the day he worked as a cutter in a large factory, and at night he sewed men's suits at home. The times were of economic crisis, when such occupations certainly didn't offer prosperity, but we lived on a reasonable standard of living, judging by working-class standards of those days. To be a good housewife demanded difficult work, what with none of the electric appliances, from vacuum cleaner to washing machine, which today ease the drudgery of housekeeping as yet uninvented and electric current unavailable at home. I was always dressed spotlessly. Years later, in 1952 or 1953, I was walking with Mama in Brooklyn when she encountered an old acquaintance from Vienna. "Ach so, this is the boy I remember from Vienna," she said in astonishment, looking at the tall man accompanying Mama, "I remember how he always wore white gloves!" She's enjoying her pleasant memory of spotless Kurti, while I'm wondering how that little boy walked in the streets, played with friends, and never forgot to keep those gloves sparkling white. For Mama this was a source of pride. I don't know if the white gloves and all the other attributes of spit and polish were habits adopted from the Austrian environment, or were they standard behavior of the Jewish mother from Poland, more exactly, from Galicia. By the way, one shouldn't forget that the "Yekes" [derisive term for German Jews] came to Israel (Palestine) from Germany or Austria, but for the most part they were the children of immigrants from the East, that is from Poland and the Russian Pale. Their "Yeke-ism" doesn't have very deep roots, except among the few whose families had lived in Germany or Austria for some generations.

The only bought toy I can recall from home is my tricycle; memories of playing with tin soldiers are connected to friends' homes, never mine. At home I did a lot of sewing of dolls' clothing, in natural imitation of Papa's work. I have clear and distinct memories of some of my books: *Struwelpeter*, an "educational" book more like a collection of children's nightmares, which has been translated into Hebrew and published with the original horror drawings; *Max und Moritz*, about the two scamps who finally meet their just (and cruel) punishment; the (in)famous Grimm's fairy tales; *Wie, Wann, Wo*, a wonderful book of science for children, which has also been published in Hebrew; a book on China pirates; and more.

Struwelpeter is an interesting case. The book was written by a children's doctor, based on stories he told them while making his round of house calls. He claims that the publication of these stories came on the basis of the excited response he enjoyed from his aural audience, and it was they (or their parents) who urged him to let a wider public benefit(!) from them. The opening story is about a boy who refuses to observe the rules of personal hygiene, and in the end is punished by having all his fingers cut off by an imp wielding a pair of giant scissors; the story's closing illustration shows the boy standing, without any fingers, dripping blood from ten stumps! Another delightful tale is about a lovely little girl who played with matches; she went up in flames, and in the last picture we can see the little mound of ashes, all that is left of her. Just in case, should any doubt arise as to the origin and meaning of the mound, the girl's two shoes miraculously survived and can be seen standing by the ashes! Each of the stories in the book illustrates some important precept like these two. According to the charming doctor, his patients "went nuts" over his tales, but what do educators and child psychologists say about them? What really happened deep down in the souls of his listeners/readers?

Mama and Papa, like most of the Europeans of their generation, knew hunger—real, physical hunger—in their youth. The experience left its mark on their behavior for the rest of their days. Food which has been served must be eaten, a holy obligation unrelated to being hungry or sated, because it is forbidden to throw out food, not under any circumstance, nor in any situation, period. One does not leave home without eating first; who knows what awaits one in the outside world? One comes home, and, of course, eats; surely outside there was not anywhere one could have eaten. "Home" meant "food." An early, vivid childhood memory is of Mama sitting opposite me at the kitchen table, commanding, "Eat!" In my case, the pressure worked; I was born with a healthy appetite and ate as required. Obviously, I became, as Mama put it, "Schoen und fett," that is to say, "Fat and handsome." A child who ate well "filled out," so to speak, and as a result of observing these important rules of good behavior, became a child who was handsome, a source of pride and pleasure to his mother.

At an early age I began (How could I not? After all, am I Jewish or am I Jewish?) taking violin lessons. Due to my young age, I started with a "half-size" violin. I can't remember anyone being swept away by my outstanding talent. After some time the lessons stopped, not due to my lack of talent, but rather because of financial difficulties when Papa fell ill. The violin was so important to Mama that when she fled Vienna in 1940, she didn't forget to pack the violin!

Papa fell ill. He had stones in his kidneys or gallbladder, and underwent an operation in the Rothschild Hospital. This was far from our home, so we went there via one of the many trolley-car routes which crisscross Vienna. Unlike at present, the procedure then was to buy a ticket upon entering the tram; the ticket was punched with details of the trip—time of entry, station of entry, planned station of exit, and the fare, which was dependant upon the length of the requested trip. Children up to the age of five or six were exempted from payment; how can the conductor judge the age of a child alighting the trolley? A ruler was affixed by the entry door, the normal height of a five-year-old was marked on the ruler, and the exemption was granted or denied in accordance with how the child measured up to this standard. Problem: not only had I "filled out" in accord with the adage of "schoen und fett," I was also tall for my age, an omen of things to come. Every time we got into a trolley (I remember the incident at the Rothschild Hospital station, returning home after visiting Papa), Mama would order me to enter with bent knees so that I would appear shorter than I was, and so squeeze under the fateful mark on the ruler.

On January 20, 1937, my brother, Herbert Joseph, who later, during his stay in Israel, decided to call himself Dani, was born. Intimate subjects, such as pregnancy, were not broached with children, so I depend on retrospective insight to surmise that Mama had difficulties with the pregnancy, and was ordered to spend the last months thereof in bed. My recollections of that period are of daily trips to the nearest Pub, pot in hand, to bring home goulash for lunch. I distinctly disliked going into the malodorous tavern. All's well that ends well, at last the baby was born, a vociferous baby, that is to say an annoyance to the older brother. I suppose that I needed the usual period of adjustment to the new situation of no longer being the sole center of attention.

Electricity came into our home in 1936 or 1937, at any rate, before the Nazi annexation. Electricity in the apartment meant technologic progress, and it made possible, amongst many new possibilities, to hear radio broadcasts. We didn't buy a radio, most likely for lack of money. I never felt poverty or deprivation; a child growing up, of course, regards its environment as normal. Perhaps today, with all the abundance and diversity in shop windows and on television the situation is different; at any rate, I felt no hardship, want, nor envy. Yet if I try to reconstruct our position during those years, it is logical to presume that there were financial problems. The economy was in bad shape during the thirties. Workers, like Papa, were happy they had a job—who argued about the wages? I remember Mama buying bread from a big factory bakery where one could buy day-old bread at a big discount; I don't think she did this for reason of dietetic preference. A neighbor across the street bought a radio and let it blare away, demonstrating his addiction to Hitler's speeches; we "benefited" from his largesse. Papa listened, became worried, and said, "War is coming." Very early on he recognized that we were sitting on top of a volcano about to erupt. Later, in his letters to me during August 1939, the dreadful tension he was under to get his family out was intensely expressed.

In our building, we were the only Jews; I don't remember any of the neighbors, but I recall talk about one of them who lived on the upper floor. He was, so I heard, a member of the Austrian Nazi Party; when the reports of assaults on Jews in Germany reached Vienna, he told Papa that he didn't believe the stories, but in any case, "Don't worry, I'll take care of you." Sure thing, somebody to count on.

On the 12th and 13th of March 1938, the Nazi Army entered Austria and the Anschluss, annexation, became a fact. This was preceded by years of diplomatic and political processes. The first mention of the idea of union between Germany and Austria was after the end of World War I, when the two empires, of Germany and of Austria, departed from this world. At that stage, the major support for this idea came from the Social-Democrats. When Hitler came to power in Germany in 1933, the Social-Democrats abandoned this, but now the Nazis, in Germany and in Austria, began to propagate the program of union. They had an important interest in pushing the idea. Hitler was born an Austrian, and the inclusion of Austria in the German state would add legitimacy to the new regime which was looking for ways to secure its rule over Germany.

In July 1934, the Austrian Nazis tried to topple the Dolfuss government, in order to bring about the unification of Austria with Germany. Dolfuss was killed, but the Putsch failed, and Germany and Austria concluded a pact of noninterference. Toward the end of February 1938, Hitler reneged on the pact, one in the series of pacts violated by him on the road to World War II. He renewed the pressure on Austria, and summoned the Austrian Chancellor to Berchtesgaden, his country residence in the Tyrol Mountains, five minutes from the Austrian border. Schuschnigg was compelled to agree to abrogate the restrictions on the activities of the Austrian Nazis. After his return to Vienna, Schuschnigg renounced the agreement forced upon him in Berchtesgaden, and proclaimed that a national referendum would be held on the question of Anschluss on March 13. German pressure to revoke Schuschnigg's new decision was to no avail. Then, on March 12, a German agent sent Hitler a telegram from Vienna, pleading for "military aid to restore order." Schuschnigg knew what was coming, resigned almost immediately, but not before signing orders to the Austrian Army not to resist German troops which will cross into Austria. The enthusiasm which greeted the German Army was so great that it convinced Hitler to proclaim full annexation at once, without any interim period of "Occupied territories" or other euphemism.

I don't know if all Austrians were happy that day. I can testify to what I saw that day—everyone who could move was out in the streets of Vienna, cheering the German troops marching in. Hitler's decision melted what political opposition to the Anschluss which had existed up to that point, whether in the Fascist government or in any other circles. There was no military opposition, nor were there any protest demonstrations; Schuschnigg's last official act had neutralized the Army, and over the years his government had crushed and scattered both Socialist and Communist opposition. The referendum on Anschluss was held a month later, under Nazi auspices, and the proposed unification was, surprise, surprise, approved by an overwhelming majority. After the end of World War II, Austria's official contention was that the country was conquered by Germany, the first conquest of the War. Formalistically, the claim can be documented; in fact, the "conquerors" were received so warmly that even the Nazis themselves were surprised. The welcome was so overwhelmingly friendly that Hitler was encouraged to change his planned tactics and hasten the procedures for formal unity. The behavior of the Austrian populace in March 1938 exposes the sham in Austria's claim to status of victim.

Assaults on the Jews began at once. The second semester of the school year was already under way, not an apt moment to make radical changes in the schools. Nevertheless, we Jewish pupils were separated from the others, and our classrooms were concentrated in one of the school building's wings. We were assigned only Jewish teachers, and they, of course, taught only Jewish pupils. At the start of the following school year, in September 1938, we were transferred to an all-Jewish school, and the separation of Jewish pupils from the Aryans was completed.

The Nazi youth movement, the Hitlerjugend, flourished, and every day more and more children could be seen in the streets wearing the movement's uniform. In my street, there were also some of these, neighbors who knew me as a Jew, and I started to fear going down to the street. I was afraid to meet one of these young bullies who were equipped with a "Scout" knife and had an unlimited permit to pester, intimidate, and assail me. The major "hunting grounds" of the Hitler-jugend and their adult counterparts of the Nazi militia, the S.A. hooligans in khaki uniforms who had already achieved infamy due to their rule of terror in Germany, were in the neighboring Second District. This District, which was also the territory of Vienna's famous amusement park—the Prater—was the principal domicile of Vienna's Jews, including virtually all of Orthodox Jewry. The Orthodox are easier to identify in the street than other Jews, so that "naturally," if one may use that term to describe a very unnatural, inhuman phenomenon, the Orthodox suffered most of the aggravation. At the time, the encounters were mainly expressions of vulgar masochism—cursing, beating, debasing—"good clean fun" for brutes.

In this way, exploiting the anti-Semitism which permeated the populace, the regime led the public to collaborate in the implementation of Nazi policies to separate Jews from the Christian population, to accustom the gentiles to regard Jews as inferior beings, neither fit nor deserving to be part of Aryan society. It began with small things, at times even ridiculous rules, such as the edict to attach the name "Israel" to every Jewish male and the name "Sarah" to every Jewish woman. Slowly, but surely, the Nazis got used to the changing situation, the general public grew accustomed to it, the world tolerated, even the Jews acquiesced. One step, another step, and yet another, until. . . .

On November 10, 1938, we were already in the separate school for Jews. Suddenly, the school principal entered my classroom and announced that we are being released to go home. We pupils had no inkling as to the reason for this, but his behavior signaled that something was seriously amiss. We were sent from the school building in small groups, so as not to arouse attention in the street. I got to our Treustrasse, our street, but instead of turning toward home I walked on a bit. Two blocks ahead, I encountered a big crowd in front of the synagogue. The building was in flames, firemen were at work trying to control the blaze, and I am watching along with all the people. Later I learnt the meaning of this occurrence; it was part of the pogrom which was called "Kristallnacht." A few days earlier, a young Jew named Herschel Grynspan shot a German diplomat by the name of Von Rath in the German embassy in Paris, and had inflicted mortal wounds upon him. The German died on November 9; that day, the Nazi leadership was gathered in Munich to commemorate the Nazi uprising of 1923, the "Beercellar Putsch" of Munich, which was suppressed. The leaders grasped the opportunity to honor the historic event, and from Munich sent out orders to start riots against Jews and Jewish property throughout the country, "an expression of popular anger against the treacherous attack," etc., etc. Rioting started during the night between the 9th and 10th of November, and on the following morning, our school principal was informed of what was happening.

It was a violent outburst that spread rapidly and widely, until hardly any Jewish institution was left intact. As suddenly as the violence started during the night of the 9th, it stopped a day later. The happenings of that day marked a drastic shift in the attitude of the Nazi authorities toward the Jews. From that day on, the Jews were systematically dislodged from the general economy. The regime set into motion the removal of Jews from physical proximity, by concentrating them in particular areas (not yet in sealed ghettoes); some men were arrested. In Austria, that is to say mainly in Vienna, 8,000 Jews were arrested. Among the detained, my Uncle Jusio, Arye's father. Jetti, his wife and Mama's older sister, collapsed. Quite understandable, and Mama undertook to handle the matter of Jusio's release from Gestapo clutches. For some days the detainees were held in improvised jails, such as school building cellars, and then were transferred to concentration camps. On one of the days, while Mama was at Gestapo headquarters trying to find the key to Jusio's freedom, there came a knock upon our apartment's door.

At the door stood a young couple. They held an official document which awarded them the rights to our apartment, and they had come to arrange the immediate transfer of residence. We out. They in. It wasn't some official who came to dispossess us; officialdom had granted the right, but implementation was left in the hands of the beneficiary, the little guy with a vested interest. The regime had placed the bait for the citizen to collaborate in the expropriation of Jews, and he did so willingly, perhaps even gladly, not letting any discomfort inhibit him. Papa was abashed; I have the feeling that his ability to analyze political developments was not helpful at this juncture, which requires negotiating skills of the victim cutting a deal with his hunter. I think he was about to agree with them on evacuation within days, when

Mama walked in. What, have you gone crazy? I have a baby here
(Herberti was less than two years old then), and we have nowhere to
go; we need time. Now they feel embarrassed; it will take time to get
used to the reality in which Jews have no rights at all, not even the
most basic of rights. They agree to a delay in the transfer of the keys
to the apartment.

Some days later, we found another apartment, a couple of blocks
down the street. The new place was a store with an apartment in back
of it; the Jews who owned it had been expelled, the store closed, and
now we came to live there behind the rolled-down shutter. In one of
the rooms of the apartment, the Gestapo had stored belongings of the
expelled owners, locked the door, and pasted a paper seal on the door
and frame, to make sure no unauthorized person would enter that
room. In order to prevent accidental access to that door which might
tear the seal, the dining table was placed in front of it, blocking any
possibility of approach to the door. Three times a day, at least, I sat at
that table, the seal staring at me threateningly, and tried to eat my meal.
Fortunately, I was blessed with a healthy appetite; if not for that, I
would have lost a lot of weight during that period.

Jusio was released from the concentration camp and returned home.
Most of the detainees of Kristallnacht were freed. This time.

From the day the Germans entered Austria, we, our relatives,
friends, and acquaintances, all our circle became a beehive of activity
in search of escape routes. There was one business on hand—getting
out, in any possible direction: infiltrating into Switzerland, "illegal"
immigration into Palestine, immigration to Australia, anywhere, anywhere, and, of course, to America, the Land of Dreams which had
turned hostile to "the masses, yearning to be free." I remember the
ardent, feverish conversations, every evening, in which one guided the
other, alternatives were weighed, dangers assessed, and plans resolved.
Papa wrote to his sister Berta in America, recruiting her to our aid. His
sister and her husband Paul Bier were needy, almost penniless, labor-
ing class people, at times without a job, not the kind of people who
could supply an immigrant's affidavit, i.e., financial guarantee, on their
own. They turned to well-to-do relatives in the South, and succeeded
in eliciting their consent to supplying an affidavit. Alas, the guarantee was not sufficient for all our family, and so it was decided to utilize
the offered affidavit in the traditional Jewish manner of immigration
into America, i.e., for the father of the family and the elder son. The
intent was for them to go to America, get established there, and then
send for Mama and Herberti. We needed to move fast, but America
wanted to accept us slowly, and we had to accede.

Anyone who wanted to immigrate into the United States was required to present proof of financial support, i.e., the affidavit of an American citizen of sufficient means, which was his financial surety that the immigrant in question would be taken care of financially, so that there was no danger he would become a burden on the taxpayer, even if he found no work. Only the candidate with such an Affidavit could become a prospective immigrant, and enter the waiting list for a place on his nationality's yearly quota. Each nation had its quota, which was derived from a certain calculation, which served a dual purpose: first, to limit total immigration to about a quarter of a million people per year, and second, to tilt the number in favor of immigrants from Western European countries. The immigrant had to be of good health, and to assure his medical examinations were administered at the American consulates in the various countries.

Berthold Brecht wrote that "the passport is a person's noblest part. . . . The passport is the main thing, take care of it." The first step in preparing our migration was to collect documents to verify our existence. Papa requested the authorities in Poland to provide him with a birth certificate. Since his birth in 1899, many armies had stormed through Galicia, this way and that, with opportunities galore to pillage, burn, and kill. It seems that local Offices of Registry were not immune to destruction, and in fact they couldn't send Papa the record he asked for. Instead, they sent a document which stated, "It is reported that Hermann Roth was born. . . ." Not really certain that this man was born, but highly probable.

Some American Jews were deeply troubled by the deteriorating situation of German Jewry and the limited possibilities of immigration to the United States. Congressman Emmanuel Celler, from Brooklyn, New York, proposed a law that would enable the immigration of 100,000 Jewish children from Germany into the U.S., in addition to the regular immigration quota. He, along with many Jewish organizations, pledged that these children would be embraced by Jewish families from all over America, so that their absorption would not become a burden on public budgets. Celler hoped that a rescue plan, independently initiated, planned and carried out by the Brith Sholom Lodge of Philadelphia, would demonstrate the potential of Jewish mobilization to this cause. Brith Sholom planned to bring fifty children from Vienna to America and assign them to volunteer families. The children were to be chosen from families who already had affidavits and were on quota lists. Brith Sholom would guarantee [support] for the children from their arrival in the United States until their settlement in foster families. The children's parents were to arrive in the States

The fifty "Brith Sholom children" aboard ship heading for America with rescuers Eleanor and Gilbert Kraus, 1939. The Krauses personally assumed legal responsibility for all fifty children until and if other foster parents were found for them in the United States or they were reunited with their natural parents. Archives of One Thousand Children®, Inc.

The fifty "Brith Sholom children" arriving in New York getting their first sight of the Statue of Liberty, 1939. ©Bettman/CORBIS. Image donated by Corbis– Bettmann.

within months. While the plan worked well (Brith Sholom selected twenty-five girls and twenty-five boys, brought them to the United States, and succeeded in placing them in foster homes), the outbreak of World War II on September 1, 1939, brought an end to Congressman Celler's attempt to pass such a bill.

Back to the start of May 1939 when we were called to an interview in the Kultusgemeinde; thanks to the affidavit that Papa's sister had succeeded in obtaining for him and me, I was included in the list of candidates for the Brith Sholom project.

FROM A MEMOIR

By Martin Birn [2001]

To my son David, his wife Bonnie, my daughter Meryl, and my granddaughter Anna

The apartment in Stuttgart was very large by German standards and served as Uncle Justin's place of business as well as home. It was a third-floor walk-up with large living room, dining room, large office, storage room, playroom, and at least two bedrooms. It was beautifully furnished in a modern style. There was a grand piano in the living room, which nobody could play. Uncle Justin was in the oil import business and incidentally had a car, an Opel, probably fairly new.

Martin Birn, at age 11, with his father in 1937. Archives of One Thousand Children®, Inc.

I remember Uncle Justin driving the family to Baden-Baden in the Black Forest, not too far from Stuttgart, and me getting carsick on the way.

I don't remember how long I stayed in public school in the Fall of 1934, probably only a semester or two. In any case, I, along with all Jewish kids in Stuttgart, were expelled from public school and started going to Jewish school. It was in a building next to the synagogue. Since Stuttgart had a large and prosperous Jewish community (according to the *Encyclopedia of Judaica*, the Jewish population of Stuttgart in 1933 was 4,900), the synagogue was a large and beautiful structure and the school was in a new, modern building. In addition to the normal subjects, we all had to take Hebrew and English for at least an hour a day. Unlike the German kids who went (and still go) a half day on Saturday, we went to school for only five days a week. But of course we were expected to go to the synagogue for religious services on Saturday morning. Outside of some of these vignettes, my memories of Stuttgart between 1934 and 1938 are rather dim. Uncle Justin and Tante Frieda were both easygoing and good-hearted persons who were fond of me and probably enjoyed having a "normal" child around as a counterpoint to the more difficult job of dealing with their Kurt. They probably got lots of strokes from my father on his visits. Of course he always counseled me to "be a good boy" and on my question to Tante Frieda a few years ago, she said that I was an easy child to raise. My life was probably very similar to other Jewish kids growing up in an upper-middle-class family in the tense and stressful environment that was Nazi Germany in the 1930s. The only difference being that I did a lot more traveling, spending many vacations in Estenfeld, and also visited other relatives from time to time.

One of these visits was to Uncle Adolph, my father's oldest brother. He and Tante Sira and their daughter (my cousin) Lieselotte (Lilo) lived in Weiden an die Oberpfalz. He was a tailor, and I still remember him sitting cross-legged on a big cutting table. They emigrated to Buenos Aires around 1936 or '37. I was in Estenfeld for a visit when they came through Estenfeld to say goodbye on the way to Argentina. It was also the time when the two brothers, Uncle Adolph and Uncle Friedel, made up. They had been on nonspeaking terms for many years, neither one probably remembering why. My father used to be the go-between. I think it was then that I made up my mind not to hold a grudge against a family member for very long, no matter what the circumstances. I kept in touch with Uncle Adolph up to his death. I think their lives in Buenos Aires were not easy. Lilo married a German Jew (named Hirsch) living in Santiago, Chile, and moved there. She was widowed, remarried, and is still living in

Santiago. We had not been in touch until about 1985 or '86, when she and her husband (Joachim Model) surprised us with a short visit here in Seattle. They were on the way to visit his two sons who live in Montreal. We now keep in touch. They have invited us to stay with them and I hope to take advantage of their hospitality one of these days in the not-too-distant future.

My father came to visit me probably every six weeks or two months. His visits were eagerly awaited by me, and he never wore out his welcome in Stuttgart because he always brought with him some scarce commodity, like a couple of pounds of butter, or good coffee, or something else similarly scarce. I have no idea how he got those things—obviously through the black market—but one did not ask those kind of questions. I also don't remember how long he stayed, probably two or three days. In any case, he never wore out his welcome.

The Stuttgart Jewish community owned a camp at the edge of town. It was complete with a clubhouse, swimming pool, soccer fields, track, etc. I spent many a weekend there, participating in soccer, swimming, and track—100-yard dash mostly.

[Birn goes on to describe family medical problems: his own hernia operations and his father's intense headaches due to a brain tumor, the latter resolved by an operation in 1935.]

The next significant event I remember was the infamous "Kristall-nacht" (Night of the Broken Glass), November 8, 1938. That was the night when every synagogue in Germany was torched, windows of the few remaining Jewish stores were smashed, and every adult male Jew was arrested. Some were imprisoned in local jails, as was the case with Uncle Justin, and some were taken to concentration camps. There was a knock on the door of the apartment, and a couple of men in Nazi uniform asked for Uncle Justin and told him to come with them. I don't remember if they allowed him to pack anything. My father, who was living and working in Cham, near Regensburg, was sent to Dachau, the infamous camp near Munich, on November 12th. Of course, I didn't know where he was taken to until he told me after his release. He was living alone then without family and was not allowed to write, so I also have no idea how I found out that he had been arrested. Those arrested at that time were kept imprisoned for three weeks to two months and then released. I remember writing to the Geheime Staats Polizei (GESTAPO—the Secret Police) in Regensburg, telling them that my father should be released as he was a wounded veteran of WWI, and holder of an Iron Cross 2nd Class. I don't know if this helped. He was released on the 26th of November. (This date came from a letter I received from the International Tracing Service, a part of the International Red Cross. I had written them in 1986 to inquire if they had any information on the fate of my father. This was the only information they could find at that time.)

It should be noted that concentration camps in 1938 were—as the name suggests—large prisons, not extermination camps. There were only three or four in Germany at that time. Dachau, Buchenwald, and Sachsenhausen come to mind. Inmates were treated harshly, but not purposefully killed except through diseases. The infamous mass death camps—Auschwitz, Treblinka, Bergen-Belsen, etc.—had not been built yet. They were mostly in Poland, which was not to be occupied by the Germans for another ten months. The gas chambers in those places were part of Hitler's "Final Solution," which wasn't put into effect until 1941.

There was much despair and of course it was especially difficult for the women and children with all male adults incarcerated. And since all teachers were male and therefore incarcerated, there could be no school. The strain was too much for some. My teacher (Herr David), after his release, turned on the gas jets in his apartment, killing himself, his wife, and two young children. We heard of other similar tragedies.

Up until Kristallnacht, Jews who were WWI veterans could work or maintain their business (although they would have gotten very little business from non-Jews). But from then on, things deteriorated rapidly. Much property belonging to the Jewish community as a whole was confiscated, all businesses were closed, and Jews could not earn a living anymore except in dealing with other Jews. Also, those lucky enough to be able to emigrate were very limited in what they could take with them—not much beyond furniture and clothes, no gold, silver, cash, or other valuables.

In mid-February 1939, I turned thirteen and became Bar Mitzvah, a big celebration even in those troubled times. The religious services took place in the gymnasium of the school, which is where all services were conducted after the synagogue was burned down. The whole Jewish community would turn out, and no doubt as many of my relatives as could travel came to Stuttgart for that occasion.

Shortly after that event, Uncle Justin and family had to move from their large apartment to a small one-bedroom basement apartment. There was no longer any room for me, and I went to an orphanage in nearby Esslingen (thirty minutes or so by suburban train). My memories of life in Esslingen are rather dim. The orphanage was a large mansion on a hilltop at the edge of town surrounded by several acres of fields and fruit orchards. There were probably twenty-five to forty boys and a smaller number of girls in residence. We slept in dorms. The orphanage was strictly kosher and orthodox. Everybody went to the synagogue (chapel) three times daily for the appropriate services. School took place in the building and the teachers in the multiclass classrooms also lived in [it]. We had to work in the fields and orchards part-time, raising vegetables and fruit. I presume this was necessary for survival due to rationing rather than due to a shortage of funds. There was a small Jewish community in Esslingen, around 100, but I do not recall having any contact with them. I imagine the orphanage, like all Jewish charitable institutions, was well endowed by funds that emigrants had to leave behind. Those of us who had relatives nearby were given passes on Sunday to visit them. For me, it was just a short commuter train trip to Stuttgart. I am sure my father visited me there several times, a four- to five-hour or even longer trip for him.

Thanks to a sister of Tante Frieda living in England, Tante Frieda, Uncle Justin, and their son Kurt managed to immigrate to England in the Summer of 1939. Their belongings (except what they carried with them) were still sitting in a big crate on the docks of Amsterdam waiting for shipping to England when WWII broke out, September 1, 1939. They never saw their things again.

In October of 1939, the orphanage was confiscated by the government. I was sent to another orphanage in Stettin. This is just about as far from Stuttgart as one can get and still stay in Germany at that time. It is a large seaport on the Baltic, now part of Poland (now spelled Szczecin). The orphanage there consisted of a couple of floors in what must have been a Jewish-owned apartment building. I remember very little about life there. It was probably a very small institution, maybe ten boys and six girls. We went to school in another part of town, together with the other Jewish kids in Stettin. Stettin had a Jewish population of 2,700 in 1933—good sized. Incidentally, I still have the report card (actually a letter) from the headmaster of the school, relating how good a student I was and how they will miss me. That letter is in the safe deposit box. The letter, dated 15 December 1939, says that I started school there October 27, 1939; therefore, I was in Stettin for less than two months. The only other thing I remember about Stettin was that we had to be careful going back and forth to school to avoid attacks by Hitler Youth kids. We took backstreets and alleys and did not go in a group for fear of drawing attention. We could not defend ourselves. I remember getting shot at with a BB gun or slingshot several times. We also had to be very careful not to have any light leaking from the windows at night, since the city was blacked out due to the war.

Fortunately, Stettin was the home of Tante Selma Fischer, my mother's second oldest sister, and her two daughters, my cousins Ellen and Ilse. So I had some family I could relate to, since it was too far for my father to visit me. You [the author's son and daughter, for whom this was written] met both Ellen in Haifa and Ilse in Kfar Schmar Jahu in 1972. Ellen died a few years ago, but we did revisit Ilse on our last trip to Israel (October 1991).

It was while I was in Stettin that I got the notice that my visa to the U.S. came through.

FROM "A CHILD MUST BE SHELTERED"

By Henny Wenkart [1998]

Whatever disagreements there may have been between my parents and however different were their personalities, on this one thing they were firmly united: a child is to be sheltered. That is why I neither saw nor heard any horror during the fourteen months that I lived under the Nazis in Vienna—from the Anschluss in March 1938 until Mother's Day of the following year, when I left with a children's transport directly for the United States.

One reason that they could shield me was that we had moved when I was six from the Leopoldstadt, the Second District where the Jewish Community was concentrated, to the tonier Ninth—near the marzipan Votive Church, the fancy tourist hotels, and the University. Except on the Tenth of November (the date the Nazis call Kristallnacht), no actual atrocities of the kind that were going on in the ghetto itself took place in the streets of our neighborhood until the outbreak of the War.

My second protection was the firmness of their Rule of the Double Door: Any relative or friend or client who had been brutalized and came to tell of his experiences, or had a family member recently arrested and came for advice or help, was shown directly into the dining room.

This room had at one time been a doctor's office; it had a pair of double doors, the inner one padded. Obviously, in normal times such an arrangement provided the greatest possible nest for hiding away with cousins and telling cousin secrets. Now it closed me off from what I did not really want to hear, and what my parents were determined I should not hear. If any visitor began to speak before both doors were firmly shut, Daddy's finger would go to his lips and his eyes would flash a warning.

"The child!" I heard him murmur more than once.

Shipmates Henny Wenkart (left) and Helga
Weiss Milberg (right) at the first reunion of
"Brith Sholom children" in 1995 sponsored by
the Brith Sholom Lodge of Philadelphia.
Archives of One Thousand Children®, Inc.

And Daddy had given me his solemn word that we would be all right.

We had to go out of doors for that solemn talk, to the park in front of the Votive Church, away from buildings and away from any thick shrubbery. We two stood beside the sandbox where I played most days after school and Daddy looked at me very seriously; his eyes, which were like mine in that they changed color with his mood, were a bright, intense blue.

"I want to explain to you what has happened. The Nazis have taken over the country."

I knew that!

"We shall leave Vienna as soon as we can. Before you were up, at 5:30 this morning, I went to the American consulate and was able to get us a very low number."

Five thirty in the morning! Nobody is awake at 5:30 in the morning, only milk-wagon drivers!

"As soon as we can get an affidavit we'll go to America. We are also applying for a visa to Palestine, but the British aren't letting many Jews in there, as you know. But you must not worry. I give you my word of honor that we shall be all right."

The previous night, Chancellor Schuschnigg had gone on the air with his farewell address. The German army was on our borders. He had telephoned Rome, Paris, London, even Washington in vain for help. A German escort stood outside the studio doors that minute ready to take him away. He was NOT calling out the guard in what must be a vain sacrifice of life to try to stop them, or to try to stop Hitler's divisions. No Austrian blood would be shed.

"God save Austria," he said. With tears streaming down my face, I stood at attention on my bed while they played the Anthem: "Be eternally blessed, soft earth of my home. . . . Adorned in green of pine and gold of honor . . . Fatherland, glorious in beauty! . . . May God be ever with you, my Austria."

The next morning, I awoke to a capital city festooned in swastikas and enormous posters of the face of Hitler.

The yellow apartment building across the street, locale of my fantasies by day and object of my clandestine observations in the night-time—my property, therefore—that yellow apartment building was covered in long red streamers from the green patina copulas and gables on the roof (which composed the "village" of the stories I told to myself on rainy afternoons) to the windows of the second floor, where lived that family who forgot to pull down their blinds at night and had those delicious fights through all the rooms. In the middle of each red streamer that hung there now, there was a white circle with a black swastika.

The policeman on the corner already wore a red armband with a white-circled black swastika. Just about everybody on the street—men, women, and the smallest children—wore a little buttonhole pin of Hitler's face. Where did they get them, so early in the morning? The shops were barely open! And how could shops have stocked them, when the day before we were still Austria? That morning soured me on pins and armbands for the rest of my life.

Deliberately, my parents began to pull apart the fabric of our orderly years. Like the white linen garments of the High Priest at the conclusion of Yom Kippur, some of the pieces were folded and put away forever.

First to go was Daddy's fancy law office overlooking the Danube Canal, in a baroque-style office building on the Franz Josef's Quai called the Quai Palace. My parents judged it "too conspicuous." He moved his practice home.

I loved that office. I used to play hooky there from nursery school. I went shopping with my mother in the mornings, and in the afternoons we rendezvoused with her friends and their children in the beautiful parks of Vienna. Sometimes we stopped in at the office and I was allowed to type. Daddy always read out to me what I had written; then he sputtered so much over the multiple repetitions of fricative consonants that he turned bright red with suppressed laughter.

Now the office was gone, and Daddy's desk stood at home in a window of the dining room. That was a pity, but of course it was also true that he was home a lot more. And there was a very exciting coming and going of interesting clients.

After the matter of the office, the next question to be settled was that of the practice itself. Jews were to be disbarred *instanter* [at once] unless they could prove that they had seen front-line action for Austria, in which case they were to have six months' grace.

Daddy had served on the Lebanon with Prince Schwarzenberg; on many a night watch they had listened to the jackals together under unfamiliar stars, sharing young men's reminiscences and projects and an occasional game of chess. That was twenty years back, but Daddy was certain that the Prince would not have forgotten.

"Your Royal Highness will remember me," he wrote to him. "We often talked together in Malaga on the Lebanon in the year 1918. Now, in order to remain in practice for another six months, I need proof that I served at the front."

The Prince replied at once, on Royal letter paper done up with several impressive seals.

"I remember you very well, Wenkart. We stood watch together at the front and I certify that you were a brave soldier for Austria. I wish you well, whatever you decide to do."

"Decide!" Every visitor was treated to the envelope, the seals, the short text and the enormous signature. Together we laughed until we cried over that "decide." What choices did a Jew have, to decide among?

So Daddy got his six months' extension. Still, that did not mean that once I was ten I could go to court and see him try a case, as I had always been promised. Although I would turn ten before the six months were up.

All of my life, it seemed to me, I had been planning for that walk with him up the tree-lined Ring Boulevard, up the curving marble ramp of the Palace of Justice, past the blindfolded goddess holding up her enormous scales . . . and then to sit in a visitors' bench, very quietly, and hear him argue, with everyone quietly listening, the judge attentively weighing my father's arguments.

Such fascinating cases, about a kind of people I had never met. I knew a few fragments from half-overheard conversations. There was the landlord's complaint against a tenant who was using too much water at the cellar washtubs. This tenant had a small rubber ball manufacturing facility up in his apartment.

"And so the judge asked, 'What does he do in the cellar with all that water?'"

At this point, trying to finish his story, Daddy would always turn dark red and shake with silent laughter. He would stop to catch his breath and sputter out the finale.

"Then he said . . . he said, 'He washes his balls, Your Honor.'"

After this everyone would crack up but me. I didn't understand because, of course, I had never been to court. But once I was ten I would go, and then I would understand.

There was a sad case, too, a case that Daddy had lost. A truck driver had suffered a head injury due to a malfunction of company equipment. He asserted that as a result of his injury he was subject to irrational rages and unable to work, and claimed an award of damages, the cost of medical care, and a living for his family. Daddy couldn't get an award for such "invisible" damages. It was not a customary claim and the judge was unwilling to break new ground. A year later, the driver killed his family and himself.

I would never go to court with Daddy now. It would be "too conspicuous." Anyway, they explained to me, he wouldn't be trying cases any longer. He would only try to collect what bills he dared, from Jewish clients and from the few gentile clients he felt certain he could trust—just enough to buy our steamship tickets and to send out some of our things.

It turned out that we had no cash. The apartment building we had owned had come under forced sale, and even the token payment from that sale was forfeit to the government. So was the token payment for our heavy inlaid furniture, which we started selling off because we were given to understand that rooms in America were much smaller— and none of the ceilings twelve feet high, the height for which this furniture was designed.

Once our affidavit came through and our number came up at the American consulate, we'd have to have our steamship tickets in hand or we would be passed over. But most of the clients would no longer pay Daddy what they owed him, even in installments, because according to the Nazi laws no money owed to a Jew need be paid.

Many new clients came just to have forms filled out which they needed to submit in order to leave the country. Either the forms were too complicated, or they didn't trust themselves to do it exactly right.

But Daddy usually did not charge these people any fee; and there were fights about that.

"They'll all get out and we'll die here!" I once heard Mother screaming, right through the padded double doors. "We'll never get out, we'll die here!"

"Shh, Darling. Shh . . . shh. . . . How can they pay? They have no money either."

Both Mother and Daddy had emigrated before, each as a child, from Galicia when that was still part of the Austro-Hungarian Empire. The move to Vienna amounted to a transfer to the capital city of one's own country. But as they were passed along to me, their memories of these moves were so different that I never put the same word to them. One was a search for greater economic opportunity, the other a flight in wartime.

Daddy was born in Zaleszczicki on the Dnieper River, a modest place with two substantial estates set on opposite hilltops; one was the seat of the local Polish nobleman, the other the house of Daddy's maternal grandfather, the miller Salmon Horowitz. Three great poplar trees marked the brow of the hill; flowing down the hillside were the miller's orchards. Early in the morning, before the early morning prayer, they said, great-grandfather Horowitz would sneak down through his own orchard to leave sacks of flour on the doorsteps of the poor. His wife's name was Malkah, which means "Queen," like the Queen Sabbath who comes to our homes every Friday evening when we light the candles.

"I come of a long-lived family," Daddy used to say. Malkah's father had lived to see not only great-grandchildren, but great-great-grandchildren, and that is a straight ticket to Paradise. Malkah was in her eighties when I was little. I never saw her, but twice her daughter, my Grandmother Chajcie, went back to visit her in the summer, as I remember.

Grandmother Chajcie had been the miller's petted only child. In her late teens, she married the Talmud scholar Solomon Wenkart, giving birth to Daddy when she was twenty. Simultaneously, her mother, Malkah, mysteriously became fruitful again and bore her daughter Gusta, and later her son Shmaye. When Daddy was small, tenants inhabited the great house itself, while the family lived in a wing. There was not much of a living to be made there; when Daddy was four and his brother Simon two years old, their father went to Vienna to seek a livelihood. He came back for them two years later. That was a great adventure for the little boys, involving their first sight of—and ride in—a great iron railroad train, destination Vienna. In 1898, the Imperial

Capital was full of a beauty and glorious vitality which easily ravished especially my father, who fell in love with the ancient crooked streets, the expansive gardens, plazas, and palaces, and especially with the wooded foothills and vineyards that are the Vienna Woods.

Two years later, baby Ignaz was born (in the apartment, with his brothers listening at the door), and as soon as he could walk properly, Daddy hiked with him to the top of the Kahlenberg or the Kobenzl to gaze upon the circle of the city's spires and the broad, grey-green Danube. One time, the little lad's legs gave out and they had no street-car fare, and there was an anxious police search for them half the night.

When I was small, Daddy and I would go out on Sunday mornings, always on a different path, up a different hill or mountain. We walked in silence on the springy moss, listening to the birds. If we had to say something, it was in a still, brief whisper.

Mother was born in the Hasidic community of Otynia, near the Romanian border. Her grandfather was sort of a business manager for the Otynia Rebbe. Her parents, Jacob and Heni Stein, were first cousins; my mother was Ruchele, the youngest of two sons and two daughters. The family lived above and behind their dry goods store, a lively gathering place of the town. Hasidim from the countryside and from far distant towns would come to spend the Sabbath and the Holy Days with the Rebbe, and on festival evenings they danced and sang in the street far into the night. Getting up in the morning to find their breakfast in the kitchen, Mother and her siblings must tiptoe over members of the congregation who lay bundled in their coats and hats under the table and by the stove. Before Passover and before the High Holy Days, the stockrooms of the store would expand with new finery for the town until stock filled the rooms of her brothers Adolf and Leo and her sister Marie. Mother was Grandmother Heni's pet and often shared her bed.

The children would consumer test all the toys in the store. They got gifts of chocolate from the visiting Hasidim. Here's what you did to keep your chocolate to yourself: you licked it all over and put it on your dresser. But sometimes a brother or sister would take it anyway, and re-lick it to establish a claim.

My mother was so surrounded by people all through her youth that she needed them when she grew up; she seemed to prefer even the company of boring or unpleasant people to no company at all.

Early in the War, when Mother was eleven, the Rebbe heard that the Cossacks were moving toward Otynia. This must have been in 1915. He decided to move the community out of harm's way, to the Capital. They packed what they could into covered wagons, closed up their houses and stores, and hoping for the best, set off for Vienna. It was a slow, tedious procession. Grandfather Stein, always a lively, fun-loving man, got so bored walking beside his family's wagon that he finally declared that he must protect the store and turned back all alone, ignoring the entreaties of his wife. In Otynia he ran into the marauding Cossacks, who brutalized him, and [he] spent the rest of the War in a Russian prison camp. His family never heard from him until 1918. Then he went to Vienna, inquired for the Rebbe, and found his family living in a single room in the midst of the community. The teenage boys were doing odd jobs and the girls were in school, refugees, ridiculed for their strange clothes and their Yiddish accents.

Marie took it all lightly, as she took everything. She learned to dance and play popular songs on the piano; when she had any money, she enjoyed chatting and people watching in the cafés.

Mother was much more hedged about. She did meet boys, of course, because her brothers brought all their friends home, but there was no question of going out with any of them. Her brother Leo squired her about and showed her the city. Then every night he would gather up everyone's spare clothing and arrange it into beds on the floor. This job would occupy his mind during the day as well. In the midst of a conversation, he might break off to say, "If I fold the sleeves of your coat over each other and stick my spare shirt underneath, that would make a little pillow for your head."

It was Leo who had introduced my parents to each other. It was Leo whom the Nazis would scoop up into the concentration camp at Dachau and then Buchenwald, where he died.

The tenth of November 1938 began very early. When the maid brought coffee and the mail and the morning papers to my parents' door, I was dressed for school. I went in with her and drew their drapes, opened the heavy wooden shutters, and settled on the sofa at the foot of their beds.

First, Daddy got up to brush his teeth. Then he slipped back into bed and opened the day's report from Postal Checking, to discover whether any client had deposited money to his account. Next, he turned to his coffee and roll. And then he opened the newspaper.

"My God. A Jew has killed a German consular official in Paris."

In my whole life, I never saw my mother wake up so fast.

"Get dressed," she said instantly. "I'll call the Vandors. They are Hungarian citizens. I think they'll let you hide at their place."

Go away from us and hide? Daddy generally hid in a hall closet when the doorbell rang—and it was humiliating to see him do that— but at least he was home where we could see that he was perfectly all right. To hide far away, in another District of the city?

"What will happen? Do I go to school?"

"Don't go anywhere. Help your mother, play with the baby, stay indoors. This man is clearly insane to endanger the rest of us this way. He may not be a Jew, or there may not even have been a murder, but one thing is sure—they'll use this as a pretext. Thousands of Jews will die in reprisal, whether it happened or not."

"But this is supposed to be a safe neighborhood. Isn't it better if you just stay here? Is it smart for you to go out on the street?"

"Nothing will happen to me in the street. They never spot me as a Jew. You'll be all right here. I'll call you. Help your mother."

I watched him head for the front door of the apartment, down the long hallway where two enormous wardrobes crammed with file folders had moved in when he brought the practice home.

Just then the doorbell rang.

Daddy opened it himself. I heard his voice and another voice in the entrance hall, and then he came back into the hallway. Peering around the pink curtain in a glass panel of the bedroom door, I realized for the first time in my life that Daddy was not a tall man. His fair head, calm and erect, was less than shoulder high to the black SS uniform beside him. I cringed to see him look up so high to another man; but his voice was steady and his movements firm and deliberate.

He threw open both doors of each wardrobe to reveal the shelves upon shelves of his life's work.

"I give you my word of honor that I have no weapons. I shall show you. We can begin here."

"No, no, Herr Doktor. That will not be necessary. Of course I accept the word of a fellow University man. I'll be leaving now. Hiel Hitler."

He turned on his heel and left without putting Daddy into the usual quandary—how to return his greeting. (A Jew was not permitted to say "Hiel Hitler," but at the same time it was an illegal act for anyone to give a different greeting in response to it.)

In my hiding place, I crumpled up shaking and crying quietly. When I could dry my eyes, Daddy had relocked the wardrobes and left.

The phone calls started very soon after that. In the same way that Daddy was going to hide with the Vandors, female relatives from the ghetto were coming out to hide with us. Mixed with these calls were extortion calls. It seemed that everyone who had ever lost a case to Daddy wanted money, and wanted it that very day.

We held our breath until Daddy himself called—only an hour later, but a very long hour.

He gave orders for money to be withdrawn and then taken by the babysitter to one extortionist, by the secretary to another, by the cook to a third.

He was calling from a phone booth. The Vandors were generous with the shelter of their home; but they were sure that Hungarian or not, their phone was bugged. Hiding a Jew was a crime and what little immunity they had did not extend to being caught committing crimes.

Mother hung up before I could ask to speak to him.

When he returned from one of his trips to the public phone, Daddy found that all Jews in the building, except the Vandors with their Hungarian papers, had been arrested. He had been saved precisely because he was on the street at the time!

The guests arrived a couple of hours before the Brownshirts. Grandmother Wenkart was already living with us. Grandpa Stein's third wife, referred to by him as "the old devil" and known to us as "the stepmother," came with her daughter Rosa. Then Aunt Marie, my mother's sister, chuckling gaily over a close call she had had on her way over. She had been made to scrub the sidewalk with a toothbrush for two hours, but then released.

I felt that Daddy was all right; I had a day off from school, and all sorts of exciting visitors to be given midmorning coffee and sandwiches made a nice change. My baby sister was being her one-and-a-half-year-old cutest. It seemed a jolly, cheerful sort of female morning.

When the building superintendent came to warn us that the Brownshirts were downstairs evicting all Jewish tenants and sealing off their apartments, my immediate reaction was one of elation; for once I would get to participate in what was going on all around us. Alertness was required now, and perhaps even a degree of heroism.

My mother began by getting back into her pajamas and a dressing gown and tying a clean, folded diaper about her throat. In this attire she received the Brownshirts when they appeared at our door. They remained near the entrance to the hallway, just where the SS had stood earlier in the day—a couple of rather good-natured young locals just doing their job.

My sister, who had been walking for quite some time, took it into her head to get down on all fours. Then she did a thing she had never done before: she ran up to them on all fours, looked up with her face at about the height of their ankles, and barked.

She went, "Bow! Bow Wow!"

All five women froze where they were, but the young men only laughed.

Then they got down to business. "Where is your husband?"

"Oh, I wish I knew that," my mother fussed. "I wish I could tell you that. He left early this morning and promised to call and we haven't heard from him. I'm sure he's been arrested."

"He hasn't been arrested," one of them said.

He had no way of knowing that, with the thousands of arrests going on in the streets. Mother knew he was bluffing.

"I wish I could be sure of that. Do you know that for sure?"

"If he said he'd call you, he'll call you. And we want to talk to him when he does. Meantime you pack a few things; you're moving."

"But I am unable to leave the apartment. I am not well. I have a severe throat infection."

"Start packing. You are moving. Where does he keep his documents?"

Now this was something I did know about. Often they would come and search a place, and leave a Communist Party membership card or other incriminating paper behind. When they returned for a second search they would "find" this evidence, and the next thing was a concentration camp.

They went through the double doors into the dining room. I sort of went in with them.

"I'll show you the desk."

I climbed on a chair to switch on the big silk lamp over the dining room table. Then I circled the room, switching on every wall sconce and watching everything on the desk that the men looked at, every drawer they opened. I didn't see them put anything in, so perhaps they really were only searching. And perhaps, I told myself, they would have left something if I'd not been watching, and in any case I could report to Daddy what they had touched.

Meantime, Mother was "packing." Grandmother had got out her enormous suitcase, and Mother asked her for some room in that.

"I'm sorry, I need all this space for my own things."

That was just the reply Mother wanted. Down into the cellar she went, diaper around her throat, to get some suitcases out of storage. Then up into the attic five flights up, for boxes. All the time she was carrying several sheets done up in pink tissue from one wardrobe to another, putting them in, getting out something else.

Bewildered by all this purposeful activity, the two men kept saying, "Hurry. Hurry up. We have a lot of work to do upstairs."

When Mother told the story afterwards she always giggled at this point. "They had a lot of work to do! They had a lot of people to throw out of their homes! I guess I saved everybody on the floors above us."

She was in the cellar when Daddy called again, and I picked up the phone before the men could get to it.

It was important for them not to know it was Daddy calling. So, although it was disrespectful, I addressed him by his first name.

"Hello, Herman. I don't know where my Dad is, I'm sorry. There are two gentlemen here waiting for him, too, and we can't find him."

I hung up quickly.

"Where is he?" asked one of the Brownshirts "Who? That was a friend of the family."

He wasn't having any. How did he know it was Daddy? I didn't realize then that in some "advanced, modern" families, children addressed their parents by their given names. Apparently the Brownshirts knew it, and thought that I was such a child.

"Where is your father?"

I looked pained and confused, and they realized that I really couldn't tell them where Daddy was, I suppose—above all, they had the GI's constitutional laziness when it came to going above and beyond what they could reasonably be expected to accomplish. They left me alone.

The next thing I decided I had to do was to save my Torah scroll. I had a very small Torah, the complete five books of Moses in miniature—printed, of course, not scribed by hand on parchment like a kosher Torah. It was made with ivory handles and had a green everyday dress, and a red silk dress for Sabbaths and Holy Days. It was kept in a gold paper box. I was sure that for my Torah there would be room in Grandmother's suitcase. Grandmother was a very firm and observant Jew.

Mother came rushing in from the cellar, and stopped dead in her tracks when she saw me come out of the dining room holding the Torah aloft—I had opened the gold paper box and dressed the Torah in its best, to make it a more solemn act. Grandmother received it from me solemnly.

"Put that away! Close the box!" Mother hissed.

But the Brownshirts didn't care, or maybe really didn't know what a Torah was, or that *this* was a Torah.

"Are you almost done?" they said to Mother. "Hurry, hurry! We have work to do!"

There was a diversion while Mother went to the wall safe behind one of the great bedroom wardrobes. I tried to keep the stepmother from seeing where the safe was, and she was very happy to take me out of the room on a pretext of seeing my toys. It seems she was trying to keep the location of the wall safe from me, too. Mother tucked her jewelry in her douche bag and packed it.

She kept this sort of thing up until the janitor came to tell the Brownshirts he had heard on the radio that the *Aktion* was over. They were directed to return to headquarters. They phoned in, found it was true, and left.

The tenants downstairs from us never entered their sealed apartments again. But we and those upstairs of us were saved from this fate by Mommy.

[A continuation of Wenkart's narrative is found at the end of chapter 3.]

Chapter 3

PATHS OF ESCAPE

*O*nce *those Jewish parents in threatened communities made the decision to send their children to America, they faced many hurdles: bureaucratic, logistic, and even physical. There were many delays in the relocation process, and sometimes children spent years in transit from their original homes to their eventual foster homes in the United States. Interim relocations provided temporary havens that were in turn threatened. Finances, quotas, timetables, shifting political winds, and organizational problems directly or indirectly influenced the confidence, safety, and psychological well-being of the children, as well as their caregivers. For some, entering on the path of escape predated any decision that would enable children to reach the United States unaccompanied by their parents. Many families relocated several times to escape the growing Nazi stranglehold on the European continent, attempting to avoid Nazi clutches and ride out what they hoped was a temporary madness.*

Sometimes the children alone were relocated elsewhere in Europe in advance of arrangements that could bring them to safety in America. Sometimes parents made timely decisions and everything fell into place for speedy departures toward a new life. In the later period, a typical path would run through France and Spain to the port of Lisbon. Even later, when this path was no longer available, children escaped by first traveling overland through Russia, Manchuria, Korea, and Japan and then by ship to the West Coast of the United States. Conditions were often uncomfortable, provisions sometimes meager. Always, there was a mixed sense of loss, fear, and adventure, too.

The memories of Ruth Safrin Finkelstein, Lea Wasserman Schwarz, Camilla Tidor Maas, Richard Schifter, and Henny Wenkart provide different contexts, arcs, and facets of the master escape narrative, though each variant sooner or later requires the good fortune of accepted, official paperwork and a number that fits within an annual quota.

The story of Michel Margosis is unusual in its vivid presentation of the many way stations that eventually led to the escape voyage.

As Professor Baumel's introduction makes clear, the story of the rescue effort is one of separated families and resettled children on the one hand, and of the rescuers and rescue organizations on the other. Morris C. Troper's letter to Eleanor Roosevelt reminds us that a handful of influential Americans did lend their support to this rescue effort, as does the letter from Albert Einstein to Eduard M. M. Warburg.

The German-Jewish Children's Aid (GJCA), which initiated the rescue of the One Thousand Children, was supported primarily through fundraising by local chapters of the National Council of Jewish Women. Later, when the GJCA became the European-Jewish Children's Aid, other Jewish organizations such as the American Jewish Joint Distribution Committee and the Hebrew Immigrant Aid Society provided additional support. After about 1939, non-Jewish groups began in earnest to raise money for the rescue of unaccompanied Jewish children.

On September 10, 1941, a multi-denominational gathering of notable and philanthropic New Yorkers and Americans dined on paupiettes of sole Nantua (fish fillets rolled into cylinders with a white sauce of whipping cream and shrimp butter) with Maine lobster and breast of native guinea hen with juniper berries at the Waldorf Astoria. On the dais were Eddie Cantor, Marshal Field, Archibald MacLeish, Paul Warburg, Stanley Isaacs, Eric Biddle, Clarence Pickett, Morris C. Troper, and Fiorello LaGuardia. The audience included Dr. Stephen Wise, Joseph Revson, David Sulzberger, the Warburg family, Newbold Morris, Lotte Marcuse, Winthrop Aldrich, Fred Hirshhorn, Mrs. Frank Furstenberg, John Wharton, Solomon Lowenstein, and several hundred more Who's Who in America *entries. The event was a fundraising dinner sponsored by the United States Committee for the Care of European Children in order to raise badly needed funds for the rescue of children desperately caught in the crosshairs of the Nazi's Final Solution.*

Without such support—without the determination and generous spirit of selfless caregivers, the organizations they served, and the donors who financed these delicate operations of relocation—the fate of the One Thousand Children would be difficult, perhaps horrible, to imagine. The rescue effort depended on a large network of rescuers and cooperating rescue organizations, in Europe, on shipboard, and in the United States. W. Howard Wriggins represents the many who worked tirelessly at the European end of the rescue enterprise.

FROM "RECALLED TO LIFE"

By Ruth Safrin Finkelstein [1946]

The French did all they could to make us feel more at home. At almost every station the Red Cross welcomed us with warm milk for the children. The civilians eagerly complied with bids to bring water. It is the little, thoughtful kindness in time of need that gives one the assurance that he is not left alone with his troubles.

The night was spent restfully though not comfortably. Late morning of the next day saw us at our destination in southern France. Back into the truck once more—to Camp de Gurs. After about an hour's ride we watched the barracks and wire mesh fences fly past us. The men were soon left behind while the women and young boys under fourteen arrived at a different ilot ["little island," meaning station, district, or section]. With heavy hearts we passed the double, strong fence.

French girls, I do not know who they were, led, us in groups to the different barracks. We passed the ilot headquarters at our left, leaving

Internment camp, Gurs, France. Established in 1939. Controlled by the Vichy government from 1940 to 1942. The Germans ran the camp from 1942 to 1944 during which time inmates were deported to extermination camps in Poland. It is here that a number of the parents of OTC children requested permission to see their children who were being sent to the United States. The camp commander granted them ten minutes. Courtesy of Jack Lewin. Archives of the U.S. Holocaust Museum and Memorial.

the open-door kitchen, consisting of six iron containers with a wire compartment at the bottom of each, at our right.

Barrack 12, Ilot L became our new home. Four bare walls welcomed us. Children were sent to look for stones for the elders to sit on. Our baggage we had left at the station.

The wooden beams at about one yard's distance from each other served to hold up the sloping sides of the barrack. Thus the barrack was divided into sixty-six even spaces wide enough to permit one straw mattress. From the sixty-six persons in our barrack, only about twenty-five elderly women slept on a mattress the first night. The rest of us slept on the wooden floor. Hot so-called coffee was served later in the evening with the apology for lack of preparation since we were to have gone to a different camp that was flooded at the time. I was sooo sorry for not having been awakened when the hot coffee came.

If we could have lived on air and scenery, it was there for the wanting. The snow-capped mountain peaks of the Pyrenees glittered in the morning sun and were bathed in fire at sundown. Such majesty and beauty of nature can never be surpassed.

Our diet consisted of a piece of bread making about six slices, some so-called coffee in the morning, a thin soup for lunch, and one for supper. It may be onion soup for lunch, a concoction of chestnuts and chestnut shells at night. Once in a while there was dishwater with hard sissy peas. Tompinambour (hope I spelled it correctly) became the famous camp specialty. Tompinambour, in appearance like a potato, is originally sty feed. It was cooked in water and a little meat perhaps, and tasted like very sweet frozen potatoes. Hungry as we were, we could not eat much of it. The greater part went to the rats in the shallow ditch running around each barrack. Jelly, apples, and biscuits, as well as muddy-looking cakes of what was supposed to be soap could be bought from the canteen.

Our second day at camp was Friday. As usual, Mother lighted the Sabbath candles at sundown. Wolf [Siegie], my older brother, began to chant the Sabbath services. The barrack filled suddenly to capacity and overflowed at each of the two entrances. Wolf's clear, youthful voice set every one of my heartstrings vibrating.

Three days later, Mother became very ill, so ill that she had to be removed to the hospital barrack. "Pneumonia," I heard the doctor say. There was no medicine, no medical equipment. Nine days later, we five children were left all alone in this big, wide world.

For me, the whole world had gone under. Fifteen funerals were held the following day, a number which was to increase daily. Mother had expressed the longing for a roll with butter several days before the crisis came. Wolf, as a minor, left the camp to hunt for rolls and butter. For miles and miles around the concentration camp he trudged in vain until with some persuasion he was able to buy two jelly buns. But it was too late.

One by one, except Fanny, we followed my little sister Dora to the new hospital barrack. After that, "to be or not to be well" was the question. Life must go on, and Time, the great healer, tried his best.

Aunt Rosa, who had been with us all this time, took the place of Mother. The chef of our ilot had heard of our misfortune. We were given several articles of clothing and from now on were allowed to eat in the kitchen. She would sometimes take us for a walk and teach us French.

With the approach of winter, conditions grew worse. Coal and wood were scarce although there was only one stove in each barrack. Of blankets we had not many. Rain brought knee-deep mud. Dora spent most of the time in the hospital. Wolf became eligible for the men's ilot. Insect companionship became obvious. On the whole, elderly people suffered most. The children had an opportunity to take lessons in English and French in the children's barrack, where about twenty children also slept. The three and a half months we spent in the camp seemed eternal. Our happiest moments were those in which we received a package indirectly from America. Those days were holidays for us; like the ones when Wolf came "home" from the village with bread.

Life once more took on meaning for me as we five children among fifty other children waded through knee-deep snow through the village of Chabannes to the children's home, the Chateau de Chabannes. At a snail's pace the days of quarantine in bed passed. Our clothes had to be disinfected, our stomachs to be gotten used to food gradually, and our limbs to be given a chance to thaw out. No one minded sharing his bed with another since those who were to have gone to a different chateau were retained on account of the high snow.

We five—Wolf, fourteen; Fanny, twelve; Max, nine; Dora, six; and I, thirteen—were regarded as a little family. Wolf acted as the father, I as mother, Fanny as the governess, and Max and Dora as the children. And it almost was that way. Wolf would often spend an hour in consultation. With the money Aunt Rosa sent us from the camp, we bought groceries for packages. Very often [we] had to wait because we could not buy paper or string. We decided that one lump of sugar was enough for our coffee; the other lump we saved until enough sugar had accumulated to be sent away.

I always enjoyed school immensely. Learning French was a pleasure. My teacher enjoyed teaching me French as much as I enjoyed teaching Hebrew to Dora.

I took my onus seriously. I saw to it that the smaller ones, Max and Dora, were faithful to their religion, and that their clothes were always clean and mended. It did my heart good to watch Dora's suppressed ebullience gain full freedom. Food was not to be had in abundance; at times we hungrily left the dining room, but we did not complain. Many a pleasant evening was spent singing to the tunes of a piano.

Hopefully we looked toward America and we were not to be disappointed this time. It was on a Saturday, May 18, 1941, when the director of the Home called me into his office.

"Congratulations! You are leaving for America in two days, the twentieth of May; the five of you, Carla, and Margot."

Happy is not descriptive enough for our feelings, though I had my unuttered doubts, paradoxical as it may sound. Twice before, the day of departure had been postponed.

Sunday was a busy day from early morning till late at night. We were allowed to carry no more than two sets of complete wearing apparel and a blanket.

At last May 20th arrived. After having hardly touched our breakfast, we took leave in regular French fashion. Each one of the personnel, from the director and the doctor to the cook and the maids, received two kisses, one on each cheek.

Soon we had left Chabannes behind. In Limoge, we met the rest of the children's transport. How happy we were to recognize some of our old friends from Germany among them!

> Friend is a word so mellow and rich;
> Friend is a word so pleasant to each;
> Friend means frankness, friend means gold;
> Friend means someone in love to behold.
> A friend is a mirror presenting your image undimmed.
> A friend is a column with ornamentation untrimmed.
> A friend is your hand reaching out in your need;
> Like a cherub from heaven in word and in deed.
> Blessed is the man, who possesseth a friend.

One hundred and eleven children with a story of hunger, cold, and a little wooden sign that marked a mound of earth! No gay laughter rang from the hearts of these little men and women as they marched from the restaurant back to the train in Toulouse.

Ruth Safrin Finkelstein (top row right) and siblings upon arrival in America June 21, 1941. Archives of One Thousand Children®, Inc.

"I wouldn't care if I should die or if our ship would sink. Life is not worth living," a fifteen-year-old girl told me. At that time I agreed with her.

The transport was chaperoned by a doctor and his wife.

I shall never forget Aunt Rosa's face as I saw it in Pau for the last time. Her red eyes said one thing, "Try to help us when you get to America."

Marseille was our next stop. The boys remained in the city, whereas we girls stayed in a Spanish home for girls in the outskirts of the city. Of Marseille we saw nothing except the streets through which the trolley passed on our daily trip to the city. I had never seen the ocean. Knowing that Marseille is a seaport, I longed to see it. But I had to be patient for some time longer. Though I could not stop to gaze, it was the first time in my life that I ever saw a Negro.

The beautiful scenery did not coincide with the not-too-clean home, especially in regard to their otherwise tasty food. After supper about one hundred voices would rise in a French tune; we were thoroughly amused at their pronunciation.

Ten days flew by; all papers were ready and in order. Our last night in France was spent in the train that left early the next morning. In groups of four we had been divided. The leader of the group was responsible for the division of the food. My little group consisted of Fanny, Dora, and a tomboy of nine. And did she keep me busy.

Perhaps the only time in my life that I became oblivious of my identity and all else around me was while we traveled through the Pyrenees Mountains. The winding train suddenly became part of the snow-capped giants, which seemed to scoff down upon us as if to mock man's attempt to outsmart nature by digging tunnels and pulling themselves up the mountainside on a wire. The sun smiled brightly at the glittering snow, while narrow streams of water skipped gaily from rock to rock. Peace reigned over all.

Spain made quite a different impression upon me. For some reason, the first impression can only be modified but never be changed. After passing the customs house, we boarded probably the oldest train that ever rolled on rails. Straight-backed wooden benches with piles of rubble underneath, broken doors that had to be fastened with wire, and rattling windows contributed to our discomfort and made some of us throw up. Fortunately, we changed trains shortly afterwards. Even then, shabby-looking, filthy beggars, mainly women, jumped on and off the speeding train to collect pennies from the passengers. The scenery remained always the same, nothing but lowland, here and there interrupted by a small town or city.

At about ten o'clock the following morning, we reached Madrid. Chartered buses took us to a monastery in the heart of Madrid, where we spent the rest of the day. How kind everyone there was to us! And yet, I was frightened stiff for no obvious reason when the priest addressed Dora in Spanish, at the same time motioning to the sisters who were coming that way. Aside from that I was worried about Fanny, who was being treated for a high fever she had contracted from an infected scratch on her leg.

Lined up two by two we took a walk down the main street in the afternoon. A very wide street it was, outlined by the most modern buildings. I was all eyes and ears admiring the exotic beauty of the Spanish women and their daintily dressed babies. Open-mouthed, I gazed at the gorgeous costumes several women wore as they rested on the benches on the lane that divided the wide street. I still do not know why they were dressed differently in high collars, long, ruffled skirts, and dangling earrings.

We said goodbye from Madrid that very evening. At noon of the following day we crossed the Portuguese border. From now on we

Ruth Finkelstein (née Safrin), Siegie (Wolf), and Fanny (on left), and
Dora, Ruth, and Max (on right) with foster parents and siblings, 1941.
Archives of One Thousand Children®, Inc.

Ruth Safrin Finkelstein (first on left) with brothers and sisters, 2002. Archives
of One Thousand Children®, Inc.

traveled by bus. The picturesque beauty of Portugal fascinated me, the dense forests, the rich farmland, and the uniform houses of white and blue, and the farmers with their wide-brimmed hats similar to the sombrero.

For lunch we stopped at a hotel, while supper was served in the next city under the flashes of camera bulbs. Then fatigue got the upper hand in me. In Lisbon, I beheld the ocean for the first time from the window of the children's home. I must have watched the rolling waves for at least one hour, when my sister woke me up by telling me to go to bed.

The grandest treat that could have been given us was a big dinner served in the largest hotel in Lisbon. What a beautiful sight was the long table, decorated with roses laid out in the center. Even the silverware looked unfamiliar. In amazement, we watched the waiters balance big platters in artistic array. Even the individually packed rolls were handled with forks. Upon leaving, each girl was presented with a red rose. A moving picture at the Casino—we five did not see it because we were in mourning—and souvenirs topped off the day.

Reminiscing about Portugal brings back to me the taste of string beans cooked in oil and fried fish, which made up our daily supper. On the tenth of June we embarked and were ready for anything—mines, shooting, and sinking. . . .

FROM "ABOUT OUR FAMILY, FOR OUR FAMILY"

By Lea Wasserman Schwarz [1982]

For my daughters, Elaine and Susie

The first time my father came face to face with the reality that he would have to leave Germany was in 1937. At that time, they passed a law forbidding Jews to do any kind of work or hold any kind of job. He was immediately terminated by the large company he had worked for for many years, and now had no choice but to think of coming to America. At the same time, all Jews had to turn in all valuables such as gold, silver jewelry, expensive cameras, and binoculars to the Gestapo. My best girlfriend, Hilde Elkan, gave me her gold ring. Since we were not German, but Polish Jews, that law did not apply to us. However, we did have to turn in our radio because it was a shortwave receiver. It was almost new and our parents bought it especially to listen to foreign news stations, our only means of communications from countries outside of Germany. Each night after dinner our father turned on Radio Luxembourg very softly and listened with his ear to the speaker. Listening to foreign stations was, of course, forbidden.

In the 1930s, the radio was to our generation as much of a novelty as television was in the 1950s to the young people of America.

With his ability to earn a living coming to an end, our father finally registered with the American consulate and received a waiting (quota) number. Our number was 637 on the Polish quota. Our friends, the Brenner family, also registered and had the number 638.

Our parents wrote to Tante Gisa in America for an affidavit. She went to the Balsam branch of the family because they could afford to vouch for us. Anyone giving an affidavit had to be wealthy enough to support us if we could not find work so that we would not wind up on welfare. As I understand it, it was quite an ordeal for Tante Gisa, but she managed to get all the papers together and send them to us. My mother wrote her the following letter, which was given to me by Tante Gisa many years later:

> My dear sister-in-law,
> A thousand thanks for your golden heart. I cried for joy when your letter came. God will reward you as well as the other relatives. You have rescued four people from a critical situation. I hope, dear Gisa, that you will derive much joy from our family. My dear Simon is a fine and competent person. Also my two children are both competent and I myself do my part, so that we have a harmonious life together.
> Should fate allow us to unfold our energies in a free land, it would be our greatest happiness. I hope the reality will soon follow this letter. Until then, we hope for a happy reunion. With many sincere regards and kisses,
>
> yours,
> Etka Wassermann

There was no date on this letter, but I would assume it was written in April of 1937. We fully expected to immigrate to America by the end of that year. However, as we waited and waited, we found out that the American consulate only allowed about six people a year on the Polish quota. On the German quota, hundreds, if not thousands, of people got their immigration visas each year.

Some people, especially those who had a lot of money, waited in other European countries for their visas. Some people were able to get into Cuba, as did your dad [the author's husband, as this is written to her daughters] and his family.

While my father was not ready to pull up stakes and leave before 1937, he tried much earlier to prepare himself for earning a living in a country where he would not know the language. He learned how to make down quilts. He made a few that came out very well. When

Gisela and Rudy Piehler visited Germany in 1936, he sold them one. There was nothing my father couldn't do once he set his mind to it.

Early in 1938, my father went to Italy where Tante Fanny was living at the time, to see if it would be possible for our family to wait out the German situation. He took my sister, who was fourteen years old at the time. They had a wonderful time. I remember picking them up with my mother at the train station. They both looked wonderful. My sister looked so grown up with a new coat and hat that I hardly recognized her.

At the consulate, our number was coming close. There was nothing else for us to do but stick it out. Because my sister and I were born in Germany, our parents switched us to the German quota so that we could get out as soon as possible. It now meant that we would have to go with a children's transport rather than with our parents. We thought it surely would not be long one way or another before we could leave.

In the meantime, we tried to live as normal a life as possible. None of the public recreation areas were available to us Jews, so we took advantage of some empty lots on the Jewish cemetery and made it into a sports field. We had competitive sports there with Jewish organizations from other towns. [Your] Daddy tells me that he came a few times from Augsburg with his group. He was a plumber's apprentice there because it was important to learn a skill that could be used to earn a living until one learned the language in a new and strange country. Of course, at that time we did not know each other; even if we had, he was seventeen and I was eleven years old!

On October 28th, 1938, there was a knock on our door in the middle of the night. There were two Gestapo men outside; they told my father to get dressed and come with them. Our questions were unanswered and we were not told what this was all about. The following morning we found that both grandmothers, our uncle Chaim and Tante Annie, as well as all our relatives and friends had been picked up, except mothers with children. Through the grapevine we heard that Poland had issued a proclamation to the effect that all its citizens that were not within its borders by October 31st would lose their citizenship. The following evening at 9 o'clock they came for my mother, my sister, and me. They brought us to the "Palace of Justice" (where later the war crimes trials would be held) and put us in jail. There were about twenty people to our jail cell, with one toilet for all.

In the morning we were put on trucks, taken to the railroad station, loaded onto trains going to the Polish border. There were mothers with babies who were crying—there was no milk for them—and I don't remember getting any food except for a square of cheese the night in jail, probably towards morning. By the time we arrived at the border, it was after midnight on October 31st, and the Polish authorities did not allow the train to pass. The train stood for hours. When it finally began to move again it was going back in the direction from which it had come. After three days, we arrived back in Nuremberg and were allowed to go home. However, the first transport, the one our father was on, never returned. They were taken off the trains in "No Man's Land," an area between the German and Polish borders with the Poles shooting at them, not allowing them into their country, and the Germans behind them chasing them. There was nowhere to go but set up camp right there. It was near a town called Zbaszyn.

They were able to write to us from there, and life went on as well as possible. Barely one week after we returned from the Polish border, the morning of November 10th, 1938, the woman living downstairs from us rang our bell to tell us what had gone on during the night. She told us the synagogues were burning. Everything Jewish was destroyed. The rabbis as well as other Jewish men belonging to B'nai B'rith, were being made to crawl on all fours to eat the grass on the ground as animals would, and then they were dragged off to concentration camps.

We had only to look out the window to see other windows broken in Jewish homes. We went to our friends, the Brenner family. Their home was a shambles. The breakfront had been knocked over. All their beautiful crystal and china was in pieces on the floor. The mattresses and featherbeds had been slashed with bayonets; there was not a piece of furniture in their entire home that was left intact. Feathers were flying all over the place.

We thought it was a good thing that our father and the rest of the family were at the Polish border and did not have to go through this heartache. Since our apartment building was not touched that particular night, we fully expected them to finish the job the following night. After dark, there was a knock on our door. When we answered, it was our father's good friend and customer, Hans Spanner. He was not Jewish. He came to pick the three of us up and hide us in his house, as he too expected the Nazis to finish the houses they had not gotten to the first night. Of course, this put his own life in jeopardy. I have never forgotten that. We huddled on the floor of his car so that no one would see us. When we got to his house, we huddled in a dark corner of a dark room there. He told us that the Nazis were holding a meeting that night in the town square and he would go and let us know what was decided. He may have been a member of the S.A. (the brown-shirted storm troopers), as life was difficult for German men who did not belong to the party. We did not, however, see him in uniform when he returned from that meeting. I have often wondered if he had anything to do with the fact that our building was spared when Jewish apartments all around us were destroyed. At about 1 a.m. he came into our room and told us that the pogrom had been called off and he took us home.

After that, of course, any Jews who could leave Germany left as quickly as they possibly could, and we were hoping that we would be next.

As weeks turned to months, our mother, who had been a pillar of strength, sold everything she could turn into cash for us to live on. She sold the expensive Leica cameras and binoculars, which my parents bought to sell in the States so we would not be penniless. This, of course, would have had to be smuggled out, as no one was allowed to take out more than ten marks. Since we needed the money for what food we could buy, that was no longer an option. She also sold our good china, silver, and gold.

If I remember correctly, the Jewish Federation subsidized those who needed help. While at the Federation one day, our mother found a woman who was totally distraught. Her husband was also at the Polish border and she had a five-year-old son who was retarded. She had no money, no place to live. Our mother offered her our home to share and brought her home with her, thinking that our immigration number would be called any day. The last number called was only fifteen to twenty numbers below ours.

The child did not talk but screamed incessantly. Our mother's nerves were too frazzled to take it, but she did not have the heart to tell the woman to leave; so she decided to give up our apartment and rent a room for us at the Brenner family's apartment for the few more weeks we expected to need it.

In the meantime, another "Nuremberg" law was issued: Jews would henceforth occupy only one room per family, and if they had no place to share an apartment, they were assigned a room. The rooms they assigned were located in the red-light district of Nuremberg, facing the wall that surrounds the old city. Both Paula's and Martha's mothers were forced to live there. Martha's mother could no longer handle it and suffered a breakdown.

Mrs. Brenner had a sister in Holland who arranged for her and her children to go to England by way of Holland to wait for their American visa there. Mr. Brenner, who also was at the Polish border, asked our father to go further into Poland—illegally, of course—and from there, they would find a way to get to Holland. Our father's answer was, "I cannot leave the two old grandmothers and all our people here and save myself. Whatever will happen to them, will happen to me." Mr. Brenner sneaked his way out of No Man's Land into Poland by himself, and from there was able to make his way to Holland. Reunited again with his family, they all went to England to await their American visa. Fortunately, they arrived here in the U.S. before the war broke out and were spared the "Blitzkrieg," where some people I knew lost their lives.

In the meantime, our mother sold more of our furniture and belongings. Belongings and valuables she could not part with were packed into a large wooden crate and stored in the basement of the house at Camerarius Strasse 6, where we last lived. Among the things stored there was a large charcoal drawing of Theodor Herzl, the founder of Zionism. It was an interesting work of art; what looked like the tweed fabric of his suit actually was the complete text of one of his writings. (I am no longer sure which one.)

I have often thought of going back to look for it, but always knew I could not handle that. It would be nice to have and pass on in the family. I have hardly any mementos from my family. I was allowed to bring only what I could carry in one suitcase. My sister, being the older one, did not allow me to bring many of the family's pictures; I felt sorry for her having to stay behind and did not want to fight over it.

The apartment on Camerarius Strasse 6 had five rooms and a kitchen; therefore it had to be shared with four other families. There were three maiden sisters who were quite old living in one room. One of them was always talking to herself. Then there was a very religious family of three: parents with an adult daughter in her thirties. The father always hogged the one and only bathroom in the apartment. He always went to the bathroom carrying a coffee mug, presumably for a religious ritual having to do with pouring water over your hands. Then there was an older man who left no doubt in anyone's mind that man is a descendant from apes. The fourth family had a young daughter. Usually after supper, she, my sister, and I were in the kitchen cleaning up. Unaware of the sadness of the times, or perhaps because of it, I can remember having some of the best laughs of my life there. We usually talked about or mimicked the other people who shared the apartment.

Of course, there was no such thing as buying new clothes or anything else. To begin with, there was no money, and even if there were money, Jews did not get rationing stamps for anything. We spent a great deal of time fixing, altering, and making useable what we had. The Jewish Federation had a "Kleiderkammer"—a clothes closet where people could exchange something they could not use for something they could.

One day in July of 1939, we received a telegram from our father. It said he was on his way home from the Polish border. They were given the choice of going into Poland or returning to where they had lived. Those who had no immediate family left in Nuremberg, like our grandmothers, aunts, and uncles, returned to the villages they had left so many years ago, hoping they would be safe there.

After nine months in a camp at the border, our father came home. Needless to say, we were in ecstasy. We surely thought that the worst had been behind us now, and it would not be long until we would get our immigration visas.

The joy of having our father home with us did not last long. On September 1st, 1939, Germany declared war and marched into Poland. All Jewish men who held Polish citizenship were arrested and taken to jail. I assume non-Jewish men were also interned, but not in jail. When at the end of September Poland surrendered, all Jewish men were sent to concentration camps. Our father was sent to Buchenwald. He was able to write to us from there every two weeks. The letters were all censored. We learned to communicate by writing one thing and meaning another.

Our mother went to the Gestapo and asked what it would take to get my father released. She was told that if he could leave the country, he would be released. Tante Fanny, who was in Italy at the time, was able to procure a visa to Siam (Thailand). It was counterfeit and bought on the black market; however, it would have helped him to get to Italy.

Our mother went almost every day to the Gestapo to push for our father's release. It took a lot of guts on her part, because if the Gestapo didn't come looking for you, nobody went looking for them. Our hearts were in our shoes every time until we saw her home again. By that time, many families had received containers of ashes of what had once been a husband or a father. Among these was Paula's father.

One day in April 1940, we received a telegram that originated from Munich. We were scared out of our wits, but when we opened it we found a marvellous surprise. Our father was released and on his way home. It was like a miracle. He was the only person I know of to have been released at the time. It was also the first day of Passover. I will never forget how he looked: his head was shaved and we could see every bone in his body. He told us that before he left the concentration camp, he had to sign a paper to the effect that he would not speak to anyone about what he had seen or experienced there; we knew not to ask him.

Around the same time, the immigration numbers for my sister and me on the German quota came up. We had to go to the American consulate in Stuttgart for a physical and we both received our visas. We now had to wait for our boat tickets.

After spending nine months on the Polish border and eight months in Buchenwald, our father wanted to spend the few days of Passover with us before going to the Italian consulate for his transit visa. Our mother kept urging him to leave immediately. She said they would not hurt us women and children, but he must get out at once. He said he would go after Pesach. After spending the holiday week with us, he went to the Italian consulate in Munich. As he was about to enter the building, they closed the door right in front of him. Italy had entered the war. There were no more transit visas issued.

In the meantime, my sister and I had received, with the help of HIAS (Hebrew Immigrant Aid Society), passage on the Italian liner, SS *Rex* and were scheduled to leave on May 11th from Trieste. Needless to say, that departure was also cancelled and we could not get to Italy either. The HIAS tried to arrange an escape for me and my sister by way of Siberia. Of course, the Russians entering the war ended that opportunity. So once again we waited. Our father was told that he could not get his American visa unless he had his hernia operated on. He went to Berlin, where there still was a Jewish hospital, to have the hernia repaired. In the interim, the American visas that my sister and I had received expired—they were valid only for four months and only to age sixteen. My sister had turned sixteen in July of 1940. Our mother took us both back to Stuttgart, to the American consulate, to try to get both visas renewed. It seems that the clerk who handled the renewals would never have noticed that my sister was now sixteen years old if our mother, with the best of intentions, had not asked him to renew it "anyway." Unfortunately, that called attention to the fact that she had passed the age limit for children's transport visas and the visa for my sister was denied. A few weeks after my visa was renewed, we received notification that a transport on a sealed train was being put together to leave from Berlin anytime after Jan. 3rd, by way of France, Spain, and Lisbon, where passage on a ship to America would be arranged.

My mother had a girlhood friend from Rzeczow, where she was born, who lived in Berlin. Mama wrote to her and asked if I could stay there until my transport left, as there would be very short notice. The woman was a very nice person and said she would be happy to put me up. Unfortunately, her husband was also in a concentration camp, being a Polish Jew. She had an eighteen-year-old daughter who was a beautiful girl. While I was living there, the Jewish Federation arranged for me to have private English lessons twice a week.

Our father was arrested again two weeks after his operation, directly from the hospital. They never gave him a chance to recover. At first he was kept at Fuerstenwald Prison near Berlin. When my mother brought me to Berlin to stay with her friend, we were allowed to visit him in the jail yard, and I said goodbye to him there.

After a four-week stay in Berlin, I was notified that the transport would leave early in February. My mother came back to Berlin to take me to the station. The group was to gather in an air raid shelter at the Anhalter Bahnhof. Only people who were leaving were allowed inside, and I had to say goodbye before going in. I barely got through the door when it hit me that I was actually leaving. I went back outside to see my mother again, but she was gone.

I don't remember how many hours we waited to board the train. While waiting, I met a girl who was also travelling alone from Nuremberg. She and I were what made up the "children's transport." Her name was Eva and she was eleven, almost three years younger than I. Eva did not have parents. She was raised by a grandmother. We got along well on the trip and of course being the older one, I felt responsible for her. There are only a few things that I remember about that train ride. As we approached the German border, I was concerned that I might have a problem getting across the border with the gold ring my friend gave me. I decided it was not worth the risk and threw it out the window into a field.

As we passed through some of the large cities, the Jewish committee passed some lunch boxes with food through the window. No one was allowed on or off the train. In Paris it stayed in the railroad station all night. French bread was passed to us through the window by the Jewish Federation in Paris. The first time we were allowed off the train was in San Sebastian, Spain. We were put up in the hotel Santa Maria overnight and given dinner. Dinner was rice with clams on the half-shell. I decided to eat the rice only, but then found what must have been a loose clam in my mouth. It was all I could do to keep from heaving right then and there at the table. Early in the morning we had some time to look around the fishing village, and I will never forget the beautiful view. It was the first time I saw the ocean. Although it was only a bay, I was very excited.

Spain at that time was a very poor country, as it was ravaged by a civil war that ended only in 1939. The country was so poor that the dogs we saw from the train were so thin they looked like skeletons. We fed them from what we had left of the stale French bread. Then the children ran after the stale pieces of bread, competing with the dogs.

I do not remember ever feeling hungry. That may be because as a child I had no interest in food. Or one just accepted the fact that one ate what one had. During the past few years, certain food items were available based on food stamps only. Jews did not get the same rations Germans did. Meat, especially kosher meat, was totally unavailable and I doubt that our mother would have bought any other kind. I do remember standing in line for hours to buy a fish or herring or even to get a bag of potatoes. Sometimes by the time we got to the end of the line they were all sold out. The availability of food in the U.S. really impressed me when I first arrived here. So did the public display of anything Jewish, such as the Yiddish press or kosher butcher signs.

From San Sebastian it was just one more day's travel to get to Lisbon. Once there we were taken to a boardinghouse which belonged to a Captain Dacumba.

Eva and I shared a room. It was impossible for us to sleep. The bed, which had a straw mattress, was infested with bedbugs, and we found out from experience that bedbugs do bite. I remember taking the blanket and trying to sleep on the floor. That helped somewhat. The next day we complained to our representative of the Jewish Committee. The place was fumigated and we got different beds. That took care of that problem.

I spent three weeks in Lisbon during which I had a good time. Had it not been for the concern about my family I could really have enjoyed it. . . .

On April 1st, 1941, we were allowed to board the ship that was to bring us to America.

[Years later, Lea received information about the deaths of her parents and sister.]

FROM "FOR THE NEXT GENERATION: UPROOTED DURING THE HOLOCAUST"

By Camilla Tidor Maas and Sarah Cudzillo [2001]

Upheaval and Uncertainty

In October of 1938, my father was arrested by the Gestapo and imprisoned in Frankfurt. I remember the knock at our door in the early hours of the morning; it was the Gestapo who took my father away. I was only seven years old. It would be eight years until I would see my father again. Dad was later transported to Buchenwald concentration

Camilla Tidor Maas and her
brother reunited with their
father, 1946. Archives of One
Thousand Children®, Inc.

camp, then to Auschwitz, then deported back to Buchenwald where
he remained until liberation in 1945.

On the day that my father was arrested, my mother took us on an
evening train to Poland. Father was a Polish citizen and at the time,
the Jews with Polish passports who had been arrested were transported back to Poland. My mother was hopeful that we would find
out information about my father. However, Nazis at the border blocked
our entrance into Poland and we were not able to continue the search
for Dad. We returned home and resumed life without him.

After his arrest the Nazis confiscated his business. He was taken into
custody just prior to Kristallnacht, the "night of broken glass," which
took place in early November. I remember overhearing my mother
converse with acquaintances about the night of chaos, yet I do not recall viewing any of the destruction.

The three of us tried to return to our day-to-day activities. Mother
tried to find some work outside of the home and we continued to go
to school. Our mother was able to receive some correspondence from
Dad in which he urged her to send the children out of Germany. In
December of 1938 or early 1939, while I was walking home from
school, a stone was thrown at me and I was knocked unconscious. This
incident prompted my mother to send my brother and [me] out of Nazi
Germany.

I was eight years old in March of 1939, when my mother placed
both my brother and [me] on a train to Belgium along with other
Jewish children. Little did I know that I would never see my mother
again. We were escorted from Frankfurt to Belgium and placed under the supervision of an organization aimed at helping refugee children. Today, this movement and protection of children is known as
the *Kindertransport*. Numerous children from Europe were sent away

by their families with the hope that they would be saved from Nazi persecution and war.

I was placed with a family living in Brussels, Belgium. My brother and I became separated because he went elsewhere in Belgium, to a children's group home. Thus, we lost track of each other. The family that welcomed me also sheltered two other German Jewish girls. The foster family had a son, Jean-Marie, who was about eleven years old and a very handsome boy. They were a Catholic family and operated a Catholic day school within their townhouse. I remember sitting in on classes and learning French. Occasionally, I went with the family to church, but only if I wanted to go. I recollect Jean-Marie curiously asking his parents why I could not be Catholic and they answered, "[B]ecause she is Jewish and we are taking care of her for her parents." This family exemplifies that kindhearted and generous people existed during the war.

I remained with this caring family for approximately fifteen months until the Nazis invaded and occupied Belgium in May of 1940. During the aerial bombardment of the city, we hid in the basement of the house. While we listened to the bombing, the foster parents decided that their family (including myself) should flee to France. The two other Jewish girls were to be sent to a refugee organization before we fled the country.

I shall never forget the trip from Belgium to the Southern part of France. We went by car and the highway was jammed with thousands of others who were fleeing as well. At first we rode in the car and progress was slow, at the rate of five to ten miles an hour. We soon found we had to push the car a great deal to save on gasoline. Then the Nazis began strafing the cars and people who were on the road and it was no longer safe to stay on the highway. The first couple of days we spent out of sight, in the ditches along the road, driving or pushing the car when there were no German airplanes in the skies. The last part of the trip to the French border was made on foot during the safety of the night. At the border we abandoned the car and took a train to the interior of France.

It was then that this wonderful family who had brought me to safety with them realized that I, as a Jew, was a danger to them. They turned me over to authorities of Oeuvre de Secours aux Enfants (OSE), a children's aid service.

Reunited and Exodus

Eventually, I was taken to Masgelier, a castle in Southern France, which had been bought by the OSE and converted into a children's

shelter. The daily routine included some classroom education, however, this was complicated because the backgrounds and languages of
the children were so diverse. We first had to learn a common language,
French, in order to communicate. After living in this residence for
about a year, I finally heard that my brother was alive and living in
France. He had lived in Belgium. After German occupation he was
transported along with other children to Southern France. He was living at the Chateau de La Hille, another shelter for refugee children.
With the aid of social workers, it was arranged that he would join me
at Masgelier.

The OSE, American Friends Service Committee (AFSC), and the
United States Committee for the Care of Refugee Children (USC)
were some of the refugee and resettlement organizations. They attempted to bring children out of danger from the advancing war.
My name had been placed on the second list of children who were
to be evacuated from Masgelier to the United States. However,
when it came time to leave, and my brother had not yet been sent
to be with me, I adamantly refused to go. When he did arrive, we
were both scheduled to leave in August. We became part of the last
major transport of children (organized by the USC) sent to the
United States.

In the middle of August 1941, my brother and I, along with fifty-
one other refugee children from Masgelier, left by train for Marseilles.
On the 19th of August, responsibility for care was relinquished from
the OSE to the AFSC. At the embarkation point in Marseilles we received inoculations and vaccinations necessary for emigration, and
affidavits that secured our travels. We then traveled by train to Lisbon,
Portugal, and boarded the SS *Serpa Pinto* on September 9th, destined
for the United States.

FROM "MEMORIES OF YOUTH AND WAR (PRE AND POST): HOW I ESCAPED THE FATE OF SIX MILLION JEWS"

By Michel Margosis [1995]

War! War! War!

As a Zionist and a newspaperman, my father uncompromisingly
opposed all forms of dictatorship, left or right, and wrote passionately
and vehemently against them. He used the medium effectively to pursue this path by berating Communism as well as Fascism at every
opportunity. After the bloody emergence of Stalin, he viewed with
great alarm the rise of the Black-shirts under Mussolini and of Nazism

Michel Margosis, March 2002.
Archives of One Thousand
Children®, Inc.

and the takeover of Germany in 1933 by Hitler and his advocates like Léon Degrelle, the Rexist leader in Belgium, Pierre Laval in France, and Francisco Franco who led a Falangist group into an utterly devastating civil war in Spain.

I remember the third of September 1939, just as I finished observing my 11th birthday, browsing with mother through the flea market near the Rue du Lavoir in the old city of Brussels proper, when church bells began to peal to announce that France and England had declared war on Germany because it had attacked Poland two days before. That marked the official onset of World War II. Just at that time, my father was in Geneva, covering the International Conference on Zionism as an operative of the fourth estate, but the outbreak of hostilities delayed his return to Brussels by several weeks. My mother had to tend the family business in my dad's absence, but I was old enough to help on occasions. I recall once during that time mama was distraught and I felt alone and hungry upon my return from school, and did not know where my siblings were nor what they were doing, but I knew well enough to peel and boil a kilo of potatoes and fry them for dinner mixed with two eggs. This was repeated on several occasions, as my parents became more preoccupied with the newspaper business. . . .

As winter advanced, my father's attempts to obtain passports and exit visas in Vichy and then in Marseille, failed. As a Jewish newspaperman constantly editorializing in support of Zionism and irrevocably opposing any form of despotism, particularly fascism and communism, his life was in mortal danger, and he had to flee swiftly out of France through to Portugal, where he eventually was settled in Caldas da Reinha by the authorities. An occasional letter from him informed us of the lack of progress to get exit documents on our behalf, but even that communication ceased until we reached Spain. . . .

[Margosis next records his family's several relocations on the road to freedom. These include sojourns in Toulouse, to the farmhouse of a family friend, in Marseille, and in Gerona. Each relocation keeps them a step ahead of Nazi encroachments, and each involves the constant search for safety and the official papers that are the keys to safety. Margosis does justice to the economic and cultural circumstances at each state of the journey. The escape from France involves a secretive and difficult crossing through heavily wooded mountains.]

Spain: Gerona

We had been heading downhill for a long while, and as dawn ultimately approached, we entered a small and quiet village where everyone surely must be asleep. Our guides led us surreptitiously into an inn in the middle of Puigcerda, a town inside Spain. In the barely visible main dining room of the inn, we gathered several chairs together as a barricade, and we immediately fell asleep behind it. When we awoke, daylight had penetrated the inn through the shutters of the windows, but most of the chairs were stacked upside down on the tables and the shop was closed although it seemed to be about ten o'clock in the morning. As we rubbed the sleep from our eyes, a stranger approached us and in a thickly Spanish-accented French inquired if we were interested in proceeding on our journey to Barcelona. After we paid for our first Spanish meal in French francs and we ate our bread, we discussed our next plan of action. The two gendarmes (who had been our guides) had disappeared and had apparently returned to France presumably to assist someone else in need, no doubt. Again, mother took some American currency out of a hidden purse, and paid this guide in advance. We moved out again under cover of darkness after recuperating from our previous march in the inn during the day and resting. The terrain was flatter and easier to step on, this time, as we hiked downhill through several woods and grassy fields. We trekked through without seeing a soul. As another dawn appeared, we stumbled onto a railroad track and followed it for two or three hours presumably until we could reach Barcelona, many more miles down the road. We were finally spotted by two uniformed men wearing hats that strangely resembled a typewriter. We became particularly apprehensive because before the complete occupation of France by the Nazis, those seeking refuge in Spain were not generally given asylum and were forced back over the border.

The Guardia Civil arrested and searched each of us and confiscated my mother's purse containing the American bank notes, and Willy's straight razor, along with all our other possessions. They then escorted us to a country inn in the vicinity of Figueras where we were treated to dinner and were informally introduced to Paella Valenciana, a surprisingly delicious mixture of cooked rice and various seafood delectables. We were warmly welcomed and advised by the locals that Paella is indeed a highly regarded national dish of Spain. We were then invited by the authorities to stay as their guests at the inn overnight. The following morning, we were routed in separate directions: my brother, mother, and sister to jail for men and women respectively in Barcelona, and I to the Hospicio or orphanage in Gerona. It was there that I met the spindly Georges Flasschoen, who was about a year older than I but well over two feet taller too. When he told me that his dad had been serving as consular attaché in the Belgian Congo when he, Georges, was born, I expressed astonishment that he was not black like all the Congolese people I had ever seen. We presently became friends, and later with the other French-speaking refugee children who had also been recently welcomed into Spain. Any communication with the staff in the old orphanage had to be arranged only through the local or resident priest. He tended the non-Jewish refugee children too, because the sisters remained mute except during mass and the mealtime prayers. Breakfast was served in a large refectory at about seven o'clock only after the morning mass and the procession of the sisters. Lunch was less formal and fairly brief, but dinner seemed to take forever because of the length of the religious services. The food was adequate from what I recollect except that it seemed to me to consist much too frequently of beans, possibly the navy type, or what were labeled munjetes in Catalan or abichuelas in Spanish. That did assuage my hunger, by and large, but it also caused frequent uproar within my still growing alimentary system.

According to my mother's passport that covered the four of us, we claimed citizenship of the Persian empire. Thus, as a citizen, I had requested assistance from the Legation, but a British representative showed up instead and presented himself by the fence surrounding the play yard of the Hospicio explaining that Persia was a British protectorate. He maintained he could do absolutely nothing for me, but he kindly gave me several pesetas bank notes as pocket money so that I might buy little things. Within the next day, I spent the money on roasted onions sold through the fence from a cart on the street. They were sweet and quite good and provided me an altogether wonderful respite from those munjetes.

Caldas de Malavella

After a week or two or three, I really don't remember, at the Hospicio, I was transferred with my mother and sister to a hotel in Caldas de Malavella, a small spa town in the region, while my brother was dispatched to a concentration camp in Miranda de Ebro just south of Bilbao in the Northwest region. I believe the hotel and others like it had been especially subsidized and retained by the American Jewish Joint Distribution Committee, [which] we simply referred to as the Joint, an organization that was entrusted with the care of refugees that were pouring into Spain at that time. The Joint had been founded in 1914 to help Jews during World War I, and later on during World War II, to emigrate and settle. It must have been just around Christmastime, as the hotel staff arranged a delightful feast of Spanish fares, including Arroz con Pollo [chicken and rice], Paella Valenciana [rice dish originating in the town of Valencia], and torrones [nougat candy made from honey, sugar, almonds, egg whites, and orange or lemon flavoring], the superb domestic specialty, [and] Halva, a sweet treat made with almonds rather than sesame seeds. I suppose we chose the right time to emigrate! The place was clean, we were well treated, and we had freedom of the town. I do not recollect any shower or bath nor toilet room as part of the accommodations. But showers were indeed available but provided to us, that is young boys, with a garden hose against the wall of a very spacious white-tiled room. That became great fun. I did complain of a toothache at one time, and the local dentist gave me a shot of anesthetic and removed it, the tooth with the ache.

Georges kneaded a chess set with the soft doughy part of some extra bread. White bread was not readily obtainable, but the dark variety was handy for the purpose. He taught me to play the game, and as we had nothing but time, I spent much of it playing with anybody I could challenge. But it was not until I could devote more science to the game as I did several years later at college that I learned to play more competently.

The priest occasionally came from Gerona to engage us in various activities, to introduce us and to educate us on the fertility of the local lore and the Roman baths built many centuries ago, and the country-side where Napoleon overran the natives. He was particularly warm, friendly, tolerant, and gentle to all the children, and apparently well learned too, as he strove to speak a little Hebrew to one of the kids. He taught us to climb pine trees to sift cones for the delicious nuts within. The Padre treated all the children with utmost decency and respect, Jew and non-Jew alike. We always looked forward to an outing with him, for it was always a pleasure and an education to attend his discussions. After several weeks of replenishment in this resort, the Joint arranged with the authorities to subsidize our relocation to Barcelona. Willy was finally released from the concentration camp and joined us in the city and we were reunited at an 80% level, although still fatherless for the time, but this allowed us a new freedom.

Barcelona

We were lodged at a Pensión on Via Layetana, where we were furnished two clean bedrooms with linen. Meals were served regularly at fixed times in the dining room with the other guests. We were yet to become acquainted with even more delightful Spanish and Catalan gastronomic tastes, even though the country was itself still in its fourth year of slowly recovering from a traumatic and most painful civil war. Anna became friendly with local young adults, one of whom she had met in jail in Gerona where Carmen had been sequestered for a month for not rendering the arm forward fascist salute of Viva Franco at an athletic competition. These friends took Anna under their wings and became guides for her. Occasionally, I would benefit from her friendships by accompanying them to a local dairy bar to taste nata [a delicious sweet cream] and other tidbits, and occasionally attending the Barcelona Symphony concerts, which was so easy for me to love. We soon learned some of the local Spanish traditions such as clapping your hands when you got to your building front door late evenings to hail the sereno [night-watchman who went from building to building checking doors] clanging a bunch of keys to unlock the door. Thus, we did not have to carry front house keys. After a short while, the American Jewish Joint Distribution Committee gave mother an allowance so that we could find more reasonable accommodations. Thus, we relocated to Calle Paris with a Catalan family of three, an artist painter who was particularly fond of Rubens and copied him freely, his wife, and a tall beautiful blonde girl of about my age. I became interested in art such as sketching in pencil or charcoal, while my new friend taught me Spanish. One of the main activities in Barcelona, it seems, is to stroll late evening on the Ramblas, where we were bound to see friends, towards the statue of Columbus standing by the port and looking outward to the seas. One picture that sticks vividly in my mind and moved me immensely was the fluttering of the Stars and Stripes from the balcony of the American embassy on Plaza Cataluñas, while another flag with a Swastika was hanging similarly from the German embassy nearby. The beaches were also crowded about that time of the year because the city is hot and does not cool off well in the evening. I often visited another Pensión where many refugees were housed, so that I could practice and improve on my playing chess, while someone was playing Brahms's Hungarian Rhapsody. Those days I developed more interests, like picking tunes up and replaying them on a piano with two fingers, and picture drawing with pencil or charcoal, and strolling through the philatelic market and the Barrio Chino, the fascinatingly picturesque ghetto and red light district of the city. As I walked along the Avenida José Antonio, I noticed from the big marquees that the movie of the day playing [at] the huge first-run theater was *Rebecca* with Lawrence Olivier and Joan Fontaine.

The Joint, headed by Dr. Sequerra in Lisbon, was organizing to save children under sixteen years of age and sponsored special groups to ship to the United States. My mother enlisted me into it, and then had me fitted for a new suit with knickers by a local Jewish tailor who had settled in Spain in 1933 after escaping from Germany via Turkey. Apparently, Willy did not qualify for this venture even if his birth date had been altered on his "official" papers. Fairly soon I was on my way to the railroad station to catch a train for Lisbon along with a group of children numbering probably two or three dozen ranging from a toddler to barely young adults. Members of families were wiping tears away as they were saying their goodbyes, not knowing when they would see each other again. The children boarded the train and they all chattered until the wheels began to move. The train made a stop in Madrid to refuel and to collect several additional children. Some of the young passengers had been with me at the Hospicio in Gerona and in Caldas de Malavella, and it was good to see Georges again. Jacques Russman, a Southern French Jew from Montauban, came aboard in Madrid along with Daniel Rosenberg.

Portugal

The train ride to Lisbon was uneventful, but as soon as we had arrived, father was waiting by the rail station to greet me. I had not seen him in nearly three years, for he had been in Caldas da Reinha a small spa outside Lisbon hiding for the duration, since Vichy became the non-occupation capital. One instant especially captured in my memory bank is when I gave him a small package of cookies that only my mother could bake, the type that though it might likely fracture your toe if it fell on it, tasted quite good particularly with Russian tea. Well, he just opened the package and stared at the contents, then longingly admired and tenderly kissed each cookie before slowly crunching them away. It wasn't until November 1944 that mother found a way to smuggle herself into Portugal to rejoin him. By then, Anna had sailed to Palestine pursuing a Sabra beau she had fallen for in Marseille and saw again in Barcelona. My father forcefully suggested that Willy was to accompany his sister as a protector or chaperon and they left Europe by way of Cadiz, sponsored by Youth Aliyah.

I had apparently matured and as he took me over and around, he exclaimed "You are a big boy now!" and offered me a cigarette from an etui and a light. He bought me a fedora and we paraded along many of Lisbon['s] wide and well-kept tree-lined avenues, stopping at a café for a pause now and then, but just strutting around like two grown men. I stayed with him for a week, and we strolled much through town, the park, a movie, and we talked and talked at length about everything, from the war, the history of Portugal, the earthquake in Lisbon in the seventeenth century, to the teaching of Hebrew, Yiddish, and the Torah in Caldas da Reinha. He also turned over to me four or five rare old volumes of the Bible in Latin with footnotes and commentaries in Greek and Hebrew. He believed that I might be able to sell them in the U.S. for a very good price to a collector, or possibly to Cardinal Spellman of New York or one of his cohorts. A movie whose title I have forgotten but impressed and stirred me, starred Paul Lucas as a new immigrant into the United States who gets highly emotional about defending his new country from enemies within. It was simply marvelous and glorious to be with him and to have him all to myself, just the two of us, for a whole week before embarking for America. Furthermore, as an omen of good fortune, the sun shone even more brilliantly during my stay in Lisbon and the day we departed. On a leisure trip to Mexico in 1989, Anna and Andre met the Comte Armand de La Rochefoucauld, Duc de Doudeauville, who is pictured in the group photo taken with dad in January of 1943 in Caldas da Reinha, where he too had sought refuge.

Sailing Away

The *Serpa Pinto* was a fairly small Portuguese steamship that
looked like it had been fitted to take on passengers as well as freight.
I presumed it took on no more than forty to fifty passengers and a
big load of cork, a customary commodity exported from Portugal. It
seemed to me that better than half of the passengers belonged to our
bunch of children with four out of five likely Jewish. We stopped for
several hours in Oporto to load a cargo of the reputed local wine and
we moved on again to the open seas. The cadre for our group kept
us fairly busy with morning and evening exercises and games of
every type including shuffleboard, chess, checkers, and they even had
ballroom dancing on occasions, although I do not recall any live
bands. We made another stop and anchored offshore in the Azores
where native lads swam about and would dive competitively alongside the ship to catch coins that some passengers tossed overboard
one at the time, specifically to enjoy the sport. Some young lads were
vociferously hawking and advertising pineapples for sale from small
boats loaded with the fruits, and as my mouth began to water from
the thought of feasting on it, I bought two large ones. I waited pa-
tiently for the appropriate time through to the following morning,
and as the fruits had been ripening fairly rapidly, I cut into one then
into pieces and with juice dripping all over, I devoured each and all
of them. It was the most succulent and delicious fruit I recall ever
consuming, and as I wiped my mouth, I began carving the second
one. When I had finished it, I got up from the seat and I wobbled off.
The fruits had ripened so well, that the fermentation juices had actually made me tipsy.

Some days the sea was so absolutely calm, we could discern the
faintest ripple in the water, especially in the early mornings. After supper, we would often gaze into the waters, watching mainly for flying
fish as they would soar alongside the boat. At one point, perhaps at
halfway point in the Atlantic, a young lad from our group noticed a
distant pinpoint metallic reflection in the water and informed an officer of the ship, who quickly disappeared. He reappeared on the
bridge shortly afterwards with the captain. The reflection soon became
a reality, actually a periscope which slowly surfaced atop a submarine
marked with large black iron crosses alongside. The steamer slowed
down to an eventual stop, when sailors from the U-boat boarded us.
All the officers were escorted by the protective squad of armed sailors and disappeared for about an interminable hour. Everyone else
remained standing on the deck very quietly for a very long time, when
we suddenly heard a splash, then quiet again. The ship's officers finally

reappeared as the captain intently observed the German navy leave just as efficiently as they had appeared. Apparently, the only disturbance was a soft splash and the mysterious disappearance of a cook.

The ship resumed its voyage and completed it uneventfully. . . .

FROM A MEMOIR

By Richard Schifter [1992]

One day that I have never forgotten was October 27, 1938. It was my parents' nineteenth wedding anniversary. They had gone out for the evening. I was home alone. It must have been about 9 p.m. when the doorbell rang. I went to the door and asked who was there. The answer was: "Police. Open up." The next voice I heard was that of the janitor's wife, who said: "Don't be afraid, Richard." I unlocked the door. A burly man in civilian clothes stepped into the apartment. The janitor's wife stayed outside, in the corridor. The man who had identified himself as a policeman held a batch of papers in his hand, which I recognized as the police registration forms, which we and all other residents of the city were required to fill out at regular intervals. He asked for my parents. I explained that they were not at home. In a stern voice, he told me that I should tell them as soon as they returned home that they had to report to the nearby police station.

More than half a year had now passed since the Nazis had taken power. We had felt the consequences of that event all along. But now it had really hit home. In a state of agitation, I awaited my parents' return. When they came home, less than an hour after the policeman's visit, I told them of the instruction he had left with me. My parents took the news quite calmly. They looked at each other, said they would indeed go to the police station and left.

A friend of my father's from his days in Rochester, NY, a non-Jewish native of Vienna and naturalized citizen of the United States, was staying with us at that time. He came home some time after my parents had left. I told him what had transpired. He said that there was nothing we could do but wait and suggested I go to bed.

I went to bed and waited. Our grandfather's clock would strike every half hour. I was thus aware of the hours passing without the familiar sound of my parents, returning home. My teeth started chattering uncontrollably. I could not even think. I was totally gripped by fear. I may have dozed off every once in a while. But when I awoke, my teeth were chattering again.

In the morning, my father's friend went out to make some telephone calls. (We had had a telephone at the store, but not at home.) When he returned, he told me that he had found out that there had been a large number of arrests the previous evening and that my parents were probably at the Rossauerlaende police lockup.

The Rossauerlaende police station was not very far from where we lived. I decided to go there. By the time I arrived, a crowd had assembled across the street from the police station, in a park-like area adjoining the Danube Canal. I joined the crowd and asked questions. All the others in the waiting crowd were relatives of persons who had been arrested the previous evening. We could not think of anything more useful to do than to stand in front of the police station, occasionally talking to each other, most often totally silent. The crowd thickened as the day wore on. The word had gotten around about the location of those who had been arrested. As I stood there, just staring ahead, I said to myself that this is a day I shall always remember.

Sometime after 5 p.m. there was some commotion in the crowd closest to the entrance to the building and the word quickly passed that a handful of prisoners had been released. Gradually more of them started coming out. I was able to get close to some of the released prisoners and asked whether they had seen my parents. One of them told me he had and that everyone would be released that evening.

It must have been around 6 p.m. when my mother finally emerged from the building, erect, calm, and collected as always. She greeted me with a kiss and told me we should go home now. My father, she explained, would be released shortly and would join us at home. As we walked back to our apartment, my mother explained that they had all been treated politely, had been told that they must emigrate quickly and had been required to sign a paper certifying their intention. The irony of this occurrence was not lost on us. For more than seven months, all our thoughts had been singularly devoted to the objective of emigration. It was not that we lacked the will; we lacked the required entry permits.

My father rejoined us before long. His experience had been the same as my mother's. We certainly had been through a frightening night and day.

We subsequently learned that all over Nazi Germany tens of thousands of Jews who were expatriated Polish citizens had been picked up that night. My parents had gotten off relatively easily. In other parts of the country, the persons arrested had been transported to the Polish border. When the Poles refused to admit them, the German police forced them into the no man's land between German and Polish border posts, where they then camped for days. In quite a number of instances, children had been picked up together with their parents. The families stranded along the border therefore included many children. (One of them, then nine years old, was Max Frankel, the present Executive Editor of the *New York Times*.) In light of the seriously adverse international publicity, the Germans relented after a few days and allowed the return of the expellees.

The son of one couple arrested on October 27 had previously immigrated to France and was living in Paris. That young man, Herschel Grynspan, was so upset about the news involving his family that he decided to buy a pistol and to proceed to the German embassy, where he shot one of the junior diplomats. Severely wounded, the diplomat, Ernst von Rath, died a few days later. The abuse which the Nazi press now showered on the Jewish people knew no limits.

On November 9, I was ill with the flu and confined to my bed. I have no recollection of learning anything that evening of what was going on in Vienna or elsewhere. The following morning my father left the apartment to do some errands. He returned before long, ashen-faced. What we heard was that a nearby large synagogue had been seriously vandalized the night before and that the police had just stood by. Bands of storm troopers were roaming the streets again, picking up Jews left and right. My father was afraid that they might come after us. It was decided that he would crawl under my bed, with the covers draped in such a way as to obscure him. It was hoped that if the apartment were invaded, the fact that there was a sick child in the bedroom would cause the invaders not to conduct a search. As for the errands that had to be conducted, my mother decided to handle them. Her deep blue eyes and her general appearance made it possible for her to pass as non-Jewish and she was going to take a chance.

My mother was able to complete the errands and our apartment was not invaded in the wake of what has come to be known as Kristallnacht (Crystal Night). The newspapers were now full of new decrees against Jews and further orders of collective fines and confiscations of Jewish property. To us it did not make a lot of difference. We just wanted to get out. We were, of course, aware of the damage done to synagogues and other destruction of property. We were also aware of the fact that there had been another wave of arrests. We did not receive any reports, to the best of my recollection, of the fact that some of those arrested had been killed. (In the United States, special note has been taken of Kristallnacht as a major atrocity. It has never seemed to me to stand out that much in light of the far more horrible atrocities which began about two and a half years later. It may be that Jews in Austria had since March 1938 become used to Nazi excesses, so that November 9/ 10 did not mean to us what it meant for Jews living in the old Germany, for whom it marked a sharp break with the milder form of repression which they had experienced since 1933.) For us, the focus remained on the single question which had been with us since March 11: how can we get out of here?

Around this time I received word that I should report for my physical examination at the U.S. Embassy. Shortly thereafter I received my U.S. immigrant visa. I recall taking an oath before a U.S. Vice Consul, whose name was Frederick G. Reinhardt. (In later years, I followed Reinhardt's career. His last position was Ambassador to Italy.)

I then had to obtain various German exit permits, including one from Gestapo headquarters in the Belvedere Palace. I remember standing in line when someone suddenly hit my left shoulder hard from the back. I turned around and saw an SS man standing near me, simply staring past me. I then realized that he wanted to pass through the line in which I was standing and wanted me to make room for him. Rather than speaking to me or tapping me on the shoulder, he hit me. Even after I turned around and looked at him, he did not deign to speak to me or even look at me. To him, I was an animal that had to be shooed out of his path.

Finally the day arrived for me to depart for the United States. It was December 4, a Sunday. All my luggage had been packed beforehand. In the morning, my parents and I got into a taxi, a rare event for us, to take us to the Western Railroad Station. Although it was December, it was a pleasant day. The sun was shining.

As I was a fifteen-year-old traveling across the ocean, my parents had searched for someone to look after me on this trip. They found a couple scheduled to leave on the same day and to take the same ocean liner. We met them at the train station for the trip to Rotterdam, the Netherlands. After I had been properly installed in my seat, my parents left the train and stood on the platform, right next to my compartment. The compartment window was open and through it my father was giving me last-minute instructions. To prepare me for my future, he had decided to speak to me in English. Although I had by no means mastered the language at that time, I did recognize the substantial difference between the accent I had learned in school (British) and the one my father used (very much New York). My mother stood behind him. She said very little. She had her handkerchief out and cried quietly, wiping her tears from time to time.

Finally the calls announcing the train's imminent departure were heard and the train started to move. I was standing at the window now, exchanging last-minute words with my parents. As the train rolled on, I waved back at them. They waved with handkerchiefs as the platform gradually receded. Then the train came to a bend and they were out of my sight. I was never to see them again.

FROM "A CHILD MUST BE SHELTERED"

By Henny Wenkart [1998]

It was spring once more.

A year had gone by since the Anschluss; we had our affidavits, and our number was inching closer, even on the "Polish quota." Mother and Daddy had been born in Austria during the Empire, but both Zaleszczicki and Otynia were across the Polish border now, and that was the way the Americans reckoned. Eastern European immigrants were much less desirable than German ones; people born in Vienna were now German. Since Uncle Igo and his wife, Aunt Elsie, were Viennese by birth, they had joined her brother Alex in Providence, Rhode Island, where he was an engineer. He had sent exotic presents from time to time, like Hawaiian pineapples, and used American idioms. One such idiom caused a scare in the family: when Uncle Igo's income had stopped, Alex began sending money every month with a little note. In one such note, he said, "I'm really sorry that I can't make it more." Hurried, frightened family conferences, until "our" American medical student, Mr. Glenn, explained that Alex was merely sorry it was so little, and couldn't *make* it *more—not* that he was going to *stop* sending money. Not that he couldn't *do* it anymore.

To enter the United States you had to have an affidavit from someone financially able to support you, who guaranteed that you would not become a public burden even if you failed to find work. In practice, none of these guarantors ever had to contribute to the support of their immigrants since the Jewish community saw to the support of the refugees, distributing them across the country. Despite this, it was difficult to get people to give affidavits. Most people of means were loath to open their financial resources to Federal scrutiny. Affidavits from close family members counted for much, even when there was little income, because the Americans assumed that families would share what little there was. So Uncle Igo had sent us his own affidavit as soon as he had a job, although he only earned ten dollars a week for himself, Aunt Elsie, and little Ruthie.

Aunt Elsie had started a cottage industry cookie-baking business in addition, but that didn't count for an affidavit. Every morning before work and every evening at dinnertime, Uncle Igo nagged Rabbi William Braude of Temple Beth El for papers. "My mother, my brothers," he would say. "My brothers, my mother."

Rabbi Braude in turn nagged his congregants, and persuaded the pediatrician Dr. Waterman to send us his affidavit. Between these two affidavits we were probably alright. The difficulty was that we couldn't be sure until our number actually came up, which would probably be in August or so. Insufficient papers meant fatal delay. No one we knew had yet succeeded in getting out by supplementing papers that had been insufficient in the first place.

And there was bound to be war soon—how many more countries would the Allies hand over to Hitler? Once the war broke out, we would be trapped. Nobody told me these things, but more and more they were so much in the air that I could not help knowing them.

It was at this time that word began to sift through about a new, small children's transport direct to the United States. Kids I knew had been sent out on Youth Aliyah to Palestine, and others to Holland and England. Each time my parents explored these possibilities with me I refused to consider them. My parents had no visas for any of those countries. How could I go there without them, when I got homesick the four hours away from them in school?

But here was a group going to the United States. It seemed that the Brith Sholom Lodge of Philadelphia had built themselves a guesthouse for twenty-five couples in connection with their children's summer camp. The idea was a congenial vacation with Lodge brothers, where they could catch the occasional glimpse of their children. They had dedicated the building, and then had decided that a good way to inaugurate its use would be to forgo those vacations for a year, bring over fifty refugee children; and house them there for the summer. They had gone first to Berlin, somehow had not found there what they were looking for, and were now coming to Vienna.

They had no wish to wind up with fifty orphans on their hands. So what they wanted were children whose parents had papers for the United States and a low number—people, in other words, who were likely to make it out of Greater Germany before the war. They had affidavits for all the children: to maximize the good they could do, they were looking for families whose papers were just barely inadequate, but would surely be enough once they were unburdened of one family member. We qualified on all those counts: the affidavits we held would rescue my parents if they had only one child, and maybe even with us two—but maybe not.

I wasn't told directly, but I began to realize that we were going to go to the Jewish Community Office to be interviewed for that transport. As the days went by, I started to feel cold in my middle, stopped eating, and began to shake inside uncontrollably. I thought about the thirty-one endless days at Alpenhaus, the one sleep-away camp I had ever been to. If I went to America, there would be thirty-one days like that, and then another thirty-one, and God only knew how many more. Kuki would learn dozens of new words every one of those days, and start to talk in sentences, and say none of them to me. She might even forget me by the time she saw me again, and not know who I was!

There was another side to it: I was big now, big enough to be a heroine. I could save Kuki's life by giving up hearing her first sentences. I could save Mother and Daddy if I took myself off their affidavits. Furthermore, if I was impressive enough, seemed big enough, maybe I could take Kuki with me, and then I wouldn't be alone. My precious older cousin Edith was in America. I would see Edith. I remembered her train pulling away, with me screaming and screaming on the platform. After that one episode in the terminal, I had never been taken to see off any more relatives, but I felt the trains pulling away out of all the stations every day, as every day we continued not to leave Vienna. I tried to get myself to imagine getting on one of those trains myself, leaving the station on it, out to safety. But I couldn't do it.

We arrived at the Jewish Community Office at the end of the week and I saw to my enormous relief that there were hundreds of kids waiting with their families. Confidently, I took both my parents' hands. The odds were so slight that I would be taken from them, with all those other families already waiting. For the first time in a week, the cold in my stomach dissolved and I felt comfortable. I had Mother and Daddy to myself while we waited, we were together; I even began to feel a little hungry.

The American team consisted of a lawyer and his wife and a pediatrician. Since she spoke German, she conducted the interview.

"Would you like to come to America with us and wait there for your parents?"

"Can I take my sister?" I heard myself say. Out of the corner of my eye I saw identical expressions of alarm pucker my parents' faces.

The doctor looked at me very keenly, and kept looking at me hard while she said, "No, your sister is too little. We aren't taking any babies."

"She's almost out of diapers. She'll be out of diapers in a few weeks. And I can take care of her, really. I can take care of her completely, I really can." I turned away from my parents, who were trying to signal to me.

"You can't bring your sister. But if you decide that you want to come, we'll be happy to have you with us."

Then she turned to Mother and Daddy.

"We want only children who really want to come. Please put no pressure on her of any kind. If we find that she has been pressured, she will be dropped from the list. She must make the decision, one way or the other. Please come back with the decision a week from today."

We went home and I took to my bed. All week long I stayed there, nauseated, sleeping as much of the time as I could, huddling close to a hot water bottle that was refilled every few minutes all day long. The misery in my parents' faces filled me with shame.

"The poor child," I would hear them whisper to visitors. "They are making her take this terrible decision upon herself. We are not allowed to help her. It's so terrible to see her suffer. She can't keep a bite of food in her stomach."

It was like pretending to be asleep when they came home from the opera, long ago, but it was so much worse. This time I had them both fooled, not just Daddy; and this time I could not make up for my deception by resolving to be really asleep in [the] future.

For I had no decision to make at all. The shameful thing was that the minute that doctor said I could go, I knew I was going. And it was no use repeating to myself that for someone like me, who suffered so from homesickness, it was really a brave thing to do. Nor that I really was saving my family's lives, probably, anyhow—at least I was making certain that they had good papers.

It was no good. I knew that we were all in peril. No amount of shielding me from the details had kept this overarching danger a secret from me. I had begun to feel the city like a trap closing on me, was conscious of the trains leaving in every direction without me. What I was doing, no matter how anyone chose to interpret it, was to save my *own* life and leave Mother and Daddy and my baby sister in a danger I refused to share with them any longer. I knew that I might be judging myself too harshly and that though they couldn't say so, my parents wanted me to go, for their sake as well as to know that I was safe.

But I stayed in bed all week long *without* a decision to make. I was going. I didn't know what my real motivation was in going; there was no way of sorting it out. I also knew, even then, that I would never be able to sort it out.

We took a taxi to the Jewish Community Office, instead of walking to the streetcar. The pediatrician looked at me closely and asked me if I had decided.

"I want to go."

"Are you sure? Is that what your parents want? Have they told you what they want?"

"Nobody has told me anything. I want to go, please. I made the decision."

The faces of my mother and my father cleared, the doctor hugged me, the lawyer and his wife shook my hand, and various arrangements were put in motion over my head.

It all happened very quickly once I had finished speaking, and soon we were leaving the room. Halfway to the door, all my movements began to slow down. No one noticed this, but everything around me had switched into slow motion. My feet did not really touch the floor. The dark blue Persian carpet, the desks, the windows were not really there. Nothing was really there, not my parents and not—once I thought about this, I suddenly saw—not I myself. I knew very well that it was an illogical, nonsensical thought, but I no longer believed that I existed.

It was a condition I could not describe except in this paradoxical language, and I made no attempt to describe it to anyone. But I left the room in that condition, and I have been in that condition ever since.

LETTER TO ELEANOR ROOSEVELT

By Morris C. Troper [1941]

AMERICAN JEWISH JOINT DISTRIBUTION COMMITTEE
European Executive Committee
Lisbon

June 7, 1941

Dear Mrs. Roosevelt,

Knowing of your deep interest in the work of the United States Committee for Children and how greatly our present success in rescuing one hundred and eleven children many from internment camps in unoccupied France, had been due to your active efforts, I thought that the least I could do would be to tell you about the children now that they are here and awaiting departure for the United States aboard the SS *Mouzinho* early next week.

They are really a fine group of boys and girls and they have endured much in the last year or two. They arrived completely exhausted after a gruelling trip from Marseille that took four days and five nights. Through the kindness of the Lisbon newspaper *O Seculo*, who placed at our disposal the paper's beautiful seaside children's colony, we were able to bring the children to quiet, restful surroundings by the sea where they could play in the sun and regain childhood spirits.

When they came here they looked like tired wan, broken, little old men and women. None dared to laugh aloud and few smiled—even the youngsters of seven and eight. Their clothes were in tatters. The more fortunate of them clumped around in wooden-soled shoes. The others had improvised sandals and pitifully worn slippers with paper and cardboard stuffed in to serve as soles.

One of the most pathetic sights I have ever seen was that of these children freed of restraints, trying to learn to play again. After their experiences of the last few years they simply didn't know how to relax. They played grimly as though fearing that at any moment the sun, the beach, the food and this new unaccustomed liberty would be snatched from them and they would be thrown back into the misery and distress from which they have just escaped.

Through our Quaker friends we secured some new clothing and shoes. Whatever can be done for them physically is being done. An eminent Viennese specialist, himself a refugee, has taken over the responsibility for their health. They will arrive in New York a bit bronzed and looking fit. But it will take more than this week of care to erase the imprints of their bitter experiences.

After a few days here they smiled and laughed a little—but apprehensively, as though they might be punished for it. The results of experiences which no child should ever have to go through cannot be shaken off easily. I hesitated to call them over and speak to them individually because of the look of panic that swept their faces when they were singled out.

The memories some of these children must have! They were permitted to say farewell to their families—those still bearing relatives. The train on which they travelled from Marseille stopped at the station of Oloron and the fathers and mothers interned at the Gurs Camp were brought to the station under police escort and given a last three minutes with their children. And these kiddies, knowing they were to see their parents, refused to eat their breakfasts on the train that morning but wrapped up bread and rolls and bits of sugar and handed them to their parents whom they met.

There is one tot in the group, a wan undersized girl of seven whom we haven't yet been able to make smile. She had been separated from her mother for over a year. When they met at Oloron for the last time, for it is most unlikely that they will ever meet again, they were unable to converse for the child had forgotten her native German in the effort of learning French and English and they had no common language except tears.

There is another girl of thirteen busy mothering her four younger brothers and sisters. Her father died in the Buchenwald concentration camp. Her mother died of pneumonia at Gurs. I found her writing a letter to a woman at Gurs encouraging her, "because she befriended my mother when she was sick." Lisa is taking her brood to live with their grandmother in America.

And the little boy who was smiling when the train pulled out of Oloron while all his comrades were in tears. "It is my birthday," he explained, "and I've just had the nicest gift in the world—I saw my mother."

Everybody will love Bobby Bergmann. He is ten years old and has written poetry in French and German. He wants to be a writer someday and I think he will be. He is chubby and can be made to smile, and I think I detected traces of childish devilment in him.

I could go on for pages telling you about these children. There is something about each of them—as there is about every child. Bruised in spirit, most of them. Frail in body, many of them. And they are the fortunate ones. I know that in America they will get the sympathy and understanding they need, and I hope that with the passing of time the scars each one of them bears will be healed, and they will recapture the spirit of the childhood stolen from them, and will have the opportunity to grow up into normal men and women.

I recall with pleasure the interesting discussion about the refugee situation we had at the time of my visit to the White House with Mrs. David M. Levy last April and I am grateful to you for your continued activity on behalf of European child victims which has been so largely instrumental in the achievement of the results we have had.

Sincerely yours,
Morris C. Troper
Chairman

Mrs. Franklin D. Roosevelt
The White House
Washington, D.C.

LETTER TO EDUARD M. M. WARBURG

From Albert Einstein [1941]

THE AMERICAN COMMITTEE OF OSE
24 West 40th Street
New York City

June 25, 1941

Mr. Eduard M. M. Warburg, Chairman
American Joint Distribution Committee
100 East 42nd Street
New York, N.Y.

My dear Mr. Warburg:

As the Honorary President of the OSE I wish to thank you on its behalf for your aid to the OSE work and express our sincerest gratitude to you, to the whole Joint Committee and to your European office for organizing the transportation and bringing to this country a group of children from the OSE homes in France.

By this action you have helped not only this group of children but you have enabled us to take into the places of the evacuated children other children from internment camps, you helped to relieve their inhuman misery and suffering and give them a new lease on life. What tragic experiences these children have undergone in the past several years! Torn away from parental care and love, thrown from country to country, from place to place, delivered out to senseless persecution. And upon reaching sixteen years of age having to face the dreadful confinements in a concentration camp.

Efforts to save these children must not slacken. It is not only a question of bringing them to the United States, other countries must be opened to them, among them South America. The settlement of older children (over fifteen) in Santo Domingo must be considered. In all these efforts the aid of the Joint Distribution Committee is of the utmost importance.

I therefore turn to you with the urgent plea to keep the problem of the evacuation of refugee children in the forefront of your attention and to continue your efforts on their behalf. With all best wishes for your worthy endeavor, I remain

Very sincerely yours,
Albert Einstein

"MY TIME AS A RESCUE VOLUNTEER" FROM "PICKING UP THE PIECES"

By W. Howard Wriggins [2002]

(Bryce Professor Emeritus of the History of International Relations, Columbia University)

[For five years during World War II, W. Howard Wriggins served overseas with the American Friends Service Committee (AFSC) helping victims of Nazi persecution. He began this work in Portugal helping to rescue the group of OTC children who left from Lisbon for the United States. The following is excerpted from his paper given at the One Thousand Children Reunion and Conference in Chicago (June 30, 2002).]

I was in Lisbon from May 1942 to August 1943 with AFSC. Thinking back to that awful period, I was what you might call a young, twenty-four-year-old refugee social service caseworker. Every day perhaps a dozen or more destitute, pursued, confused, and lonely people came into our small two-person office. They had fled originally from Germany, Austria, Poland, Hungary, and who knows where, but most recently from France.

They often came to Portugal without documents. In those days documents were almost as important as food to eat, shelter over your head, and clothes to wear. Many had fled from France, crossed Spain, and entered Portugal illegally. If they didn't have documents, these people could be jailed, and the jails were quite medieval institutions.

They needed money in addition to documents to pay for lodging, food, clothing, medical attention, postage to send letters to families or other possible sponsors in the U.S., U.K., or Latin America.

After all they experienced, we believed they also needed the hand of friendship, of someone who cared. And my job was to listen to their tales of woe and quiet heroism and help steer them to others who might help them more than we could or for us to take on responsibility if the other committees couldn't.

We were not alone. There were other organizations far more important than the AFSC. The most important, of course, was the American

German passport of "Brith Sholom child" Helga Weiss Milberg, page 1. Note large "J," which was stamped on the passports of Jews. Archives of One Thousand Children®, Inc.

German passport of "Brith Sholom child" Helga Weiss Milberg, pages 2 and 4. Note middle name "Sara," which all Jewish females had to add to their names. Archives of One Thousand Children®, Inc.

Jewish Joint Distribution Committee (JDC). The European head of the JDC, Joe Schwartz, was a wonderful man. He was my hero at the time. I considered that the burden of that generation's Diaspora lay on his broad shoulders. He traveled to France often and often on his return, he included me on his debriefing.

Herb Katsky, one of his aides, was more nearly my age, [and] became a good friend. HIAS [Hebrew Immigrant Aid Society] and HICEM [acronym for three Jewish organizations dealing with immigration] were there. The Unitarian Service Committee was also there. Dr. Joy and the Dexters were supportive too. They specialized in dealing with special problems of political refugees. I'm not sure when we first heard about the large number of children's visas somehow pried out of the U.S. government in response to the awful deportations from France that had begun in the summer of 1942.

The United States Committee for the Care of European Children, supported by the JDC, the French, and others somehow worked wonders. And they were planning on sending some thirty social workers and doctors to escort these children from the Portuguese frontier to Lisbon, care for them until the necessary shipping could be arranged, and to sail back with the children's escape ship.

As I recall, we and the other agencies began planning how to take care of so many youngsters in transit. Three days in those trains at that time from France through Spain and to the Portuguese frontier would be exhausting to anyone, but even more so to those undernourished and no doubt distraught children.

We sought help from the Portuguese Red Cross, from nunneries, from summer camps that might be reopened in September or October. It was all pretty hypothetical since we didn't know when these children would come and, of course, always in the back of our minds was the anxiety about whether any children would be allowed to come at all.

In the meantime, in southern France, Quakers, Unitarians, and JDC representatives and HICEM were crisscrossing the country visiting orphanages and children's colonies where hundreds of children were being cared for. Many were lost children or children whose parents had disappeared or been deported.

One of our workers recalled how he, one French social worker, and a French medical person interviewed children. As he put it, in one of his letters, some of them had even walked all the way across Europe from Poland and without adults. A few had a suitcase of stone-hard stale bread they had been able to save when they were fed regularly as a kind of psychological security measure for the time when they would not be fed regularly.

These staffers faced the heartrending task of deciding who should have the opportunity to live and be saved and who should remain and have to take their chances.

In October, we learned that the escorts finally would be sailing from the States on one of the Portuguese ships, I think it was the *Nyassa*, scheduled to arrive about mid-November.

In the meantime in France, a group of some 150 children gathered in Marseilles to get their papers together for the U.S. consulate. But they couldn't be moved because the French had closed the frontier with Spain. During this period illegal crossings into Spain greatly increased. I don't know how many came through Spain and stayed in the Spanish refugee camps, but a lot were able to get that far.

Numerous children in France were identified as candidates. In early November 1942, the American and British allies landed on the beaches in Morocco and Nigeria. The military tide began to turn and there was much excitement in Lisbon. A huge sigh of relief went up from Portugal and Spain. But all our rescue plans were abruptly stalled. The German Army immediately occupied the rest of France. Jews held in internment camps became more anxious. All previous agreements regarding sending children abroad were canceled. No more children would be authorized to leave France. French border controls became more severe.

About ten days later, twenty-eight escorts from the United States Committee for the Care of European Children arrived in Lisbon. They had no way of knowing how long it would take for us to be really sure about developments in France. We could give these people who just arrived from the United States no assurance that there would be any children for them to escort home.

You can imagine their sense of deflation. Remember, the United States was then engaged in a major war. All these people held responsible positions in child care, human resource and assistance institutions at home. Their professional and personal lives were focused on service. They had all come overseas with the expectation of being of even greater service in escorting young victims of Hitler's madness to the safety of the United States. Suddenly these energetic, high-octane, dedicated people had nothing to do and they had to do an emotional about-face. This was not the time in history for a leisurely holiday in a Mediterranean climate, but that's what they had to put up with.

But of course their disappointment was nothing compared to that of the children or their families who thought they had seen a way out only to have it snatched away.

One of our tasks as the organizational post was to find them alternative ways to expend their energies. We and the other relief committees, the JDC, the Unitarians, as well as the HICEM and the AFSC, organized tours of historic sites and trips to beaches. These distractions were some help, but not much for these highly energetic people. More than once I overheard such remarks as, "Mental hygiene, Ruth, mental hygiene." Or, "Let's take a fast walk down to the river, Mary, that will help."

Indeed, after they had been waiting two months, I had an encounter I shall never forget. I was alone in the office late Saturday afternoon preparing urgent mail about individual refugees needing sponsors, getting ready for the next day's departure of the Pan-Am clipper. A quiet gray-haired lady asked me if she could talk with me. I was a very young man at the time feeling beset by the bureaucratic deadline of getting mail ready. I was still insensitive to the signs of serious depression.

I showed her the mess of unfinished correspondence on my desk. I shrugged my shoulders in a gesture of helplessness and said, regretfully, "I can't see you now but I'll be in all day the next day, Sunday. We can talk then." She thanked me and quietly left.

She didn't appear the next day. Several days later, her shoes were found on the rocks neatly side by side above high-tide mark on the beautiful Portuguese coast.

Already Americans and staff members of relief agencies in France were being rounded up and taken to Germany for internment. It was finally decided that we in Lisbon could do nothing for the children in France.

After some negotiations in Washington, it was agreed that available visas could be used by children in Casablanca, Spain, and Portugal. There were children whose families were stuck in Casablanca and so still under the Vichy regime and in internment camps in Spain under Franco.

It's hard to imagine now just how fearful people were that Franco might yield to Gestapo pressures and deport Jews back to France for further deportation to Poland. In any event, the visas originally obtained for refugee children in France were no longer usable.

I have not found out when that decision was made, but I do recall that suddenly refugees in Portugal concentrated in Caldas da Reinha began to consider whether they should send any of their children.

Several heads of family came in to talk with me about this terrible decision. How much longer would the war go on? Would America be more open to immigration after the war? Was Portugal likely to continue to tolerate their presence? Would the relief committees continue refugee support as long as the war lasted? What kind of foster homes would they find in America? Was American school education as inadequate as it was said to be?

Deep down of course was the fear of losing touch with one's own children. As one distraught woman plaintively put it, "We have already lost so much. Must we now give up even our children?"

We of course stressed it was their choice. There was no "must" about it. But even to raise the question was obviously terribly disturbing.

Some families were enthusiastic about the possibility of seeing at least one member of the next generation get a foothold in America and quickly identified the oldest as the one to go. Others were more deeply ambivalent or were not interested unless brothers and sisters could go and be placed together.

In the end, I think some 30 children left from Portugal at that time. I've seen a copy of the list containing about 30 names that I sent to Clarence Pickett, executive secretary of the AFSC about that time, but for the life of me, I cannot now find it.

The date was firmed up for the *Serpa Pinto* to arrive with the children from Casablanca and Spain on the way to New York. Now the USC refugee team went into high gear. I was their administrative assistant. We arranged interviews with interested families in Caldas da Reinha, which was the refugee settlement, for those who couldn't travel on the Sabbath.

Dr. Rosa Frank took their medical histories. Marion Nicholson and others talked at length with the parents to learn their wishes for foster family care and with the children to gain some impression of their character and interest.

Dr. Baruel, head of the Jewish community in Lisbon, obtained from the police the necessary permissions for families and children to come to Lisbon. The JDC, as usual, footed the bill for the Lisbon stay.

Later there were interviews and medical exams in the consulate and two stenographers filled out the necessary immigration forms. This was before the days of Xerox and every office with its own copier. So I was the one who ran up quite a taxi bill that day rushing back and forth between the consulate and the photostat shop taking newly completed forms to be copied, picking up those already copied and returning the originals and photostats in triplicate to the consul, the kindly but scrupulous Mr. Miller. For those who have not had preliminary interviews, the formalities took only five hours. That seemed miraculous at the time.

On January 9, 1943, we finally saw actually thirty-one children walk off the gangplank, each with his identification card hung around his neck with his picture and name showing through the glass window there. There were twenty-seven escorts who went home with them to help care for the some 300 other children from Casablanca and Spain. Those were a hectic, uplifting, and distressing three months—thinking about, getting discouraged about, and in the end sending at least some of the thousand children. We reminded ourselves that over 300 had been given opportunities for new lives away from what was then an accursed continent.

We then returned our attention to those who were having to stay and make the best of it.

Chapter 4

COMING TO
AMERICA

*T*he rescue efforts that brought more than one thousand European (mostly Jewish) children to the United States included a transoceanic voyage by ship to the east or west coast of America. Children arriving in New York harbor relate the special experience of seeing the Statue of Liberty and perhaps enjoying a sightseeing trip around Manhattan Island before going on to their foster families. Others remember the trip to government offices in order to be examined for fitness to immigrate. Many of the children remember their shipboard passage vividly, while others only recall the sketchiest details. Some recall those who took care of them in transit.

Manfred Goldwein's two-part narrative highlights his trip to the American Consul in Stuttgart in order to be approved for entry into the United States under the immigration quota. Young Manfred's journal is filled with the excitement of youth. Is it simply that he does not understand the causes and consequences of his adventure—or is he putting on a brave front because he will be sending the journal to his parents? In any case, "Freddy," as he came to call himself, provides a vivid record of the ship's apparent splendor, a snapshot of the daily routine, and a charming expression of his excitement in his new home. Perhaps the tone of his journal is so upbeat because he fully expects to be reunited with his parents in a relatively short period of time. As we follow Freddy to his new home, we get a taste of the transitional experience detailed in chapter 5.

Ilse Hamburger Phillips's diary, translated from German, gives us a much more detailed understanding of the children's day-to-day shipboard experience. Filled with references to time, as well as to food and activities, her simple and direct narrative reflects a young girl's attempt to take control of her experience by pinning it down in words. The diary continues with Ilse's *impressions of New York and the trip to her final destination in Arkansas. One of Ilse's return trips to her first home is recorded by her daughter, Rose Marie Phillips Wagman, in the journal "Returning to My Roots," excerpted in chapter 7.*

Perhaps no other contemporary documents of the children's voyage to America have the ring of youthful exuberance and the sheer joy of life that can be found in the emotive, image-laden letters of Ruth Schlamme Schnitzer. Dramatically center stage in her letters to the "dear ones" back home, Ruth revels in each observation and revelation. She has a keen eye for detail and a flair for making her presence felt. It is a joy to see the voyage through her eyes, though a joy that must be tempered by our knowledge of the larger, encompassing tragedy. Ilse and Ruth were passengers on the same voyage.

As we might expect, not all of the voyages to American were smooth and pleasant. Excerpts from writings by Lea Wasserman Schwarz and Walter Kron reveal that discomfort, danger, and doubt were likely experiences as well.

FROM "MY TRIP TO STUTTGART AND USA"

By Manfred Goldwein [1938]

[This journal by Manfred Goldwein was sent to his parents, who put it into the hands of a Gentile friend who held it at great risk during the war. Eventually, she returned it to Manfred, along with the accompanying letters, when he was on military duty in Europe.]

To my dear parents as Freddy,
Begin: Wednesday, 5 Jan. 1938
Ending: Sunday, 9 Jan. 1938

"Everything is ready!" The local train I'm on leaves Korbach at half past six in extremely cold weather. It's still dark. Out of several houses falls a ray of light. The train is too hot and the wagon is shaking. This is a little foretaste for the sea voyage. I do not feel well.

After Frankenberg, it gets lighter. In Marburg I change trains with a half-hour wait. When the half hour is up, the conductor says, "30 minutes' delay." That is unpleasant. I am waiting on the platform. My legs could freeze off. Finally, after another fifteen minutes' delay, the express train comes. I board and start getting warmer. Finally, a decent train.

Giessen—Friedberg—Bad Nauheim—Vilbel. I am already quite warm. Frankfurt must be coming soon; I almost got off at Frankfurt-West. "Frankfurt-Mainz main railroad station. Everybody out!" I left the train and I am really frightened. Wow! When I was here in the

Manfred Goldwein with his foster
brother Richard Greenstein, Delaware,
1938. Archives of One Thousand
Children®, Inc.

summer, the buildings did not seem as tall. When I stood behind the
Opera I think everything is falling over me. Irma is standing at the gate.
I didn't recognize her at first. We take the streetcar to the Feuer-
bachstrasse.

On the next day at 12 o'clock noon I go to Stuttgart. The D-train is
overcrowded. Only one car goes to Stuttgart. Until Heidelberg, I sit in
the dining car and drink a cup of coffee. The trip goes through the pine
tree forest. To the left of the train are snowed-in vineyards, and on the
right, rolling plains, white and dreamy. It goes through the Odenwald
with the famous mountain route. The rivers Main and Neckar are frozen over. After 20 minutes we arrive in Damstadt. The trip goes further south through Benzheim, Weinheim, Bergstrasse, and Heidelbert
"change trains!"

I can't see anything of the city or the famous castle. Now I'm thinking that there are other Jewish kids traveling to Stuttgart. I'm going
to look for them immediately. There I'm going to see quite a few of
them, and they all have Jewish faces. Wow, I missed completely, they
aren't Jewish. The boys are all traveling to Ulm. Now I'm going to skip
trying to figure who is who. Bruschsaal—Two railcars are added on
because the train is overcrowded. I have been standing since
Heidelburg. Finally I can sit down.

The train continues on through the wintry landscape. Bretten—
Mulacker—Bitigheim—Ludwigsburg. We are almost there. I quickly
take out my white handkerchief. An electric locomotive pulls the train
into the station: "Stuttgart Main Station, Everybody exit." I hold my

white handkerchief in my hand. At the gate I look for others who also
have handkerchiefs in their hand, but I do not see any!

I walk around the station for ten minutes and look my eyes out.
Don't see anybody. Now, for the first time, I admire the train station.
Then I telephone the Hilfsverein (traveler's aid). "Hello? Who is
there?—Please?—Please?—Please?—Is that the Hilfsverein? Here is
M. G. I am at the station, etc., etc." To come here, you travel on the #2
streetcar to the old "Postplatz" and go from there to the Garten Str #15.
Short and sweet, so I take the #2 tram to Old Postplatz and I walk from
there to the Hilfsverein. In the waiting room is another young man the
same age as I am who is also going to the USA. He is from Karlsruhe.
We immediately become friends. Then a third boy arrives. He is from
Elbersfeld and his name is Stefan. We are given instructions for
tomorrow. The three of us shall leave Hamburg on 16 January with the
SS *Manhattan*.

Then we go to the youth hostel to eat and stay overnight. There we
find more nice boys. We are served macaroni with creamed corn. At 9
o'clock, we must be in the Youth Hostel. There we are creating all kinds
of nonsense and the hostel father gets angry, telling one another jokes,
and, finally, fall asleep at 12 o'clock. At half past six the next morning,
we get up. We wash up and go to the trade school where we drink coffee. The cook quickly relieves us of one mark then we go to the Consulate, where we meet Mrs. Kaufmann.

In the waiting room stands a tall fat guy by the name of Fuechs, with
whom we register our names. I am the second to register. "Are there
any people here who have small children?" He yells half a dozen times.
About 9 o'clock, I was called.

I am first measured with shoes. Then a young lady takes my personal information. I go back into the waiting room. After a while I am
called by a lady doctor. I must first read for her and then must enter a
booth where I must completely undress. Another doctor comes and
listens to my heart and lungs and asks me in German with American
dialect, "Do you speak English?" and "where are you going?" and then
"dress." The end we come to the Consul and must swear that we have
answered all the questions truthfully. Then we must pay our 26 RM
[reichsmarks]. Now we're done. It is approximately 10 o'clock. We go
to the Post and send telegrams to all of our relatives. From there we
take our friend from Elbersfeld to the train station. We, the other two,
don't leave until 12:45.

Bruno just catches his train, which goes to Karlsruhe at 11 o'clock.
There I see that at 10:58 there is a train that goes to Frankfurt. Because
I already have a ticket, I enter the D-train, which goes past Mannheim

and I think I shall see the Rhine. Just as the train leaves, I sit down in the dining car and I order a hot chocolate and 8 rolls because I'm terribly hungry. This spass (joke) costs me 1 m [mark] 20 p [pfenning].

. . . [W]e travel to Mannheim. In Mannheim, I see the huge factories. Everywhere you see these plants making steel, glass, ceramics. I keep looking for the Rhine, but I see no trace of it. At 2 o'clock, I arrive in Frankfurt. I go immediately to Irma's apartment. The next morning, Saturday, the 8th of January, I go to the West End Synagogue.

There is an organ and a mixed choir. It is a very beautiful choir. In the afternoon, we tour the Old City and look at the Roemer from the outside and the Goethehaus from the inside. The old things and in particular the clock which stands on the floor impressed me greatly. This clock shows years, months, days, hours, minutes, seconds, and the position of the sun and the moon. Five hours before the clock runs out, a bear falls on his back and it is time to rewind the clock. Unfortunately, on a Tuesday, the year, month, and days, and therefore the position of the sun and the moon, had stopped.

In the evening, I saw a wonderful film: *Die Fledermaus* (the bat) by Johann Strauss. I particularly liked Frosh (the frog) played by Moser.

The next day I go home. I liked it very much in Frankfurt and Stuttgart. At Irma's I had a great hospitality. Father picked me up at the railroad station. END OF THE TRIP TO STUTTGART.

My Trip to the U.S.A.

Beginning the trip: 7th February 1938
End of trip: 17th February 1938
"Everybody board."

For the second time my train leaves Korbach and this time forever.

My parents are with me in order to accompany me to the ship. This is the last time that I see Korbach, the city in which I have lived for eight years, in order to travel to my new home, in the USA. After an hour and a half we reach Warburg where we have to change trains. Scharfade—Rimbarp. Again we have to change to a D-train to Kreinfen. In Kreinfen, we change trains for the last time to Hamburg. At about 5 o'clock we arrive in Hamburg. We get off and go to the Wormser Haus, where I will sleep. There I meet more nice boys. There are ten boys and six girls (on the next morning). Then we must go to bed. We misbehave quite a bit and, finally, one gets thrown out and must sleep in another room. The next morning we have to do all kinds of things. We have to go to the U.S. office and take care of several things and then, at half past two a bus takes us to the ship. My parents have also a ticket for the bus trip and may see the ship. After half to 3/4 of an hour we arrive at the pier. We must go to the passport and money control and from there to the baggage control where our hand luggage is examined. Then we can get on the ship. That makes a great impression. Everything is beautiful. The walls and everything is paneled with wonderful wood. We are taken to our cabins. We sleep four in a cabin. Everything is beautifully built in. Ventilators, ice water, cold and warm water, life jackets, and emesis containers are included. The ship is not moving. "In such a ship we will never become seasick," we shout happily. We then go to the dining room and have a wonderful evening meal. At approximately 8 o'clock, I say goodbye to my parents. Then we go to bed for the first time on board the ship. At 5 o'clock in the morning the ship is supposed to sail. As we awake, we are already under way. In the morning, we drop anchor because it is very foggy and we are still in the Elbe. Towards noon, the ship again gets under way but we are not moving because while the ship was anchored we got stuck on a sandbar. The ocean giant which so quickly counters the might is now powerless. In the evening, ten small tugboats, dwarfs, must pull the ship out of the sandbar. The ship is now under full steam. The next morning we are surprised to look out of the portholes—nothing but ocean, we are surrounded by waves, which almost reach to our porthole. At noon comes the first surprise! The first feeds the fish in form of seasickness. In five minutes, no less than seventy percent follow the first. I, too, feed the fish. At 5 o'clock we dock at Le Havre. We go ashore and are surprised that the city consists of old, dirty buildings with old stores. We return to the ship and are in Southhampton the next morning.

Here we see many ocean liners. Unfortunately, we cannot go ashore because the ship will stay only a few hours in the harbor.

Approximately 3 o'clock, we are leaving for Cobh (Ireland).

We stay there until the next morning and then continue our trip. Cobh is a beautiful city surrounded by green mountains. She lies in a cove. A beautiful green that the Irish love so much forms all the surroundings. Then we are now on to the high seas. I am again getting seasick and the stewards are mad because they must clean up the mess.

Let me continue in English here, for I now come to America. We had a few days very cold weather, the decks are frozen and you have to wear an overcoat all the time. For my seasickness, someone gave me a green pill and you should have seen the results. Sure, it was much easier for me to vomit, but everything I secreted had a dark green color. Even till the first days in America it lasted. Well, in spite of my seasickness, I only missed one breakfast, one lunch, and one supper, and

I think that eating helped me a lot. On Thursday, February 17, traffic became heavier, ships here and there. Around noon, we could see the skyscrapers and the "Statue of Liberty."

Oh, what a magnificent monument that is, the symbol of personal liberty.

Then at about 2 o'clock, we docked and it took more than 5 hours before we could leave the boat. Entering the pier, I heard a voice calling, "Freddy." It was Aunt Julia who had recognized me from first sight. We got our baggage examined with little trouble and went to our hotel "George Washington." What traffic in New York City! The taxi often was going fifty miles per hour. We had supper and then went to the roof garden on the eighteenth floor. From here, we could see New York City by night. All tired, we finally went to bed. Next morning, after breakfast, Norma and Uncle David came and took me to Wilmington.

Wilmington, Delaware

My new home is in Wilmington, a city of about 110,000 inhabitants. The part I live in is called Brandywine Village, named after the Brandywine Creek flowing nearby. There are three main rivers in the city: the Brandywine Creek, which flows into the Christiana River, which flows into the Delaware River. The main industry of Wilmington is chemicals, headed by the "DuPont Company," world famous. Its main plant is located across the Delaware River in New Jersey. There are two main railroad lines going through Wilmington: the Pennsylvania Railroad and the Baltimore & Ohio (B&O) Railroad.

The streets in Wilmington running in East and West direction are named with numbers (1st, 2nd, 3rd, 23rd Street, etc.). Those running from North to South have names (Franklin St., Monroe St., French St., King St., etc.).

Market Street is the main street of Wilmington. It runs in North-South direction and divides the city into the East and West part. The numbered streets are also divided into North and South part. They are separated by Front or 1st Street. The streets running perpendicular and parallel divide the city into squares or blocks; each block starts with a different number adding a hundred each. Therefore, 903 W. 23rd Street is: nine blocks West from Market Street, twenty-three blocks (North) from Front Street. The city has many parks, the main one being Brandywine Park. Opportunities for sports are great for there are many stadiums, open for everyone. The traffic is controlled very well due to the many traffic signs, one-way streets, etc. Trolley cars are networked all over the city, but they will be substituted by many trackless trolleys in the future.

Opportunities for education is great; there are many schools including three or four senior high schools with about 1,600–2,000 pupils each.

There is also a free public library from which books can be borrowed entirely free for four weeks each.

My Home

My home is a little nice house with nine rooms. Before you enter, you come on the front porch, which is in the open and the favorite place on summer evenings. Entering into the front door you directly go into the living room, for halls are not common here. The living room is very comfortable; it has no large table, but 3 easy chairs, a bench, a bureau, a bookshelf, and four very small tables. From the living room, you go straight into the dining room, from there into the kitchen, pantry, and breakfast room. The stairs go from the dining room. Upstairs are three bedrooms and the bathroom with a bathtub, a shower, and a toilet.

My Country

It is great—

My dear Mother and my dear Dad,
I hope that you will like this book, though it is a little late. Thoughts of me and everything else you may write in yourself. Though I send you this book, I hope that you will be over here soon; we are doing our best as you are, for there is a lot of trouble.

But meanwhile, may God bless you and keep you in good health. May he think of you and free you very soon—from all your troubles, so that we may be together, in a country that is too great to describe, too good that it is almost impossible to put it into words. Keep your chins up and keep smiling.
I am proud of you.

Your faithful son,
Freddy

My Gifts For My Trip To America

Person	Gift
Congregation	150 RM [reichsmark]
E. Mosheim	100 RM
B. Neuhause	2 RM

(continued)

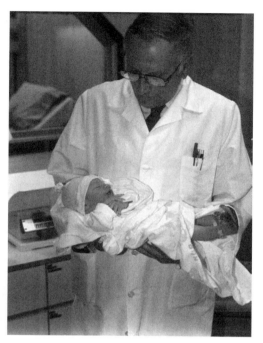

Pediatric hematologist
Dr. Manfred Goldwein, M.D.
Archives of One Thousand
Children®, Inc.

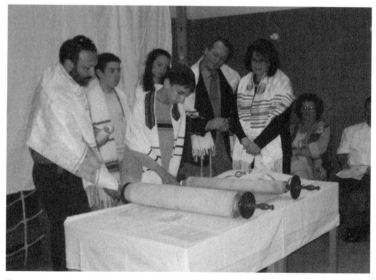

Bar mitzvah of Eric Goldwein (third-generation OTC) in 2003, in
Korbach, Germany, the town where his grandfather, Manfred
Goldwein, was bar mitzvahed before he left for the United States
in 1938. Archives of One Thousand Children®, Inc.

My Gifts For My Trip To America (continued)

Person	Gift
Sallberg's	2 Sweaters, 2 Chocolates
Alte Katz	Sweat Pants
Junge Katz	3 Ski Shirts
H. Strans	2 Gym Pants, Pocket Mirror
S. Stahl	Tie
I. Schnellenberg	120 RM, 2 Suits, 2 Coats, Shirts
M. Eldoch	Camel Blanket
M. Brannsberg	Handkerchief
_. David	Socks
M. Hamberg	5 RM, Tie
G. Mosheim	Travel Bag
M. Mosheim	Shoe Bag
M. Hamberg	5 RM
L. Mosheim	Shaving Utensils
Fr. Schild	Pocket Knife, Chocolate
Frau Markhoff	5 RM
Lebensbaum	Handkerchief
A. Lowenstern	Letter Paper
G. Lowenstern	Cigarettes Holder
Kohlhagen	Apples, Stationery
Fannigen?	Nuts
Weizenkorn	Diary [the book Ilse writes in], Sweets
W. Fischel	3 RM

Letter from his father in English, on the next-to-last page in the diary:

My dear, dear Boy!
When you receive this book, it will not be sent through us, but by others. So you must not be sad, for we are in God's dear Hand and really in God's own Land. I want you to walk His ways, for you are a son of the Chosen People; you are a link of the long chain that began in the past and reaches into eternity. Be a worthy man, a good and true Israelite and so I hope to see you again.

I love you forever and ever.

Your true Father

Letter from his mother translated from German:

My Dear Good Boy!
This book I send you through a good friend who was always good and brave to us and in our need and pressures always stood by our side.

My thoughts are with you day and night, my dear boy. Perhaps if the dear God will let us live and grants us that we can be reunited. But if it should not come about, may dear God protect you. Remain good and brave, as you have always been.

I know that you and all the dear ones over there have done all to save us but fate decided otherwise. You know that we have always done good deeds and that we have remained in God's path.

Don't forget us, my dear son, as we shall never forget you.

Once more, remain a good mensch, do your duty.

Regards to all the loved ones from us.

Farewell, my dear child. I hug and kiss you fervently.

Your Mother!

"MY DIARY!"

By Ilse Hamburger Phillips [1936]

October 26, 1936–November 12, 1936

Day 1

It is the 26th of October, the last day in my native home; it is the last morning! I have a lot of company. In the morning I still made several farewell visits, after lunch I went to Aunt Rosa who today has her 90th birthday.

This evening we will reconcile with Aunt Anna. At 7:30 came Hamburgers, Neustadters, and Mrs. Dreifuhs. My dear father will accompany me to Hamburg. The auto will come that will take us to the station.

(I take my leave from all my loved ones.) Hamburgers, Neustadters, Mrs. Dreifuhs, and Rudi Strauss will go with us to the station. I take my leave from all my loved ones and drive to the station.

I climb into the train, the station gives the sign, the train begins to move, and one more time I wave out of the train, and then it goes into the wide world.

Goodbye!

Day 2

It is Wednesday, October 27.

The train rolled into the Hamburg train station. It is 7 o'clock and we went to the restaurant for breakfast. After breakfast we went sightseeing in Hamburg. There is much activity even though it is still early in the morning.

My dear father looks for a school friend who he has not seen in 20 years.

At 10:30 we went to the Jewish German Children's Help. We took a car and drove to the Hapag Luggage Hall. There I met all the children who I met at the consulate in Stuttgart. The checking of my luggage went quickly.

At 12:30 we went for dinner. After dinner I slept. At 4 o'clock we went to town to a few places. At 7:30 we went to Kanders. Regretfully they were not at home.

We went to a restaurant in the evening and at 10:30 to bed.

Good Night!

Writings and 1st day on ship [Day 3]

Early at 7 o'clock my dear father awakened me. At 8:30 we must be again at the Hapag Luggage Hall. My dear one was not allowed to come to Cuxhafen (pier); therefore already at 8 o'clock he left. At 9 o'clock we drove to Cuxhafen. Already on the train we began to sing. After 2 hours, we arrived at Cuxhafen. As we stepped into the hall, our ship SS *New York* stood before us. Right away we could go aboard.

After the United States entered World War II, many OTC children were required to register with the government because they were not U.S. citizens and had come from countries with which America was at war. Upon registration, they were then given a certificate with their photo and fingerprint. These "foreign aliens" had to observe travel limitations in addition to other restrictions. Archives of One Thousand Children®, Inc.

First we were shown our cabin. I was given mine together with a little girl my age, Ruth Freudenberger, from Eberbach, near Heidelberg. The cabins are small, sufficient for 2 people with 2 beds—naturally, I sleep on top—a washstand, and a wardrobe.

We went on deck after the cabins were distributed. The weather is very pretty. Slowly, at 1 o'clock we sailed. At 1:30 we needed to go to dinner. After dinner we went again on deck. Already at 3 o'clock we could see Helgoland standing like a ruin in the middle of the ocean. We have a rough sea; therefore I don't feel so good. The other children feel the same. At 5 o'clock was an announcement for tea. Already at 7 o'clock this evening I go to bed.

Before I go to sleep I say my prayers.

Good Night!

Day 2 aboard Ship [Day 4]

I wake up and realize correctly that I am on the ship. Suddenly comes a familiar melody—it is a piece from "Trumpeter from Sechingen," the daily wake-up call. My cabin mate is also up already—it is 7:15. I take my prayer book and pray. Already the 1st call to breakfast is sounded. I must go on the 2nd call to breakfast. I get up and get dressed. The 2nd call to breakfast is sounded. Breakfast is very good and plentiful. I eat one egg, 2 little rolls with sausage, and tea.

After eating I go again on deck. Already one can see the coast of Southhampton.

I asked a sailor something: is it possible that you are also from Bad Kissingen?

We sail ever closer to the coast. In the middle of the ocean stands the ocean liner SS *Bremen*. Now our ship stops as well. A smaller boat brings and delivers passengers. After resting three quarters of an hour, we continue to sail again. Slowly we approach Cherbourg (France).

We play nicely on deck and at 5 o'clock I go to tea where music plays. After tea I go to the lower deck (Deckhalle). We play games. Slowly we sail along the coast. At 7 o'clock we anchor. Cherbourg can be seen very well all lit up. At 7:30 we sail again out of the canal. We now have very high tide. At 8:30 I go to bed. Before I sleep I pray again.

Good Night!

3rd day On Board Ship [Day 5]

It is 6:30 in the morning and we are having a storm. Our ship rolls badly. All are seasick. My cabin mate said, "I have a fever." At 8 o'clock the Steward came and asked what we wanted for breakfast. I ordered tea, zwiebach, ship's cookies, and fruit.

At 9:30 came our 2nd chaperon—our 1st chaperon is sick also since she sails for the first time. My cabin mate complains that she has fever.

At 11 o'clock the nurse came to my cabin mate, and at 11:30 the doctor came, who diagnosed that she had a throat infection.

The ocean has not calmed down and therefore I won't get up. So went the entire day. In the evening once again the ocean is rough. During the night it is still.

The children who travel with me to America. They are:

Friedel Heillsun, 15 yrs., Ziegenheim near Kassel
Ruth Schlamme, 14 1/2 yrs., Wurzburg
Ruth Kaufmann, 14 1/4 yrs., Frankfurt
Ruth Freudenberger, 13 1/2 yrs., Eberlach near Heidelburg
Ilse Hamburger, 13 yrs., Bad Kissingen
Betty Libovsky, 12 yrs., Tilsit
Lotte Phillips, 9 yrs., Urna
Sally Penner, 15 yrs., Urna
Ludwig Wolf, 14 yrs., Dormstadt
Kurt Salamon, 14 yrs., Hamburg
Rudolph Gross, 14 yrs., Mannheim
Heinz Lewin, 13 1/2 yrs., Tilsit
Gerhardt Badasch, 13 yrs., Berlin
Meinhardt Braunschweiger, 9 yrs., Wustensachsen
Werner Sommer, 7 yrs., Wustensachsen
[Ernst Stein was also in this group, though not listed by Ilse.]

Our lady traveling companion was Mrs. Lublind and our own private steward.

4th Day Aboard Ship [Day 6]

We have a storm again. It is 6:30—I pray. So goes this day exactly like the previous one. My cabin mate is still sick also.

5th Day Aboard Ship [Day 7]

The sea is still not calm, but nevertheless I will get up, that is if I can.

I get up . . . but what is it with me? Everything is spinning around me. I sink down and go to bed again. I console myself, for my cabin mate is sick as well.

At 10:30 a young girl comes and wants 20 ch; Ludwig Gross has a birthday and we want to buy him a pretty book.

In the afternoon our steward came by and asked how we were feeling. And so too passes this day just like the previous days.

6th Day Aboard Ship [Day 8]

Today I won't get up as soon or as quick, but up I'll get up, so I think. Said—done. At 8 o'clock I got up and at 8:30 I went for breakfast. There will be a children's festival this afternoon said our steward.

Every morning at 10 o'clock there is a morning concert. Also, every morning at 10 o'clock there is bouillon and pretzels. Today at noon there is chicken on rice, salad, and for dessert three flavors ice cream. We can have ice cream every day, in the evenings as well as in the mornings.

At 2:30 the "Kinderfest" began. First there was cocoa and cookies. Then each child received 2 balloons, 3 trumpets, and other toys. Then we all went on deck, where we were photographed by the captain and then it was over.

And so passed this day as well and soon the good time on the ship will be over. I forgot to write that today we were shown the entire ship. We needed two hours to see the entire ship. We went from the crew's housing to the commander's bridge, only in the machine rooms we were not allowed.

7th Day Aboard Ship [Day 9]

Today, again, I got up. Already, during breakfast I learned that this evening would be a costume celebration, which made me very happy. We have very lovely weather, the sea is very still and always we find ourselves on deck.

For lunch we had a breast of veal with young vegetables, potatoes, and for dessert various compotes. We were playing on deck all afternoon.

At 3:15 we could see the mast of the speed ocean liner *Europa* approaching more and more on the ocean and soon we will see all the ship, but before we could see her it began to rain very hard and like a water rat there I stand at 3:30 and the *Europa* passed by us. It took only a minute, so fast is she. Completely wet I went to my cabin to change.

After supper I put on my costume. I took a pair of pants from Ernst Stein, a tie and cap from Kurt Salamon, a shirt from Ludwig Stein and thus I will masquerade as a boy at the masquerade ball. At 12:30 I went to bed. During the evening I danced 6 "touren" [times], once even with a boy masquerading as a girl.

8th Day on the Ship [Day 10]

Today will be the last day on the ship. Since 12 o'clock midnight we are in the Gulf Stream and this evening we can see some land already.

Today we must pack. I needed two hours, for everything to be packed.

Today we have tongue and pear pomfrity [perhaps pear fritter] and 3 puddings with fruit sauce. After eating I immediately go back on deck, for today the weather is so beautiful and one has to take advantage since it is the last day.

At 7:45 is the farewell dinner. We have duck baked with red cabbage with potatoes, ice cream, fruit compote, coffee.

After dinner we continued to sit together in the writing room and played and amused ourselves and ate sweets, for who knows when we will find each other again?

At 10:30 we all go to bed after looking one more time whether we can see land and something can be seen already.

Good Night

Last Morning and Departure from Ship [Day 11]

Already at 5 o'clock a little boy shouted "we see the beam towers." I don't feel so good awakened with the screaming of that little boy. At 6:30 I, too, get up. Already at 7 o'clock there is the call for breakfast.

Now we can see New York quite clearly. We go on deck and from ship's end we can see the freedom statue "Liberty." At 12 o'clock we sail into New York harbor. Next to us in the harbor stands the ocean liner *Europa*. Once more we go on deck, after which we all must meet in the 1st class. At 1 o'clock the committee ladies come quickly, we are examined once more by the doctor, at 2:30 we are allowed to leave the ship.

On the pier stood Uncle Adolph and Mr. and Mrs. Seelig; my luggage paid quickly at customs; Uncle Adolph quickly sent a telegram to Germany.

Right away on the pier I eat a chicken salad. Uncle Adolph asked me, "Where do you want to sleep, at Seelig's or with me at the hotel?" Naturally, I say at Seelig's.

After we left the pier, one could plainly see the highest house in the whole world.

We drive by bus for one hour and then we stepped into a streetcar and drive around. Streetcar means strassenbahn. After another hour's travel, we are at our destination. We immediately saw many blacks.

In the evening we all eat at the Seelig's. At 8:30 Uncle Adolph leaves and at 9 o'clock I go to bed. I am so tired.

Sleep Wohl!

Pleasant Sleep!

1st Day in New York [Day 12]

It is a Saturday at 9:30 when I wake up. After breakfast I go shopping with Aunt Else. After lunch I go with Uncle Adolph to Archie Strauss and at night Uncle Adolph shows me the city of lights. Something like this I have never seen before—a sea of lights. Now we are going to Aunt Johanna's relatives.

At ten o'clock we went home.

Thus passed as well the first day in New York.

2nd Day in New York [Day 13]

After breakfast a friend of the Seeligs took me to the Negro Quarter, which is very interesting; a father strolls his children and at every corner sits a shoe-shine man.

At 11 o'clock I went to Lotte Hamburger, we were 1 hour on the way before we came to Lotte's house. We had to go by elevator to the 10th floor. Lotte was not at home, but she came shortly. We were so happy with each other. We ate with Lotte and I had to report everything to the smallest detail about Kissingen.

I stayed also through the evening meal and then we separated again—for how long we don't know. I still went to Nellie on this night. Uncle Adolph took a taxi and we drive to [the] Seelig's. As we come to them Mrs. Zimmerman, whom I know, is there. Today I go to bed shortly before 11 o'clock.

Good Night

3rd and Last Day in New York [Day 14]

It is Monday, the 9th of November, and today we want to travel to McGehee [Arkansas]. At 10 o'clock I paid a visit to Aunt Elsa, and she showed me the largest park in the world. After eating I went with Uncle Adolph to Broadway to the largest department store in the United States. It has 20 floors in it. The escalators are the nicest, the best, in this department store.

At 6 o'clock we depart. We are taking a sleeping Pullman and at 8 o'clock Philadelphia can be seen.

Already at 7:30 I go to bed since I can't tolerate train rides.

One Day in St. Louis [Day 15]

Early at 8:30 I get up, we still have a very far trip before us. At 1 o'clock we hope to be in St. Louis. I only eat fruit for breakfast. The trip is pretty boring, always only fields and very seldom a village.

At 1 o'clock we are in St. Louis. First we go to eat at the station hotel, after which we see St. Louis. Uncle Adolph has been in St. Louis so often. After that we go to the committee. Once again in the evening we go to eat at the train station hotel.

At 6 o'clock we continue riding further with the pullman.

Arrival in McGehee [Day 16]

At 5:30 my uncle awakened me—in a half hour we will be in McGehee. It is still deep night. At 6 o'clock the train pulls to the station. Uncle Wolffgang and Regina are at the station. The little one cannot speak a single German word.

The dear ones live on 3rd Street. The house is white on the outside with a pretty garden. The inside of the house is very cozy.

Little "Bettyle" still sleeps when I arrive, but awakes shortly. She is a precious child, blue eyes and blond hair. After breakfast the children and I go to the garden, we cannot understand each other at all.

Afterwards Jean Sue, who is Regina, goes to school. She is in the 2nd grade. I unpack my suitcase and take a bath.

After lunch Aunt Joan (Johanna) drives us to the mill, which is mighty big. She also drives me to town to show me the stores.

After the evening meal we go to town again and Uncle Bill (Wolffgang) buys me several dresses and overshoes.

At 10 o'clock we go to bed—Jean Sue sleeps with me.

Good Night!

McGehee's 100th Birthday [Day 17, plus later days combined in single entry]

Today is the second day in McGehee and also McGehee's 100th birthday. It is Thursday, the 12th of November.

In the morning there are big parades in town. After eating we all went to the movies finding a "Baby Show." Betty Ray (Betty) is with us as well, afterwards there is a film.

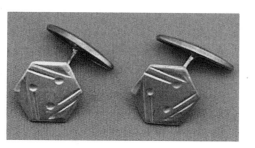

Mementos of home—a pair of cuff links, among the few possessions brought by Werner Zimmt to the United States in 1935. Regulations and circumstances usually limited to very little what OTC children could bring into the United States. Archives of One Thousand Children®, Inc.

In town are exhibitions. I have three sweaters, 2 won first prize and one 2nd prize.

In the evening the Dreifus family visited (Aunt Joan's uncle, aunt, and cousins). So passed also the second day in McGehee.

After 14 days' stay in McGehee, I moved to Little Rock, Arkansas (main city of Arkansas).

I came to a German family—Simon, from Frankfurt am Main.

I live at 510 East 5th Street.

On the same day I came to the Jewish school, which meets once a week. I met also on this day Mr. and Mrs. Sam Block and daughter Leatrice and other relatives of Aunt Joan.

In the afternoon we went to the zoo and to the movies. At night I sleep at the Simons.

On Monday it rains and it is not at all a pretty day. The dear ones from McGehee are still here.

We visit the town (sightsee) and I was registered in school and I will be in the 6B in grammar school. On Tuesday I went to school for the first time.

Miss Evans is the principal of the school.

My teachers' names:

Mrs. Lee—English
Miss Koch—Arithmetic-Geography
Miss Darr—Librarian
Miss Dr [name obscured]—Singing
Mrs. McVay—Spelling and Drawing

I love school and for Christmas I will go to the dear ones in McGehee.

Fini!

End!

LETTERS

By Ruth Schlamme Schnitzer

On board, 8:30 a.m., 10/29/36

My dear ones!

This is the first bit of quiet I've had to write to you. I'll start at the beginning. So, I said goodbye to Rosenbusch and Mr. R. brought me to the train, where we got on a special train to Cuxhafen. A gentleman who had accompanied us that far explained my camera to me. Heli R. had done that too, but then I didn't really understand. We could already see the ship from the train, but when we approached it directly through a hall, our jaws dropped and we couldn't believe our eyes. None of the luggage was searched. We boarded immediately and I received Cabin 491 with little 9-year-old Lotte, who likes me so much and was beside herself with joy.

The weather was wonderful. We went up on deck immediately and were soooo happy. At 12:45 the ship left, you didn't even notice that it was moving. Then we looked for the various entertainment rooms, but couldn't find them. They aren't for 3rd class passengers anyway. At 2 o'clock we went to the children's room to eat. There was a little soup, a small kosher sausage and sauerkraut, and then pudding. While we were eating, the ship started rocking and we got dizzy. We went straight up to the deck and lay down on the deck chairs. Ilse started vomiting first. I felt so terrible, but I didn't throw up. It was so terrible. Once I went inside, but I felt sick again immediately, so that I wanted to spend the whole afternoon outside. People were standing around everywhere and . . . the bell rang for coffee. Mrs. L. said that I should drink some. I tried, but I couldn't stand it and went right back up to the deck. I didn't eat dinner either.

The bigger children sat on deck a little longer and now I'm sitting here and writing, while most of the others are lying in bed, sick. Lotte threw

Ruth Schlamme Schnitzer (second from right), 1936 shipmate of Ilse Hamburger Phillips, with foster family, the Luries (left to right) David, Lillie, Mordie, Judy, Rochester, N.Y., ca. 1937. Archives of One Thousand Children®, Inc.

up too. I have to sleep on the upper bunk because I feel so bad at night. Mrs. L. is sick too, her suitcase with my packages isn't there yet. The other fat woman is the stewardess, an Aryan who has traveled back and forth often. There are very many passengers. You can hardly turn around in the cabin, and it's an interior cabin. This trip is awful. The children are very nice, though, and we are trying to be cheerful. I can't promise you that you'll get mail again, because it's impossible to stay upright in the rocking ship, so I can't write any cards, either (also because of money), so I'm asking you, dear mother, to get these things. Don't be afraid, though—these 8 days will pass as well. Please greet all our friends and relatives and extra greetings and kisses for you from your,

Ruth

On board the *New York*, Friday, 10/30/36, 9:30

Dear ones!
Since I feel wonderful at the moment, I want to report immediately. So, yesterday evening, after I wrote you, I climbed into bed. I didn't even notice the rocking anymore and fell right asleep. At 2:00, when I woke up, I noticed for the first time that my card from you had arrived, and I thank you for it. It was terribly hot in the cabin. At 7 o'clock we were already awake and visiting each other. Gradually some got up, including me, and we went up to the deck at 8 o'clock, were all terribly hungry and waited for the trumpet to call us to breakfast. But when we looked at the clock, it was 7 o'clock again. Of course, we were disappointed and reset our watches. We have to do that now every day (an hour back). We stayed up on deck and saw land, but we didn't know what it was. Finally we heard the trumpet and we ran down to our children's room for breakfast. It was very big, you (could) have eggs of all kinds, tea or coffee, bread or rolls; I had two soft eggs and coffee. Afterwards everybody had an orange. Before breakfast, Mrs. L. took me to her cabin and unpacked the stuff from Aunt Bronia. It was a beautiful dark blue scarf, candy, and a diary like Karlchen also gave me. It was very big and everything preprinted—I am supposed to use a page for you and one for me, but I have so much writing paper, so I don't know if I'll do that. We can already see the English coast, and at 12 o'clock we'll be in Southampton, in Cherbourg not until tonight, I think. When we are through the Channel, then it really starts. Then it'll start rocking again. Right now it's low tide. If I feel good, I'm going to go to the movies tonight. I don't know yet whether I'll mail this or continue it until New York.

1:40 p.m.

I'm going to mail the letter at 6 o'clock in Cherbourg and then starting tomorrow, I'll write in order to send the letter on November 7 with the ship *Europa*. During the morning I stayed on deck, not because I felt nauseous, but because it was interesting. We traveled along the English coast, and met many ships. I took some photos and Ludwig, who has something similar to a Leica, took a lot of snapshots of us. He is an older boy, I don't know what his last name is. We also encountered the Bremen. At 12:30 we stopped, not on land, a boat came and brought the people over. Unfortunately I couldn't see how a car was lowered down.

Then we went to eat and nobody liked it. There was a little thin lentil soup, fish with potatoes, and for dessert rice with apricot sauce. After the meal, Friedel, Ruth, and I went into the cabin and ate fruit and chocolate. Now we were moving again, but you hardly noticed it. Today I also received my 4 dollars and bought tickets and coupons with it. Today, only Ruth Kaufmann from Frankfurt was seasick. I'm already looking forward to the coffee. Now I'm going to go up on deck again. Table tennis has not been set up yet, but the younger ones were playing Tip Kik a little while ago. Otto [my brother] would really like it here. We constantly have to look for little Werner Sommer. He's always running around and is always ahead of the others. Mrs. Lubliner said the last children stayed in a hotel in New York, and she will stay with us until we are sent on. I'm sure I'll go to Rochester, many are being sent to relatives.

I completely forgot something. As we left Hamburg on the train, I thanked Mr. Chassel and he gave me a kiss. He is already an old man, but terribly nice. I'm sure I've forgotten more and I ask you—please look in your letters. Mutti, how are you going to get information to Pappele? You guys are such bad letter writers, the others have already gotten lots of mail. A few American children run around here all day and make a huge amount of noise. Did any more going-away presents come? I'm not going to send Otto a pen. Today I'm a completely different person. So, now I want to check for mail again and I think that I'll be able to write again after coffee.

4:45 p.m.

So we were up on the deck and played the harmonica and a game of tag. Then I sat down on the intermediate deck and read Henriette Jacobi. Beate inscribed the book with the following: "A very small farewell gift from your friend Beate, with great affection." Just before coffee I watched Mrs. Lubliner and Sally playing chess. The trumpet called us for coffee and I drank two cups of tea and all kinds of cake. About that time it started to rock again pretty good and I didn't feel very well. This evening, Mrs. Lubliner and Mrs. L. are going to the welcome evening with us big kids. We have to stick together, though, and go to bed at 10:30 p.m. I would have preferred to go to the movies. If I wanted to practice the violin I would have to do it in the cabin, but I don't have a music stand and no space. The only piano is in the ladies sitting room where there are always a lot of people sitting. There are Russian peasant women on this ship and many other foreigners as well. Now, Mutti, if you think this letter is interesting, you can type it and distribute it. You should especially write to the Hamburgers from me, because I only sent them a card. Otherwise, please say hello to all the relatives and acquaintances who ask about me. How do you deal with the housework? When is the *Schweinerei* [the mess related to the remodeling her parents were planning] starting? Why didn't you send me a letter to Southampton, it could be that they just haven't brought it to me, or did you think I would not get your card until S [Southampton]? Now I have to go back up on deck or I'll start feeling sick. I send you much love and many kisses.

Ruth

Sunday, November 1, early

My dear ones!
It has to work—I'm writing in bed and I can't get up without getting dizzy. So, by Friday midday you'll know. Friday evening there was a really good meal: soup (I didn't eat it), lamb, beans and potatoes, then mail was distributed and then there was ice cream and bananas. Thank you very much for your sweet card. I started feeling bad during dinner, but I still got dressed up and went to the reception and *Winzerfest*. A lot of people had already gone to bed voluntarily. There was dancing and none of us knew how. But I was encouraged a little just by watching. At 10:30 a buffet was set up and there was everything you could imagine. Everything arranged beautifully, you could take as much as you wanted. But I didn't touch anything. I drank a water with lemon, that cost 35 pfennigs [a former monetary unit equal to 1/100 deutsche mark]. We went to bed at 11:30, actually 12:30, but nobody got up the next morning. We just lay there and vomited. Since Friday evening I have not eaten a bite, but I'm not hungry. The stewardess said that I should get some fresh air and I'm going to try. I don't know yet when I can write again.

Sunday evening

The day went by pretty quickly. I pulled myself together this morning and went up on deck. Then I ate some soup and just a little bit at the midday meal. There was meat and asparagus and almond pudding afterwards. The food keeps getting better and I can't eat anything. Tomorrow is Rudolf Gross's birthday and we all contributed 20 pfennigs and bought him a book.

Ruth F. is lying in bed with a temperature. This afternoon I played a little table tennis, but the ship rolled so much and we went up on deck until suppertime. It was wonderful, but I could hardly swallow anything—soup, chicken, strawberries, potatoes, plums, apples, and ice cream. This evening is a bock beer festival, but we aren't going. If I had known that ocean travel is so awful, I wouldn't have gone to America. So I can hardly wait for Friday. Otherwise nothing important happened, so I'll write you more tomorrow. Good night!

Tuesday, November 3, very early

I haven't been able to write to you until now. But even if I felt nauseous, I would write, because today is your anniversary. So, my most heartfelt congratulations and have a wonderful celebration even without me. Are you going to have a goose or a suckling pig?

So, back to general stuff. I'm sorry that I write you such dumb letters, but that's just the way it is. So I stopped Sunday, the night was terrible and I thought I could just stay in bed Monday morning, but just before the midday meal on Monday, when I woke up, I pulled myself together and got up. And how! I wobbled back and forth and sank immediately into a deck chair that I did not leave again until evening. I wash myself like Otto, even a little more, namely my face. Getting up is a terrible job. The deck chair was not on the deck, however, but in a big airy room where many people were lying. Mama, you wouldn't be able to stand it for an hour here. Children screaming and shouting like you never heard. It's 3rd class—what can one expect? Mrs. Lubl. lay next to me and was in exactly the same shape as I was. I hardly eat anything anymore, and that's why I've gotten very weak.

I could hardly believe it that it was really me who had to be forced to eat—that never happened to me before. I was brought tea and zwieback. Because I'm still afraid at night, I thought it would pass faster if I went to a film. This was in the dining room and they showed *Im Sonnenschein*. I thought I could see it again. After that I slept like a lamb and this morning we all feel good. Last night the stewardess experienced something— she almost died of fright. Reinhard and Gerhard (who comes from Berlin) disappeared; the first one had been up on deck at 1 a.m. and the other starting at 5 a.m.—just think what could have happened! Those idiots!

Thank God, now we've reached the halfway point of this "wonderful sea journey." I'm just afraid when I think how I'm supposed to pack my suitcase with all this rocking. Everything is a mess. I haven't been able to see whether my big suitcase is there. Mrs. Lubliner says she doesn't believe that we will stay in New York. Her boy had to continue on immediately. That would be terrible. What would I do with the packages? I'm just glad that I won't have to go too far away. Most of the children had to travel another 30 or 40 hours. Money is another thing. I could have taken as much as I wanted, people pay here with German money. Other than that there is none. I've already had to use some of my dollars. Now I've had breakfast. There are always nice things for breakfast. I drank tea and ate challah [egg-rich bread, often braided] with butter and an orange.

Our birthday boy yesterday got a wonderful cake from the stewards. We gave him the book *Goli*. This evening there is a costume party; I don't think I'm going to go, I don't know what I am supposed to wear. Now enough for today.

Wednesday, November 4, 9:15

Well, my dear ones, yesterday I didn't have any more time to write. It was the best day in a long time, we all felt healthy and lively. For the first time, I enjoyed eating again. In the morning there was a tour of the whole ship. I was actually disappointed in first class. The swimming pool and gym were tiny. Down below in the ship they have one kitchen after another. There is also a printing shop, and also you can see very beautiful shops, but probably everything is very expensive. I played ping-pong for the rest of the day. We organized a big tournament and I won third place. Now, yesterday evening was a costume ball. We thought and thought about what we should wear. Friedel and I went down to the baggage room and brought out dirndls, aprons, and headscarves. At midday I was already thinking about how I should dress little Ernst Steinhe has such a girl's face. After supper I got dressed—my brown shoes and red anklets, the blue dirndl, a while apron from Friedel, and my little red headscarf. Everybody really liked the way I looked. Friedel wore a red dirndl and we looked like sisters. She's 15 and so dark, too, but smaller than me. Then I got little Ernst and dressed him in my brown skirt and the little red blouse from Papa and the brown scarf. You had to laugh when you saw him. He really acted like a girl and was dubbed Liesel. Ilse dressed like a boy and nobody believed that she is a girl. So we sat down at a table and the music began.

There were some very nice masks. The boys didn't want to dance. I couldn't stand to watch any longer, my legs were itching to dance and I got up and took Friedel, who can't dance any better than I can, and we danced bravely with the others. Every mask was given a number and then there were prizes. I had number 64. Then we had to line up for a polonaise, which was also danced. Then the prizes were awarded and what do you think, my little Ernst got the last prize. He was so happy, he won a notebook. Then we were photographed with a flash; if it turns out, I'll send it to you. Friedel and I danced a lot of rounds and trampled on each other's toes. . . . Pretty soon the little ones had to go to bed. We waited for another buffet to be set up, but they only passed out crummy platters with rolls. I ordered an orangeade that again cost 35 pfennigs. At 12 o'clock we had to leave, at the order of the ship doctor. Mrs. L. was very upset over him; it's none of his business. In the middle of the party he called Mrs. L. outside and said that he could not take responsibility for that, because we had all been seasick and our parents weren't here.

Now we're not allowed to go to the movies today either. *Weltmeister*, of all things. Maybe we'll go to the children's party anyway. It's only for the very little ones, but we are being treated like them. Mrs. L. already laid into the doctor, but we have to be obedient. Now I want to play ping-pong again. At breakfast today we all really stuffed ourselves. An observant man wouldn't eat here, because they mix things up with kosher. Today we are already in the Gulf Stream, yesterday there was one other event on board, we met the *Europa*; it overtook us and everybody was calling "hello" back and forth. It was very windy and rained and the ocean swallowed a lot of caps. Both ships blew their horns in greeting. There's a terribly big fat girl on board here who wants to make friends with us. She speaks terrible German, but she talks with us and she said that she was in Germany for three months and comes from America. I thought she wasn't quite right in the head, because she's so childish. We estimated that she was 18 to 20 years old, but it turns out the colossus is 12. So, today I've been very industrious. More tomorrow.

Thursday, November 5, 10:45

Yesterday was a beautiful day again, but still I'm looking forward to the end of our trip. We played on deck, where it's like summer, because of the Gulf Stream. You notice it in the cabin too. We can hardly sleep, it's so warm. Sometimes the food is nothing special, but we can have ice cream every evening. Because Friedel is bringing over too many packages of cigarettes, Mrs. L. said that she should open some of them and we could smoke some together. We did that yesterday and sat down in the smoking lounge. When the stewardess noticed it, she got Mrs. L. right away and there was a scene. Mrs. L. said she didn't mean it like that, that we should do it publicly, and spoke with us very seriously. We're all right with each other again. The boys acted up terribly because they weren't allowed to go to the movies. Last night we all sat at a table and played and the boys kept bringing up the subject of movies. At 10 o'clock we went to bed. I also played the piano yesterday, my pop songs and *Fantasie*. All the children sat around me, and today I'm going to get sheet music from the library.

There was a children's party again. Friedel and I stood at the door and wanted to watch. We were just pushed inside and we drank cocoa and ate cake, were given little umbrellas with balloons and while the little kids were being photographed we slipped out. Early this morning I packed my suitcase and at 10 o'clock we all had to stop by the doctor's office. There was an "examination" and I think another one tomorrow. I don't know what I should do with the card that you sent me—I can't post a 15-pfennig card in New York. But I'll finish writing it today and the letter. I'm shocked at my handwriting, I hope you can read everything. . . .

Now I'm going to close and I'll write on the card what happens the rest of today and tomorrow.

Many affectionate greetings and kisses from your
Ruth

Letter from Mrs. Lubliner

Dear Mr. and Mrs. Schlamme!
You will be reassured to hear that your little daughter, since her seasickness has passed, is looking cheerfully into the future. I am sure that she will find friends everywhere and I ask you not to take the separation from your beloved child, which I myself have also gone through, too hard. We are compensated for the sacrifice with the beautiful things the child will experience.

With heartfelt greetings,
Your Johanna Lubliner

Brooklyn, November 6, 1936

My dear ones!
Well, I landed happily in New York and already got your letter and I thank you for it. Actually, I was a bit annoyed, because you, dear Mama, reminded me of homesickness, when I hadn't thought about that at all up to now. Now I want to tell you everything about my arrival. First of all, Thursday evening we had a wonderful supper: open-faced sandwiches, soup, duck with red cabbage, green salad, and applesauce, then dishes of ice cream with cookies, all kinds of fruit and tea or coffee. After this beautiful meal we chatted a little with the sailors and then we went to sleep. Just now Aunt Betty came in and said I should finish quickly because otherwise the letter can't go with the next ship. So, quickly: At 7 o'clock we were on deck and saw the first skyscrapers. At 9 o'clock, though, we still hadn't docked. There were negotiations going on and we had to wait. First we ate a good breakfast and then the ship moved again, along the pier. Of course, we saw the Statue of Liberty first and then the skyscrapers. As I said at the beginning, I took it all in as a matter of course.

We docked at Pier 86 and two ladies from the Committee came to us and we had to wait for hours until we were let off. They only spoke English with me, they didn't know much German. By the time all the papers were in order, it was 2 o'clock and we left the ship. You feel like you're in a train station, but without platforms. I saw Felix immediately and from somewhere else a man kept waving at me. I didn't know who he was. I went to him and said, "Siegfried Westing?" and he said Helmut Sprinz! He wears glasses and I didn't recognize him. He took charge of my luggage, etc. right away, and then Riesenfeld came up. They were just as I had imagined them and they were all so nice to me. Felix was

there the whole time and R. liked him very much, and they said he should visit me and that I would be staying for 14 days. There was a lady who spoke so nicely to me and seemed so familiar to me, but I didn't recognize her. It was Miss Rosenheim from Berlin and she will tell Aunt Bronia right away. Every child had relatives there and Meinhard also introduced his mother. They didn't search my luggage at all, I only had to open the big suitcase and shut it again right away.

After I said goodbye to the various ladies and thanked them, we got into a taxi and drove to Brooklyn. Helmut didn't come with us, he's coming this evening. My big suitcase is being sent on, I think, anyway, I don't have it here. We drove for a pretty long time and talked. So, [the] Riesenfelds will certainly make sure that Otto also comes over and we will go to Joe Grabowski personally. All the ladies at the pier told me specially that my family in Rochester is especially nice and lovely. We drove through the old New York and then through Brooklyn for a long stretch. R.'s live far out in a very beautiful and elegant house. The apartment is big and modern and a Negro girl opened the door. A young Mr. Sommerfeld is also visiting from Berlin, but he is leaving this evening. I unpacked the gifts and they were all very pleased. Arthur is a devil, he never puts the harmonica down which I brought him.

After I arrived we ate midday dinner and then I unpacked. After we had coffee I went shopping with Aunt Paula and Arthur. There are wonderful shops here. There is a lot of fish. The salesgirls all look like dolls, with bright red fingernails. I am sleeping in the living room. The Riesenfelds don't have a bedroom either, they also sleep on a couch. Of course, there are built-in cupboards everywhere. I can't send the packages for the Stern's boys because they are in the big suitcase. I find that very embarrassing, actually. The other children are traveling on tonight. So, this letter is No. 1, I'm not counting the ones from the boat. The R.'s say that Opapa will come soon and that he can stay with them. Sometime please read one of my letters to Omama Julchen because I don't want to write the same thing twice and otherwise she'll be hurt. And anyhow she wouldn't believe me that I like it here a lot. I'm sure R.'s will offer me a lot, but I think 14 days is too long, because I don't have enough things for that long and I'm very curious about Rochester. That was a sad anniversary for you, Mama. Maybe we can celebrate the next one together in the U.S. R.'s say that you are also coming over soon; they are very serious about it. They'll definitely bring Otto over here. So, enough for today, supper's on the table.

Many loving greetings and kisses, affectionately, your Ruth

Postscript from Paula Westing

Best greetings! Ruth has arrived safely and is well. She looks wonderful and is just the girl for our taste. We are very glad to have her and she will be happy here.

Heartfelt greetings, Paula

FROM "ABOUT OUR FAMILY, FOR OUR FAMILY"

By Lea Wasserman Schwarz [1982]

For my daughters, Elaine and Susie

The name of the boat was *Guinee*. It was a coast liner and this was the first time it crossed the ocean. We stood on deck as it moved away from the dock. Within the first ten minutes I got seasick and began to heave over the side of the ship. There was no relief of the nausea and I was forced to go below deck to lie down. I was in an upper bunk. That was where I spent the next ten days. I was unable to eat, and what food I attempted to swallow would not stay down. There was no medication, and I grew steadily weaker. While I was lying there asking for a doctor, a big slob of a steward professed to be a doctor and abused me sexually. I did not have the strength to fight him and felt too miserable to care. After about ten days out, one of the women, her name was Lotte Samulon, realized that I was in serious trouble. She asked someone to help carry me to the deck for fresh air and requested some white meat and chicken soup. She cut it up like one does for a baby and fed it to me spoon by spoon. I recovered some strength and was able to hold up my head again.

After that I spent most of the time on deck and was able to keep down whatever food I felt like eating, which wasn't much. Fortunately, I was able to walk off the ship on my own. Had it not been for this woman, I am not sure I would have survived the trip. At the very least, they would have had to carry me off the boat. . . .

After fourteen days at sea the boat arrived outside of New York harbour on the evening of April 14th, 1941. We could see the lights of the city in the distance, but had to wait till the next morning for a harbour pilot to come aboard and guide the ship in.

FROM A PRESENTATION AT THE ONE THOUSAND CHILDREN REUNION AND CONFERENCE

By Walter Kron [2002]

On the ship itself, there were ten of us and in the afternoon there were tea dances and social gatherings. One of the passengers on the ship was a young man, a young black man, a doctor who had taken an internship in Vienna, which I gather in those days was still a major medical center, and he was on his way back to Atlanta or some southern city. He danced with the two girls who were part of our group. He did that a couple of times. And then one day one of the girls came to us and told us that an elderly lady had taken her aside and

Shipmates Walter Kron (left) and Warren Hirsch (right) meet again after sixty-five years at the first national Reunion of the One Thousand Children in 2002. They arrived in the United States in 1937. Archives of One Thousand Children®, Inc.

said, "You're going to America, you're going to live there. Well, one thing I think you probably want to know is with respect to dancing with this man, we don't do that kind of thing in America."

We'd been hearing that about ourselves, where we just came from. It was clearly understood that nobody was to talk to us or to have social contact with us and now we were faced with a situation in which there was another group that we were told we don't have any contact with, and the girl was very disturbed and I remember we met in one of the cabins and we talked about it. We got kind of scared at the time. What kind of a world are we coming to? We know the kind of world we're going from. Now look what we were coming to.

Chapter 5

TRANSITIONS

*I*n chapter 4, we saw some hints of the children's transitions to their new homeland and new families. This chapter underscores the beginning of the inner journey from European child to American adult. Sightseeing trips, visits with relatives living in the United States, and temporary lodgings in orphanages and other shelters give way, in most cases, to the foster home arrangements that were the goal of the various agencies whose combined efforts made rescue possible. Variations in experience, perception, and memory about these initial steps into a new life are functions of the child's age, personality, particular situation, and—of course—when in the decade-long history of OTC rescues an individual story occurred.

Henry Birnbrey confronts the irony of having escaped repression only to discover, among his earliest American experiences, that his new country is not free from the problems of racism.

Charles Juliusburg provides useful insights into the "selection process." In some cases, children were brought to the United States before foster homes had been found, and interviews helped match the newcomers with foster parents. Special locations were needed to house the children (and begin their Americanization) during this selection process. An interesting sidelight is his renaming from Heinz to Charles, a step that is not only a convenience, but also an obvious adjustment of identity. (Birnbrey, also originally named Heinz, adopted the American name Henry.)

For Martin Birn, we offer a somewhat wider sweep that encompasses the final arrangements for his departure from Germany and his voyage to the United States. Birn tells of the strains of adjustment, both for himself and for the family with whom he lives. Indeed, Birn's story—not altogether unusual in this respect—necessitates a removal from his first foster home and *placement in a second when it becomes clear that the Blumberg household no longer can accommodate him. (Like many of the boys who came to the United States as mere children, Martin Birn found himself in his new country's military service before the end of World War II.)*

For Bill Graham, who went on to become a major impresario in the world of rock music, the transition brought its own layer of emotional scars to those he had already suffered in Europe. Young Bill finds himself passed over time and again by those who come to select a foster child. Ironically, the town he finds himself living in while receiving such psychic pain is named Pleasantville. Another irony of Graham's embryonic American life is that of being the victim of anti-German attitudes among the schoolchildren. The refugee finds himself treated as the enemy. Graham's rapid absorption of American popular culture no doubt anticipates the mark he would make in the entertainment field.

The next section of this chapter introduces Gabrielle Kaufmann Koppell, initially through an interview that outlines her participation in the first American rescue effort (late 1934) and the consequent task of supervising children awaiting foster home selection while living at the Clara de Hirch Home in New York City. Dr. Kaufmann's memories are then followed by the voices, in letter form, of the many children who looked to her immediately as a parental surrogate. Children's parents also wrote letters of thanks to Dr. Kaufmann and to inquire about their child's health and placement. Through these documents, we gain a threefold perspective—that of the caregiver, that of the young European Jewish child in the process of becoming an American Jewish child, and that of the intense concern of the natural parents as well. Indeed, here and elsewhere, we come to appreciate the wisdom of a plan that placed these children in Jewish foster homes.

The final section, selections from letters to Thea Kahn Lindauer written by her father, Samuel Kahn, and other relatives, gives us another kind of dual perspective: the life Thea is leading in America and the life she might have been leading if her parents had not dared to send her to the United States. From their responses to her letters, we can infer what kind of news and impressions she was sending to them. Translated by Lindauer and accompanied by her commentary as an adult rereading these letters after many years, this material provides insights into both the state of mind of the OTC child and the perception of that child of those times as an adult.

FROM "MY STORY"

By Henry Birnbrey [2000]

We came over on a beautiful German ship [in April 1938], and though the ship's crew wore Nazi emblems, as did some of the passengers, we were treated with respect and encountered no problems on the voyage.

Arriving in New York harbor was just like one would expect from the movies, as we passed the Statue of Liberty and for the first time saw the skyline of New York. It was truly an emotional event.

We were met by a Mrs. Marcuse, Director [of Placement] of the German-Jewish Children's Aid, and she placed us in the George Washington Hotel on Lexington Avenue for the night. (In later correspondence, my mother indicated that Mrs. Marcuse might be a relative, but I never followed it up.) While this hotel would probably not meet today's standards, to us it was a palace. That evening we were taken to a movie, and I still remember the title, *Donkey Serenade*, which contained some beautiful and then-popular music. Also present was Mr. Armand Weil, who was the Director of the Hebrew Orphans' Home in Atlanta. He accompanied me and a young girl who was going to West Point, Georgia, on the train ride to Atlanta. I recall how he tried to explain the Mason Dixon Line and Jim Crow to me as the passengers had to change coaches as we passed Washington. The black ("colored") passengers left for the coaches designated "colored" and the white passengers remained in their seats. For the life of me I could not understand his explanation, as I really could not comprehend Jim Crow laws until I came to Birmingham. On that same train ride it was suggested that my name be changed from Heinz to Henry. Interestingly enough, this was most appropriate, as I was named after my grandmother, Henriette.

When we reached Atlanta, we merely changed trains at the old Terminal Station for my continuation to Birmingham. I had been sponsored by the Birmingham Section of the National Council of Jewish Women, and I became a ward of an organization rather than a family. This had its advantage as well as disadvantages. During my ten months in Birmingham I had more dinner invitations than most people have in a lifetime. Being the first one of a kind, I became a curiosity, but I want to emphasize, all of these people meant well. On Sundays I made the church circuit, speaking to churches about what was going on in Germany; needless to say, I could barely speak English. . . .

FROM A MEMOIR

By Charles Juliusburg [1992]

The day after our arrival in New York, we were to be taken on a sightseeing trip. It was decided that I would not be allowed to go with the group due to my fever. I gathered all my strength and limited knowledge of the English language and complained to the nurse that

Charles Juliusburg and
others at a children's
masquerade party aboard
the ship arriving in New
York, December 7, 1934.
Archives of One Thousand
Children®, Inc.

I was not sick enough to be left behind, and that "I want also go" with
the others. It was then decided that perhaps my fever was not due to
a cold or other illness but due to excitement, and I was permitted to
go.

We went on a double-decker bus, on the uncovered upper level.
Even though the weather was cold and raw, typical for December, we
did not mind the cold. We went on a street that ran parallel to the
Hudson River and were told that across the river was "another state."
Translated literally, that meant "another country" to me. I did not understand that for a year or two. We went to the Empire State building, at the time the tallest building in the world. We could not,
however, go to the top observation deck because the social worker,

Lotte Goldschmidt Magnus, dietician, in the
Army Medical Corps, Ft. Leonard Wood,
Missouri, where she helped care for German
POWs, 1944. Lotte was among a handful of
OTC women who joined the armed forces.
A shipmate of Charles Juliusburg, she
arrived in the United States on December 7,
1934. Archives of One Thousand Children®,
Inc.

who was our tour guide and chaperone, was unable to pay the admission fee and there was nobody there who could, or would, waive the fees.

We were taken to a drug store. Literally translated, that meant a store that sold drugs, a pharmacy. I found it unbelievable how much other merchandise was displayed in that store. We were then taken to the soda fountain or lunch counter, and a "soda" was ordered for me. Soda to me meant that it had something to do with soap. I did not think I would like it and resisted tasting it. I learned to like it. It was my second learning experience of many, many others. The first "new experience" in the U.S. was my first night at the orphanage, when I found out that we were covered with blankets instead of featherbeds (down comforters) used in Europe.

After another night at the orphanage, we began our rail trip to Chicago. The trip took two days. In Chicago we transferred to another train that took us to Zion, Illinois.

There, we were taken to a farm (Bensinger farm) that had two buildings that were converted into dormitories: one for boys, the other for girls. We were to stay there until a foster home was found for us. There, we met children who had come from Germany on previous children's transports.

Here, I found out about another difference between Germany and America. I needed a button to be sewn onto a shirt and asked one of the girls to take care of it. Our social worker put a stop to that nonsense and told me that in the United States it is expected that even though I am a male I had to sew the button on myself. (This was in 1934.)

Life at the Bensinger farm in Zion, Illinois, was interesting. There were so many things to learn. There were so many things that were new to me. Radio with loudspeakers and everything on radio was in English, pull-down shades on the windows, the food we ate, like Kellogg's cereal . . . and since it was the pre-Christmas season, all those Christmas songs that I thought were "German" were sung in English, such as "O Tannenbaum" (O Christmas Tree) and "Heilige Nacht" (Holy Night).

It was here, at the farm, that I was told about my mother's death. The farmer, Mr. Bensinger, was a pious Jew and he told me that it was a Jewish custom to tear a piece of clothing as a sign of mourning. He chose a sleeveless pullover sweater, but since it was practically new (as most of my other clothes were) I would not allow it to be torn apart.

We entertained ourselves by playing games, some of which were supervised by adults. My grades in the German schools had been particularly good in Art and Math courses, so I was selected to paint something, freehand, on a canvas on an easel. Mr. Bensinger gave me some coveralls to wear for the occasion. I had never seen coveralls such as these, which were customarily worn by farmers and housepainters.

A few days after our arrival, we were enrolled in a two-room school. One room was for the first four elementary grades, the other for the next four. The teacher told the classes about us and about the language difficulties we would encounter. It was a surprise to everyone that my scores in Spelling were mostly 100s. I found the other subjects very difficult, especially Geography and History, which were completely different from the like subjects in Europe. I found it especially diffi-cult to understand the concept of forty-eight states in one country or nation.

We were also given practical lessons in English, such as being sent into a store alone and told to buy something. I had a small ring binder about 2" × 4" and was asked to buy a filler for it at a 5- and 10-cent store. It took me a long time, but I got the job done.

Periodically, we had some visitors from Chicago. Families that wanted to provide a foster home for one of us came to look us over and converse with us as best as they could, considering the language problems. One of the families, whose name was Simons, selected a boy by the name of Herbert Simon, because the last names were so simi-lar. (Herb Simon had come from Germany in a previous children's group.) I thought that finding a family with a name similar to Juliusburg was extremely unlikely.

We were interviewed about our likes and dislikes by social work-ers of the Jewish Children's Homefinding Society, which was an agency of what was later to become known as the United Jewish Chari-ties. (The head of this agency was a Mr. Kepecs, whose office was in New York. I never met him. He held a subcabinet position in President Roosevelt's cabinet.) In these interviews they tried to get information from us that would help them place us with a foster family with simi-lar interests.

As previously mentioned, my greatest interests were freehand draw-ing and mathematics, so they tried to find a family with some connec-tion with architects. Heinz Neuman liked the stories he had heard about Henry Ford.

The social workers felt that it would alleviate some of my grief about the loss of my mother if a family could be found to accept two boys. We would keep one another occupied and entertained, thus we would have less time to think about other things. So, when a family was found where two sons and one son-in-law each had a car dealership (Henry Ford syndrome), and a daughter who was an accomplished artist (my interest in freehand drawing), they found a "fit" for Heinz Neuman and me.

Both of us were to go to Chicago for a weekend visit to that family, so they could look us over and we had an opportunity to look them over. We were put on a train and given instructions of at what station to get off. We wrote down the name of the previous station as well, so that we could have advance warning and look for the station where we were to exit the train. Whoever put us on the train also instructed the conductor to let us off at the proper station. Another social worker was to meet us at our destination and deliver us to the family.

Everything went wrong. We did not recognize the station nor the one before it, nor did the conductor remember to remind us to get off. Before the train's doors were closed prior to leaving the station, the social worker, who was to meet us, stopped the train, and a car-by-car search was made until they found us. And so it was, that on Friday, January 18, 1935, we were brought to the house of Nathan and Freda Katzin, there to spend the weekend.

I had been previously told that the Katzins were Russian (East European) and was therefore surprised that Mr. Katzin did not have a long beard and was not wearing a long black robe. I had a preconceived idea of what a Russian or East European Jew should look like. I probably had been influenced by the anti-Semitic propaganda in the German press.

At the Katzins that evening, we had a typical Friday night dinner. Erev Shabbat, the night before the Sabbath. I thought that the whole family was there just to look us over. It never occurred to me that this was a weekly family get-together. There was Frank, son, with his wife, Margaret; another son Sam; their daughter Lillian with her husband, Michael Braude. I think there were also some other relatives.

Dinner consisted of soup, beef, chicken, potatoes, salad, cooked vegetables, desserts, wine; a feast, the likes of which I had never seen. We communicated with one another, we spoke German and they spoke Yiddish. Yiddish sounds like archaic bad German with many words in other languages, such as English, Russian, Polish, etc. It is a language that the Jews formed from all the languages they encountered in the countries through which they travelled, while being chased from place to place looking for a homeland.

Mrs. Katzin was a typical Jewish mother. She welcomed us and told us that we must be hungry. And when a German of that era was told that something MUST be, that was an order. So Heinz Neuman and I ate and ate and ate. I, for one, thought it was the most delicious meal I had ever had. Mrs. Katzin blessed the candles before the meal, Mr. Katzin blessed the meal.

At the table, everyone asked us many questions about many things, mostly about our families and about Germany. One of the guests, Michael Braude, told us that he wanted to make a deal with us; he would teach us English if we promised to teach him some German. Of course, we agreed. And then we learned our first American slang. He told us that if anyone said anything to us that we could not understand, we should wave a hand in a certain way and say: "Oh, skip it." And then, if that person persisted to keep on talking, and we still did not understand, we should again wave a hand and say: "Ah—NUTS." We took him at his word.

After dinner, everyone except Mr. and Mrs. Katzin retired to another room, and, behind closed doors, a card game was started and cigarettes were smoked. I thought that to be very strange, because things such as card playing and smoking on the Jewish Sabbath were no-nos.

Since both Heinz Neuman and I had the same first name (Heinz), we were asked what we would like to have as our Americanized first names, and we both preferred Harry, which is the literal translation of Heinz.

Lillian Braude then suggested that in order to avoid confusion, I should be called Charles (for Karl), and since she did not like the name Harry, that Neuman should be called Henry (for Heinrich). We agreed, and so it was, even though I could not pronounce Charles.

We were taken to the bedroom where we were to spend the night. We walked through a long corridor, with doors on both sides. Not knowing that some of these doors led to closets, I presumed that each door represented one room. I wrote home (to Germany) about that beautiful apartment, with lights on the walls (candelabras) and umpteen rooms, and so much food, etc., etc. I was duly impressed. Henry and I, in a double bed together, took out the prayer books we had brought from Germany, covered our heads with our hands since we did not have yarmulkes with us, and said our prayers. Just about that time, Mr. Katzin opened our door and witnessed that. He was very pleased to see us praying.

The following day, we accompanied Mr. Katzin to the synagogue for Sabbath services. On Sunday, it was decided not to send us back to Zion . . . and on Monday, Sam enrolled us in public school. It was a very cold January day. . . .

FROM A MEMOIR

By Martin Birn [2001]

I landed in New York on Feb. 1, 1940, and was met by Uncle Max, cousin Lotte, and Ann Haas, my friend from Schweinfurt and then Lotte's girlfriend in New York. One of my first impressions was of Ann chewing bubble gum and her ability to blow large bubbles. I had never seen chewing gum before and blowing of a bubble blew my mind. Also I experienced my first subway ride and was amazed by the many blacks I saw. The handful of blacks I had seen in Germany were with the circus when it came to town.

I stayed with the Blumenthals a few days in their Brooklyn apartment. While there, I saw and ate my first grapefruit, cold cereal, "bubble" bread, chewing gum, milk shake, and was dazzled by supermarkets, drug stores, soda fountains, the subway, Macy's, escalators, and many other new and wonderful things.

Then one of the Blumbergs (I don't remember who) came and took me by train to what would be my new permanent home with them in Philadelphia. Tante Nanny Blumberg was my mother's stepsister from Grandfather Louis's first marriage. She came to the U.S. in 1905 at age twenty-five, married almost immediately, and had never been back to Germany since then.

In retrospect, living with the Blumbergs must have been quite a cultural shock. The household consisted of Uncle Morris, Tante Nanny, and their seven children ranging in age from thirty-four to eighteen. Milton was the oldest, Lillian the youngest, with Becky (her name was Rebecca, but later on she wanted to be known as Ruth), Helen, Morton, Betty (Bert), and Bill in between. The house was a typical Philadelphia row house, with a living room, dining room, and kitchen downstairs and three small bedrooms and a bathroom upstairs. The bathroom was so small that it had no room for a sink, only had a tub and toilet. One leaned over the bathtub to wash. There were two double beds in the girls' bedroom, a double bed, a single bed, and a folding cot on which I slept in the boys' bedroom. I have no idea how four people got their clothing into one small closet. Money and jobs was still scarce then. Uncle Morris had a bread delivery route, and he had Bill helping him. Milton was a foreman at a candy factory and was probably making the most money. Lillian was a senior in high school. She, Bill, Morton, and Helen finished high school. The others had to go to work before graduating. Helen was working as a beautician. I was very impressed with Milton because he not only had a large model airplane with a real gasoline engine, he also had a tattoo of his social security number on his biceps, both things I had never seen before. Uncle Morris and Tante Nanny were fluent in German and spoke that to me at first, but the others knew very little German. So it took several months before the question to Milton about the significance of the number meant anything to me. Uncle Morris was orthodox, therefore Tante Nanny kept a kosher house. However, none of the cousins ever went to synagogue that I recall. However, Bill told me recently that the three boys were Bar Mitzvahed.

It was only a day or two after arriving in Philadelphia that I started in public school: John Welsh Elementary, about ten blocks away. Like Meryl's understanding of German in Starnberg, my understanding of English was minimal despite three years of study. Therefore I was first put into fifth grade. However, it didn't take very long, perhaps two months, before my English was good enough to be put into the sixth grade, after another month in the seventh grade, and finally after a semester or two in the eighth. This put me only 1 year behind where I should have been based on my age and when I started school. I still have the report card from the eighth grade.

Living at the Blumbergs was probably the most difficult time in my entire life. Beside being a teenager with its associated normal problems, my upbringing as an only child in an upper-middle-class family was ill preparation for living in a foreign country, a small house, surrounded by nine adults, no privacy, and probably feeling very isolated. The mere fact that the Blumbergs took me in, considering their own circumstances, showed where their heart was. But that, of course, was not something I gave much thought to at that time. Uncle Morris, who was a Litvak (from Lithuania), let me know more than once his opinion of German Jews (his wife not withstanding), which was anything but complimentary. And I might add with good reason. German Jews had a great disdain for and superiority complex over Eastern European Jews. He subscribed to the *Tag* (the *Day*) a Yiddish daily newspaper, and I learned to read it a little, which enhanced my stature a bit. Of course there was no arguing about the content. If it was in the *Tag*, it was gospel.

The Blumbergs' children all had to earn their own spending money (there was no such thing as allowance), and I was no exception. So it didn't take long before I learned about the world of business. My very first exposure to the marketplace was selling imitation carnations made by one of the cousins on Mother's Day. After that, I became a soft pretzel seller. Every Saturday morning, I would go to the pretzel bakery, buy at two for a penny as many pretzels as I thought I could sell and sell them in front of the neighborhood movie at a penny a piece. In those days, the movies had not discovered popcorn, and pretzels (with or without mustard) was what one took to the movies. I probably earned twenty-five or thirty cents a week. The pretzels were sold from a picnic basket covered with a clean dishtowel, and the only other thing you needed was a jar of mustard with a paddle similar to a paint mixer and some small paper bags, which I bought from the local supermarket. Some of my classmates in school earned their spending money by shining shoes, but I was told in no uncertain terms that shining shoes is not something Jewish boys did.

I saved enough money that year (probably three or four dollars) to buy a used bicycle, a balloon-tired Columbia. Incidentally, the frame of that bike broke while being ridden the day before I went into the service four years later, and I just abandoned it on some street in Philadelphia. My first job for wages was at a small grocery store whose owner was a friend of the Blumbergs. I did everything from waiting on trade to unloading merchandise, delivering orders, and sweeping.

I have no idea how long I kept getting letters and writing letters to my father. Probably nothing after June 1940, when Italy entered the war and there was no longer any direct mail service between Germany and the U.S. I do not have a single one from that period.

As to the fate of my father, sometime after the end of the war, I got a phone call. I don't know when or from whom or how he found me. The man said he was in Auschwitz with my father and that he died there. I didn't have the presence of mind at that time to get more information. I have made inquiries through the International Tracing Service of the International Red Cross. The letter from them stated that "Birn, Sali, born in Estenfeld on 21.7.1890, Last place of residence: Estenfeld No. 29, was deported to Ghetto Theresienstadt or Concentration Camp Auschwitz in 1942" (day and month not indicated). It further stated that, "In the incomplete original records which are available here of Concentration Camp Auschwitz or of Ghetto Theresienstadt, the name of your father could not be ascertained." No other information has turned up to shed more light on his fate. Some record may still show up in the future, since the Tracing Service got a lot more records from the Russians when the Soviet Union collapsed (the Russians liberated Auschwitz) and it will take the Tracing Service's small staff a long time to translate and sort the information. But I don't have much hope.

I came to the U.S. under the auspices of the German-Jewish Children's Aid, whose representative met the ship in New York and was the major institution for settling children who came without parents and had no relatives to go to. In Philadelphia, I was a ward of the Association for Jewish Children. And fortunately, I remained under their care until I went into the Navy. I am not sure what the mechanism was, but having a social worker visit me occasionally gave me a chance to explain my side of the many conflicts that arose while living at the Blumbergs. The Association also bought me clothing, took care of my medical and dental needs, and paid a small amount toward my food costs (this only after Tante Nanny found out I had an appetite like three elephants). They also saw to it that I got a chance to go to special events sponsored by various organizations for underprivileged children. For example, during the summer of 1940, I had the opportunity to go to a two weeks' summer camp in the Poconos. The camp was sponsored by the local Elks. I was very proud to win the award for the biggest eater—it was no contest, I was the runaway winner. The award was a small shovel that I kept on my key ring for a long time and showed off at every opportunity to the embarrassment of the adults.

Ellis Gimbel, head of the Philadelphia branch of Gimbel Brothers department store, always bought out an entire matinee performance of the Ringling Brothers circus when it came to town, to be filled by underprivileged kids from orphanages and social agencies. Not only was I able to get out of school to go to the performance, every kid got a big bag full of candy, popcorn, and a soft drink.

The Association had a couple of families in Atlantic City that took in children for some R & R during the summer. So during the summer of 1941, my social worker saw to it that I got a chance to go for a week or two, I don't remember how long. But I do remember having a wonderful time exploring the town with several other kids my age. In those days, there was the Steel Pier, the Heinz Pier, and, of course, the long boardwalk and sandy beach. The trip back to Philly was especially memorable because I rode the whole way in the rumble seat of a Model A Ford. What a thrill.

I also visited Uncle Max in Brooklyn for a week or two and spent several days all by myself at the 1940 New York World's Fair. This was the introduction of fluorescent lights, television, and all kinds of new concepts in transportation, manufacturing, science, etc. And I was like Alice in Wonderland.

From the summer of 1940 on, the economy started getting better. Morton got a job at the shipyard. Helen put two of her sisters (Ruth and Lillian) through beauty school and they opened up a beauty shop. Bill went into the Army.

Prior to graduating from elementary school in the summer of 1941, I applied and got accepted at the Mastbaum Vocational School, one of three vocational schools in Philadelphia. Entrance to the school was very competitive, one had to pass a series of stringent academic as well as aptitude tests. So getting accepted was a real personal triumph. In ninth grade, they had something called "Trade Exploratory." You took classes in woodworking, auto mechanics, textile, electricity, and machine shop in addition to the regular academic subjects in order to learn what you are best at. The school day was much longer than the regular academic Jr. High School. It was there that I discovered my interest in and talent for things electrical.

About that time, a potentially tragic event turned out serendipitous. That event was leaving the Blumberg household and going to live with the Marx family.

In the early part of 1942, all the Blumberg boys were in the military. Helen, who had gotten married previously, was expecting her first child. Since her husband Morris also had been drafted, she moved back into the Blumberg house taking the second bedroom, so there was no longer room for me. One of my options was to live in the orphanage run by the Association for Jewish Children in Philadelphia; the other was to find a family to live with. My social worker found such a family in the Marxes, who ran a boardinghouse in Northeast Philadelphia, had room for me, and I guess both they and I were willing to take a chance to see if my living there would work out. It did. . . .

FROM *BILL GRAHAM PRESENTS: MY LIFE INSIDE ROCK AND OUT*

By Bill Graham and Robert Greenfield [1992]

We got to New York on September 24, 1941. I remember seeing the Statue of Liberty, but I remember much more thinking that this was gonna be the beginning. I remember we'd all been told that the one thing that would happen was that we'd all be separated. We were going to go to this place in Pleasantville, New York, to be put in dormitories. Then we would be put out for adoption or to live in private homes. We were told that people would come visit us on weekends. But we were told that we would not be together.

I went through Ellis Island, but I have very little memory of that. Space. Lines. Lots of luggage. I had my yarmulke and my prayer book. Some pictures of my parents and my sisters. I don't recall having anything else. I had no attachments to anything I can think of. No toys. To this day, I've never knowingly enjoyed a toy.

Fifty of the One Thousand Children arriving in New York in 1941, among them Bill Graham and Camilla Tidor Maas. Photographer Leo Lieb. Courtesy of the *Aufbau*.

I knew I was again going to be pulled away from something. I'd gotten used to living and traveling with this bunch of people. I guess I got used to the orphanage in Berlin and then I got used to the chateau at Chaumont. It wasn't my real family. It wasn't my sisters. But it was these same people, you know? And now I was in America, where they told me that somebody was going to take me in their house. Who, I didn't know. People *they* didn't even know. I was going to be with people *no one* knew. So I guess the question I kept asking myself was, "Who *are* these people going to be?" But it was an answer no one knew.

Of the sixty-four kids who set out from the chateau in France three months earlier, eleven made it to New York. . . .

They put us on a bus up to Pleasantville, which is a couple of hours' drive from the city in upstate New York. There were army barracks up there, with double bunks. I remember them because when I was drafted years later, it was the same thing. I had the top bed. This is my first real beginning of ongoing memory, very strong and detailed, that never left.

Families and couples would come up there on weekends and look to see if they wanted any of us in their homes. Whether they were good people or bad people or whatever their reasons might have been, there was another factor that went along with it. At that time, there was a great drive within the Jewish community in the Greater New York area to be involved with these Jewish orphans. Immigrants from Europe who were parentless.

The Jewish Foster Home Bureau offered forty-eight dollars a month to these families so it would not be limited to only people with money. Some people I know did it because of humanitarian reasons. Others did it because . . . "Hey, maybe I can net six dollars a month out of this."

It first entered my mind that it was a business venture when I saw the way some of the people who came there talked to me. At the time, I didn't even know what business was, but people were thinking about taking me in their home—judging me. You got to understand. One of the most important factors of my life, something that set it off in a certain way, was that they came there with this attitude. As though they were going to a pet shop. You know, what will *we* have to do? What are the positives and negatives of having this stranger in our house? Now I look at it much more analytically. But at the time, I thought, "Why don't they want *me*?" Because I was rejected from September twenty-fourth until the twelfth of November. Every weekend, and also sometimes during the week. . . .

Nine weeks I waited for someone to pick me out. I would clean myself up special for each and every visit because I didn't want to stay there with a lot of other strangers. It was a revolving door. Every one of the others I had come with had already been taken out. I was the last of the eleven. I'd stand by my bunk, which I'd made up very tight and clean. I wanted someone to go with, to choose me. I hated—*hate*— being up for sale. The few weeks I spent in Pleasantville were far more painful to me than anything that had happened before.

Some of the people who came spoke German, some Yiddish. But all of them spoke English, which of course I didn't yet understand. They knew the kids they were talking to had just come over on the boat. Any couple who wanted to take in a child, they would let them do so. Because if they screened them closely, how many would have been perfect?

Usually, the questions they asked were the same. "Where did you come from? How was your trip?" It was very, very limited. Usually it was me watching them talk about me in a language I didn't understand. It could be very much the way an animal looks at humans or humans look at an animal. "Well, what's *that* snake saying to *that* snake?" I didn't understand any of them. But I knew my presence was being judged and a decision was going to be made based on what kind of a feeling they got from me. You know. Like people pick out flowers or to go a pet shop, or select a dress. . . .

I don't really remember any of the people who didn't pick me. What I do remember is the rejection. It was, "You didn't buy me that weekend," times twenty-five or thirty couples.

Nine weeks. Having all kinds of doubts and the language barrier. Ironically, that was what finally got me out of there. My great-uncle and his wife, Mr. and Mrs. Ehrenreich, came to the orphanage. They got interested in me right away because their son Roy had just started going to the Bronx High School of Science. The foreign language he was taking was French. . . .

Alfred and Pearl Ehrenreich. He sold insurance. They lived at 1635 Montgomery Avenue in the Bronx. She was a very good woman. He belonged to the Knights of Pythias. I think they came up to the home to do some good for both their son and me.

If she were to be portrayed in a film, it would someone like Anna Magnani or Katina Paxinou. My sister Ester has that same kind of face and character. Very, very warm. A good, decent woman with a need to help. She took me in. I have pictures of me when I came here. I was suffering from malnutrition. I was emaciated. Almost eleven years old and I weighed fifty-five pounds. I had rickets and a bone marrow problem. She took me in and got me healthy. She rubbed olive oil into my skin every day and treated me very fairly and decently.

A few weeks after I came to live with them it was December 7, 1941, Pearl Harbor day. I kept trying to figure it out. Because now Japan and America were at war. And then Germany came into it as well. . . .

They put me in a class with seven-year-olds in PS 104, an old red brick elementary school down Featherbed Lane and Macombs Road. The first teacher I had in the library was Mrs. Leibel and she wore a toupee. I remember her only because within a few days after I came there, I was told by her through a student who spoke German that in America, it's against the law to write with your left hand. That I would be deported if I didn't stop and switch to the right hand.

I was left-handed. In a subsequent class, Mrs. Leibel caught me switching again. She ripped the pencil out of my hand and she said, "You *have* to write with your *right* hand." I kicked her and her toupee came off. I was expelled from school.

Once Germany and America were at war, I became the enemy. I had a lot of trouble coming home from school. Kids would throw rocks at me. Sometimes, a group of kids would beat up on me. I remember one fight on a rooftop. I wasn't by myself. There were three of us and about five guys hitting on us. They kicked the shit out of us and that was it. A number of times, a kid would say, "Hey, *fuckin'* Jew!" or "Yid *bastard!*" or "Go back where you came from—*Kraut!*" and knock my books out of my hand. Sometimes, I would stand there. Sometimes, I'd fight back. Other times, it was three guys and my senses said, "What am I gonna do? *Blindly* fight three guys?" Within a very short period of time, about a year, it stopped.

I was thrown out of school once 'cause I had a fight. A guy spit on me and I hit him. It was about a year after I came to the Bronx. Two guys got me in P.T. [Physical Training, also known as gym class] playing ball. They hurt me bad—in the body. They yelled, "You're a *German* Jew—you're a *Nazi! You're the enemy!* Go home!" There was *always* that. "Get outta here, get back to Germany." By then, I'd started to speak English fluently. I was *never* German. I was born in Germany. My parents weren't Germans. The point I was always trying to make even then was . . . I'm *not* who you think I am. And even if I was . . . *what* then?

What my brother Roy did, besides being my friend and then my brother eventually, because he became my brother, he was wise enough to say, "Learning English isn't enough. You'll always be a foreigner if you don't drop the accent." And he was the one who worked with me on the "THs" and the "Rs." I always think of "THs" and "Rs."

Bill Graham (Volodia Grajonca), child refugee. *Bronx Home News,* October 28, 1946.

Bill Graham, entertainment
impresario, September 1982.
Courtesy of the Bill Graham
Archives, LLC.

"*Srow zee* ball." "I can't remember *zis.*" The "THs" and the "Rs" are the
giveaways. Those are the two that stay *wiz ze* foreign*ehs* who come to
America. *Zay* always speak like *zis.* "Around *za* corn*ah.*" Roy and I
would practice after school, over and over and over. I'd write things out
in a notebook with black and white spots on the cover. The headlines.
Rommel and Eisenhower and Montgomery. Tojo and Yamamoto. I'd
copy them off the front pages. I'd write and then read them aloud and
he would correct me. In our room on the floor between the two beds. . . .

   I remember seeing their [the Ehrenreichs'] apartment for the first
time. It wasn't so much the apartment that impressed me as people
living on top of one another in the building. Six floors, with an elevator. I'd never seen an elevator before. Their apartment was a living
room, kitchen, bedroom, and another room, their son's room. I shared
his room. You had to go through our bedroom to get to theirs.

   They had the front view, we had the yard view, with the other
houses facing ours. Montgomery Avenue was two streets away from
the thoroughfare. University Avenue. Two, three blocks down was
Tremont Avenue. University and Tremont. Andrews Avenue, Montgomery Avenue, Popham Avenue, Undercliff Avenue, then the river.

   The living room was where my parents socialized. The women
played Mah-jongg in the living room and the men played pinochle in
the kitchen. About eleven, they'd break to have food. There was no
television, but we had a radio in our room and another one in the
kitchen. The radio was our route to the other world. *Gangbusters* and
The Hit Parade was in that room. *FBI in Peace and War* was in that room.
The Shadow was in that room. Coming home at lunch to listen to *My
Sister Ruth*, a soap opera on at twelve-fifteen. That was *big*. It was a
great room. . . .

   Were they my parents? She was my mother. He was never my father because I'd never had one. Also partly because of who he was.
He was an okay guy, but I can't say I loved him or cared deeply about
him. I think he was married to a wonderful woman.

FROM AN INTERVIEW WITH AND LETTERS
TO GABRIELLE KAUFMANN KOPPELL

From "Interview with Gabrielle Koppell," interviewer Gertrude Freyer (transcriber Sara Nicoll). Conducted for the Bronx Regional and Community History Project (now Bronx Institute) of Lehman College of The City University of New York, April 28, 1982. The interview gives Kaufmann's background (born 1900) in Germany. Her father was an industrialist. He and his wife had three daughters. Gabrielle was the middle daughter. She and her sisters were encouraged to pursue higher education, and by the age of twenty-six, Gabrielle had earned a Ph.D. in geopolitics from the University of Heidelberg. Gabrielle's older sister married and moved to Chile, and Gabrielle visited her there. As things worsened in Germany, they obtained Chilean passports. By 1933, Gabrielle knew that her life as a German Jew would be in jeopardy. After relocating her mother and grandmother to Switzerland (though they seem to have moved back to Berlin and later, after the grandmother's death, Gabrielle's mother moved to Chile), she moved to England. Both in Germany and England, Gabrielle worked as a magazine editor. Then, in England, she became involved in helping to resettle German Jewish professors. When the first transport of German Jewish children to the United States was organized, Gabrielle was asked to accompany them. Her own words—her own memories—are an important part of an important story.

KOPPELL: . . . I was in touch with my friends in Germany who organized children's transport to come to this country and they told me in case I would go they would like me to accompany "to chaperone" the first group of eleven [Jewish] children who were invited to come from Germany to the U.S. and to be placed in different kinds of families. And that was, I think I told you before, President Roosevelt gave the permission to bring 250 children from Germany to the U.S. And they organized this transport and the first group was ready, I think, for November of 1934. And then they asked me to bring these children here. I think that was a sign from heaven for me to go, to accept the invitation.

Q: Was there anyone paying for this?

KOPPELL: My trip was paid by this Mrs. Kuhn. For the children, I think, maybe the German-Jewish Children's Aid, which was established here. I'm sure it was paid by the National Jewish [Women's] Organization. I think it was paid, of course, from America, from the U.S.

Q: Was there any difficulty in getting the children out of Germany?

KOPPELL: No, no difficulty.

Q: How old were they?

KOPPELL: From six years to fourteen. Eleven children. Boys and girls.

Q: Tell me about the trip.

KOPPELL: Well, I joined the group in England in, I think it was Plymouth. The children were already on the boat. I also should tell you something else. I went to the American Consulate in Germany to ask; I think you needed to have permission to come on the quota. At that time the U.S. had a rather small quota for any kind of people. So he was extremely nice and interested, asked me why I wanted to leave, and said, of course, I need a so-called affidavit. You know you could not come here, you did not get the permission to enter if you did not have an affidavit of at least two people who would certify that you would never be a burden to the country. . . . So then I showed him that letter of this Mrs. Kuhn and then he said, "That's not an affidavit." And I said, alright then let me write her, I'm sure I will get it in on time, and then he said, "I told you to come next Tuesday here for your examination, and did you listen to me, come here next Tuesday." So I came next Tuesday and I came here without an affidavit. They gave me the permission to come to this country without an affidavit. I was 307. The 307th person to come from Germany to this country in November 1934. So I stayed for two months with this Mrs. Kuhn in Cincinnati.

Q: What did you do with the children?

KOPPELL: The children were supposed to be placed by the German-Jewish Children's Aid in different kinds of Jewish families who permitted these children to stay in their house, accepted as a family member. But it wasn't so easy to place these children. I think those first eleven children, two of these children were placed with a Cincinnati family; I took those children with me on the train to Mrs. Kuhn. The other children, I really don't know, but I think there were enough families at that time to accept these children as their guests. I was for two months in Cincinnati and during that time all the other 250 children arrived. And it was very difficult for them to place the children. There were enough families here to accept the children, but the children were, it was kind of a cultural shock which they experienced here. They came from Germany; in that time, Hitler had an immense influence on everybody and they came here and saw these ladies with beautiful red fingers and beautiful makeup, which was completely put down in Germany as something sinful. They just couldn't accept the change suddenly, and I think also the abundance here. When I stood first in front of a chocolate stand I just couldn't stand there. It was a horrible feeling that somewhere in the world was such a—so much to eat and so much to buy. And on the other side of the ocean there was nothing. It was very difficult times, you know. . . .

Q: What did you do in Cincinnati?

KOPPELL: Well, it was the story about the children. While I was in Cincinnati, well, there was one more girl from Stuttgart and myself and we had a wonderful time. We accompanied Mrs. Kuhn to all her meetings, we spoke at meetings, we told them about what happened in Germany, we went to all the wonderful musical parties, which were a good time given in her house. She was a very cultured person; everybody who came to Cincinnati with a kind of name in art or music visited her house. I had a really wonderful time and it was during Thanksgiving time, so I think every night we were in another home with a wonderful Thanksgiving festival with turkeys and I think I never ate as many turkeys in my life again.

But during that time I received a telegram or a letter from the German-Jewish Children's Aid organization here that told me that they are not able to place sixty of those children into homes. The children didn't stay there, they came back [to New York] again, and [they wanted to know] whether I would come back and stay with the children until they would be able to place them successfully, because they needed somebody who could really speak to them; you know, they didn't speak much English. And they came, and they asked me, and they saw that I came with the first group. And they saw my relationship to the children and they asked me whether I wouldn't come here and stay with the children until they would be able to place them.

And the children stayed in a home in New York City, which was called, I think, Baron Hirsch Home [actually, the Clara de Hirsch Home]. I don't know if you know the name Baron Hirsch, he was a very wealthy South American, Argentinean Jew. And he bought this house for young Polish and Russian girls who came here to this country, and he wanted them to have a home until they could establish themselves and find work here. So this home, it was the sixty children who could not be placed, they were placed in this home. The German-

The Clara de Hirsch Home for Working Girls in New York on East 63rd Street was the temporary "home" of a number of the One Thousand Children in 1934 and 1935 waiting for placement with foster families. Dr. Gabrielle Kaufmann, Ph.D., was their much beloved "housemother" and escort on the first ship in 1934 to bring unaccompanied children to the United States under the plan carried out by the German-Jewish Children's Aid, headed by Cecilia Razovsky. JewishEncyclopedia.com.

Jewish Children's Aid rented two flights in the house and placed children. But they needed some kind, like a housemother, and they asked me whether I would come here and stay with the children. So I stayed with the children. That was my way back to New York again.

[Kaufmann, soon to be Koppell, gained work in Jewish social service organizations and successfully pursued a master's degree in social work to advance her career. After marrying, she and her husband—who had been a major publisher in Germany—began a publishing enterprise in the United States. This was only one of many intriguing and adventurous endeavors in Gabrielle Kaufmann Koppell's long, productive life.

The letters to Gabrielle that follow are a small sampling of the many dozens of letters sent to her by the new Americans (and their distant parents) who were her charges, either on the initial trip of November 1934, or from her time at the Clara de Hirsch Home. The letters' tone and the very fact of their existence attests to her special "relationship to the children," twenty-six of whom signed a Mother's Day card for her. It was important to them that she knew their thoughts and feelings. And they were, clearly, quite cer-

tain that she would welcome their news—even their complaints. Unlike other material contained herein and written by OTC children, the Kaufmann letters were not contributed by their authors or their families. In courtesy to the authors of these letters and persons mentioned in them, their surnames have not been used.]

[Undated, probably December 1934 or January 1935]

Dear Miss Dr.,

Today finally I get to write you. Before I start telling you how things are here, I would like to thank you for the photo album. I was very happy with it. Now I will answer your questions. I am doing very well here. Everyone is nice to me and I have everything I could possibly wish for. I feel very comfortable just like I did at home in Germany. I have also learned a lot of English. I'm absorbing the language like a sponge. The food here is very different than in Germany, but it tastes very good. School is very easy for me and I am in the highest class where I am learning English, grade 6B. In February I will probably enter high school. I also see both the L. boys, who are the only ones I can have conversation with since no one else here speaks German. I have it very nice here also and will be together with the Ls and Hans J., who is coming from Newark. Please write to me soon. I have absolutely nothing in German to read here. I get invited an awful lot and don't have a lot of time for myself. I already have 2 letters from Germany. I am very satisfied with everything here. Of course there are many new things that I have to get used to. . . . Now I must close since I am naturally again invited and this time from the Rabbi.

Many regards for Herbert & you.

Your Peter B.

February 2, 1935

Dear Dr. Kaufmann,

First of all, I would like to apologize one hundred times for not writing earlier. It was certainly not very nice, but you can imagine that when you first arrive in a new land you are somewhat lazy when it comes to writing. My sincere thanks for the Chanukah present. I can use the photo album very well and was very pleased with it. Now I will tell you some things about my life in America.

As you know, I came to the family S, and I recognize that I really lucked out. Their house and everything they own is very well located. After spending the 1st 2 days in the house, I was enrolled in school. It is a private school where we only go home during vacation. I am of course in the same school where the S's son is. The school is fabulously located. The school is in the middle of a forest at the foot of a mountain. On one side the school is surrounded by forest and on the other side is a lake. The daily routine: arise at 7:00 a.m., 7:30 breakfast, 8:30–12:30 school, 1:30

lunch. After lunch we go into the forest to either chop wood or carry it, or ice-skating or sledding. At 6:00, dinner. From 7:30–10:30 are again classes, which I don't attend. Everything is really to my liking except for the sports. The American sports don't impress me. You can't continuously do the same things: Ping-pong playing and ice-skating. By the way, there were Ping-pong tournaments here at the school, which I won. I am on an ice hockey team and excel in high jump and distance jumping on the ice with skates. But I miss handball. In the spring it gets hot but is very nice since we have many rowboats, we can swim and above all have 16 tennis courts. I really have had great luck. After being one month in this school, one of my best friends came to America and . . . came to the same school. I call that luck. Now, one month ago a third German boy came to this school. Now we are 3 German boys.

The Christmas holiday was very nice. Aunt S. took me to NY for 3 days where I visited various people and among them Norman M. Norman and his brother liked Aunt S. very much. Norman invited Aunt and me. We met him at his hotel the next afternoon. And then he drove us with his brother's car on a sightseeing trip of New York, showing us all the most important sights. Aunt said to me that most of the sights, this is the first time that she had seen them. . . .

Gunther C.

[Undated, early winter 1935]

Very Honored Mrs. Kaufmann,

Today your letter arrived and I read it with great pleasure. It is not because of neglect that you haven't heard from me. Every day I made up my mind—today you will write to Dr. Kaufmann. Every day I had to postpone it. Since the prophet did not come to the mountain, the mountain comes to the prophet; i.e., you wrote to me. You could not have given me a better Chanukah present than the photo album. Please accept my heartfelt thanks. Since a thank you is better shown by a deed, I am sending you a drawing. (I think it depicts a horse's head.) It also is serving as a Chanukah gift. Except for Heinz L. and Gunther C., no one has written me. And I myself have not been able to obtain the addresses. Gunther is doing as well as me. His foster parents sent him along with their own son into a private school. He writes that the teachers and the students treat him fabulously. He even won a Ping-Pong tournament.

Now I would like to tell you about myself. I am living with Mr. and Mrs. S., whom I must call aunt and uncle. We have a nice one-story house in Newark. Aunt and uncle love me really like their own child. Both tell me daily I should not be ashamed to tell them if I want anything. They really don't want anything else but to see me happy. Even on the 2nd day I already felt at home. I really love the S's and I only miss the people who did so much for me up to now. I wish that all those who wished me everything good could see how happy I am. All the children who are coming over and who are already here should have it so good. Although I get homesick and Germany is so far away, I am hoping to see it again.

Today I received the first news from home. It felt like a piece of my homeland came to me. I read the letters, no, I lived them. Everyone who was mentioned in the letter I could clearly see there in front of me. I could clearly hear them speak and their wonderment. Especially [about] the menu I sent them, I heard them all say "knock on wood." All Jewish children should have it so. All the Jews from "Schwiebus" read the letter at a get-together for which some even came from other towns and my aunt read the letter to them. In the meantime, 3 other letters should have arrived. They wrote that I deserved this luck. I said in return—I did not earn it. How? However, I want to earn it.

I have been attending the Weequahic High School for 3 weeks. School! For 7 months I've had the deep desire to be able to learn again like others who were financially better off than me. Now after 7 months I am again permitted to learn with other boys and girls, no, not only that, but I am allowed to show them that I have learned something. We German students are more knowledgeable than the American students. Even though I am attending school such a short time I already love it. Twice daily I take German to learn English, 2 classes in drawing, one class Algebra, and French. It has been granted to me to show that I have already accomplished some things. The teacher and students insist that I speak English very well. On my English homework I always get a "very good." My teacher himself is German and he really makes an effort and he reigns over me. You ask if I can do as well as a born American? I answer: I can indicate that I can do better because after 4 weeks I can already speak some English, whereas a born American can't speak until he is a year old. What do you say to my logic? . . .

Something else about the S's. I wanted to write to my ex-class in Germany. I wanted to have a globe or map to explain some things. I told Mrs. S. that I would borrow a globe from one of my friends of whom I already have many. That was at lunchtime. 2 hours later I came home from school and found a globe on my table. She bought it for me without me even asking for it. Then I was asked if I knew how to ride a bicycle, and when I said yes, one was promised to me for my birthday. Tomorrow we are driving to Philadelphia only because I have 2 friends there whose names are L. You will remember that saying goodbye to those was very difficult for me.

Many Greetings,
Your Hans

Best wishes to Herbert. My birthday is on the 17th but I already received my bicycle today. You can see how well I'm being treated.

P. S. I am not very proud of my handwriting.

Very honored Mrs. Kaufmann,
I want to thank you very much for your friendly lines. Until recently, we had not received any mail for 3 weeks from our dear children. It became very worrisome. Now thank God, every week we get good reports. The girls write in every letter how nice everyone is to them. That is a very calming thought for us. Believe me, it is not easy for a mother to send two such young girls into the world. Never mind that you cannot enjoy the daily growing, the blossoming, the thriving of the children. And then you are constantly pursued by the thought of whether the children are in right hands, so that they grow up to be useful and nice people. My daughters probably have told you that we also have the intention of emigrating to the United States. Unfortunately, the consulate is giving us great difficulties because the relationship to our American relatives is very distant. Had I know this previously, I don't believe I would have allowed my girls to go across the ocean. In any case, I ask you with all my heart to really investigate the family with whom my children are being placed.

I am sending you, as well as all the other ladies who showed my children such love, many thanks.
My best greeting,

Bertl B.

[Undated, winter 1935]

Dear Mrs. Kaufmann,
I arrived here very well and I want to thank you many times for the fact that you organized everything so nicely for me. I am sorry to say however that I must disappoint you. I don't like it. I had the best intentions, but I don't feel comfortable here. You are thinking that after only a day one can't really tell and I try to talk myself into that also, but I don't like the surroundings. The people are very nice to me, but they are just very simple. I don't feel comfortable here at all. I cried the whole night instead of sleeping and that upsets me further. When I cry then it must be pretty bad. I think you know me well enough to realize that. Please do me a favor and see to it that I am placed with a different family. In Pittsburgh the situation is also fluid. Possibly you could hurry and place me there. I really could not be happy here. I don't fit into these surroundings. I will give you an example: at dinnertime, the door to the toilet is wide open, which is not very appetizing. Even so, the dishes are washed in this nice place. The store is small. They have shoes, four-year-old clothes, and laundry. The people think that I make a face because I don't like Nashville and miss New York very much. This is also true, but that is not the reason. It is not homesickness or getting used to this way of life. It is only that the surroundings are uncomfortable for me.

Please don't be angry at me that I am writing this, but I can't really write that I like it if it isn't true. Please, please write immediately and tell me what I should do. I don't think I have ever been as unhappy as now. Please try everything to place me with another family. These people say that I am quite different from the way I was described. They are very satisfied with me. Only I am not with them. They know why. I hope you can help me like you have always helped all of us.

Please give my greetings to Mrs. W. and I send greetings to you from your
Gerda R.

[Undated, spring 1935]

Very honored Miss Kaufmann,

. . . I was picked up at the train station by Mr. and Mrs. M., whom I was told to call Aunt and Uncle. They have 2 very nice boys, one 1-1/2 years old and the other 16 years. With him I go to school and am part of the time in the same class. We live in a wonderful house in the countryside. At 8:45 I go to school and at 12:45 it is finished for me. I could not take so many subjects because the semester is almost over and it is just too late. Vacation starts on May 25 and lasts until beginning of September. What is happening in the children's home? Did more of the children get placed? And who? Give my regards to all, including Gunther G. and Heinz S. Please don't forget to send my alarm clock and forward my letters. Have you found out anything about my wristwatch?

I share a room with the older boy and we even have our own bathroom. The family also has a Chevrolet and a Cadillac. I don't have to take a trolley to go to school. We are being driven there. On the way back, though, I ride 1/2 hour on the streetcar and then have another 1/2 hour walk. At school my teachers are not as nice as in N.Y., but it goes OK. I have already learned baseball and that goes well. Last night I was at the movies—*After Office Hours*. It was very nice. What's new in the children's house? Give my regards to Miss S. and tell Miss S. that the fruit she gave me for the trip was very tasty. The trip was wonderful.

Many regards, your
Rolf W.

[Undated, spring 1935]

Dear Miss Kaufmann,

I was very glad to receive your card. I am very well and like it very much here. Mr. and Mrs. M. are very good to me & help me a lot. I am always glad to hear from you. I play baseball every day but not Saturday, that day I go to Temple. Afternoon I go to movies.

Best Wishes
Manfred M.

April 21, 1935
Dear Miss Kaufmann,
I thank you very much that I came to this family through you. I have had a very good Passover. Only on the second day I did not feel good. I had a stomachache because of the roast duck and all the wine which I drank. Mr. and Mrs. L. are very nice. I was at the movie the day before yesterday. I can't tell you everything that I am experiencing at the L's. When I am with you, I will tell you all about it.

Dear Miss Kaufmann, I send you heartfelt greetings from Mrs. L. and she will talk to you personally after the holidays.
            Many regards. I hope you continue to have a good Passover.
                                                            [unsigned]

May 11, 1935
Dear Mrs. Kaufmann:
Today I received your letter and I thank you very much. You have no idea how much your lovely letter comforted me. I don't have the address of the lady from the committee. I can't really tell you that I don't like her because I don't trust her that much yet like I trust you. To you I can write everything because you know me. I had a very nice day today that I spent with a few girls my age. Unfortunately the 6 days did not go well. I was in a good mood when I returned and joked around. Mrs. E. told me to wash the dishes and I said no. But she thought I said it in earnest, and she chastised me and told me that I am not here to only go to school, to be treated with kid gloves and to be happy. I was very scared, but I didn't say anything but got homesick and cried. Even if I can take a lot . . . I would have washed the dishes, but Mrs. E. did not understand that I was joking and consequently a big thing was made of it. I wished that I was home and then wouldn't have to worry that all the things I enjoy here are charity. It is not a nice feeling. Please take care of this by the Committee so that I can go away from here. I would like to go to Pittsburgh very much because my friend is there. She is in touch with the Committee. They promised her that I would be placed in a family in Pittsburgh if I had patience and could wait a little longer. In the meantime, I was placed here. . . . If it doesn't go any other way, I'll stay here until a family in Pittsburgh is willing to take me. Of course, I would like to leave as quickly as possible.
        Send greetings to Miss W. I will write her in the next few days. I am sorry that I must distress her, but she understands me. How are things in the home? Did some others leave already? How are the 2 boys who came with me to Louisville? Please write me soon. This living together with these people is very unpleasant for me and I would like for it to end.
                                                    Greetings from your
                                                            Gerda R.
I am not going to school because the semester is almost over. There are only two more weeks of school.

[Multi-part letter, July/August 1935]

Dear Dr. Kaufmann!

Yesterday I received your postcard and I was very happy to receive it. Yesterday especially was a very good day for me. I met a girl my age. This afternoon I will go to her house. She was in the same class as myself. That way we right away have something in common to talk about. I also was not as quiet as I usually am, but talked quite a bit. She doesn't know one word of German, which is wonderful for my English. Dorothy is a very happy, energetic girl, talks a lot but is not unpleasant. She is very tall. Tonight I will tell you more about her. Otherwise, New York is N.Y., filled with stories and people who never have time and are always in a rush. It is good that I can smell good air once in a while. Hopefully you are living very quietly, go to bed early and are often outside in the midst of nature. When you return you must have red cheeks, a 10-pound weight gain, and must feel generally healthy. Otherwise I won't permit you to return.

Unfortunately, the girl was not home. I have just called Hanna R. The other Hanna is sitting down there by the telephone.

N.Y., 30 July '35

Oh Dr. Kaufmann!

Don't be sad. Yesterday I was at the dentist and the nasty man pulled one of my teeth. Tomorrow I must go back to have another tooth pulled. If at least I were O.K. now, but I have a swollen cheek and take Aspirin.

1 August '35

Ah, finally! Today I am going into the countryside. Last night L called me to tell me the good news. I will send this letter from there.

Scarsdale, 2 Aug. '35

Really, here are trees, a lot of green, fresh air. Oh, it is so pretty. I have a lovely room. The people are very fine. Everything is so right and free and of nature. This afternoon we'll go swimming. Last night we were at the theater that plays here during the summer. It was great. The child is two years old. . . . I am so lucky that I am out here. It is so wonderful to see trees and green instead of stones when one wakes.

Best greetings
And take care of Hanna
Lilli

October 8, 1935

Dear Mrs. Kaufmann,

How are you? How is it going?

Last week I was together with Mrs. L. and had her give me your address. First of all (although somewhat late), I'd like to wish you a good [Jewish] New Year. How are you? I hope well. Have you heard from everybody? I can assure you that last summer was the nicest summer I ever had with the exception of when I was traveling. I came to a nice but typical German family. The people (especially the man) are still more German than Jewish. Already 30 years in this country and still "Germany over all!" But if you don't pay attention to that, then everything is fine. I am satisfied! I have my own room (more like office than bedroom). You know me. I'm just kidding and would be happy if my parents would not give me such bad news from Luxembourg and Germany, that I can't fall asleep at night. My father is no longer allowed to work and his notice requiring him to leave the country has expired. But you can't get into another country.

In Germany, at best the prospect is a Concentration Camp, if he tries to work. My mother had to give up everything and no prospects. My relatives cannot help. I was at the Committee, but the same old story. My mother was at the Committee in Berlin, but can't get out. She'd like to go to Brazil, but no possibility. First a citizen must sponsor her. America (USA) is impossible! The rest of Europe—already tried it: Holland, England, France, Belgium, Denmark, Poland, Czech Republic, Austria, Switzerland. Everything impossible, even USSR of course. You can't imagine in what situation I am running around here. The American says, "try to get over it and make your best out of it." But it isn't that easy. Did you read the novel *The Ship of the Dead?* It's not yet that bad, but who knows? I will only again be happy when my parents are out of Europe and in safety.

I am attending James Madison High School in Brooklyn. Another 1-1/2–2 years. Then high school is over. [I am in the] 5th semester [of the 8 high school semesters] because of report cards which I have gotten in the meantime. I am learning and I find it ridiculously easy . . . only my parents! I would be very happy to hear from you soon.

In the meantime, I remain with heartfelt greetings,

Your Adolf

FROM ". . . I WANT AN OCEAN BETWEEN US"

By Thea Kahn Lindauer [2002]

[The letters from Lindauer's father (Samuel Kahn) and other relatives carry responses to the news conveyed in her own letters from America, as well as reflections of worsening conditions in Germany. As the children underwent the transition to life in America, many were kept aware of what was happening to those who remained behind. While letters from parents often disguise these conditions, Lindauer's father no doubt felt that his twelve-year-old daughter could deal with such news—and in early 1935, conditions were far from what they would become.]

Introduction

The year was 1934. Hitler had been in power just a year. . . .

Thea Kahn Lindauer at camp in
the United States in 1934.
Archives of One Thousand
Children®, Inc.

Pappa was a merchant. He dealt in beautiful fabrics, silks from
France, woolens from England, and linens from Germany. The front
of the store was all stocked with feminine attire, and the back for the
men included a tailoring department. Behind it was a windowed office that held all the business ledgers and the important papers for all
the agencies he represented: The Hapag and North German Lloyd
travel companies; the Munchener and Aachener Fire Insurance Company; and the Allgemeine Life Agency.

For a small town, it was a significant business. The house was large
and three-storied, encompassing a large street-front house [that] contained the store, our living rooms, two other three-room flats, and a
synagogue. Yes, a synagogue where Pappa gathered all the faithful
from the entire area for holiday services. Of course, Mamma fed most
of them. The right wing contained storage areas and a clay cave, a cold
cellar. The back building housed a clothes washing and drying hall and
a small caretaker's room. To the west was a high wall separating us
from the neighbor's property. The enclosed courtyard held one tree,
boxes of flowers, and a summerhouse.

Pappa went on buying trips. If it were during vacation time, he
would take me along. That's how I got to see *Hansel and Gretel* at the
age of five, in Frankfurt at Christmastime.

One day, Pappa came back from one of his Frankfurt trips after I had
gone to bed. At breakfast the next morning, he asked me: "How would

you like to go on a real journey, a long, long trip, see all of America, and have a wonderful education?" I couldn't contain myself! To see all of these wonders: New York City, the beaches of California, where my half-sister lived; of course, I would stay away from Chicago, where there were so many shooting gangsters. Yes! Bright golden visions burst into my head. Mamma kept calmly shushing me: "Listen to Pappa."

He went on to explain that while in Frankfurt he had been invited to a meeting where the Hebrew Immigrant Aid Society had a representative speak about sending hundreds of young children from all over Europe (mainly Germany) to the United States to be adopted and integrated into American families and educated to the best of the family's ability.

Since I could no longer follow the family plan of having me join my older sister Gerda, a medical student in Leipzig, this seemed like a perfect answer. My grandfather, still living at the time, asked: "[W]hy can't she go to the relatives in Sweden, or France, or Luxembourg?" I remember Papa standing, cutting the challah bread and saying very calmly: "No . . . I want an ocean between us."

In the month that followed, Pappa was held up to ridicule; a heartless monster who didn't care about his child so young, a doomsayer who didn't know all that Hitler would do for the Jews. . . .

"No!—I want an ocean between us!"

November 1934
Dear little Thea,
This is the first of what I hope will be a steady stream of wonderful letters between us. We await your first letter most anxiously. Just remember, writing is at present our only link to you as the telephone calls abroad are so closely monitored—even the most innocent ones are cause for suspicion. You looked so eager, excited, and small waving your goodbyes. I wish I had thought of taking a picture as some of the others did. What awaits you in United States of America? We cannot say. We can only hope that wherever you go, people await you eagerly and will be kind to you. I have the fullest confidence you will not disappoint them. This is my fervent hope in our shadowy future.

The card you sent from New York mentions being seasick and in the infirmary all the way across. Please explain. Apparently you were in New York a very short time before you took off for Chicago. Only six of you were to go on to the Midwest. There are so many questions that we need to have answered, but we know you will put our minds at ease. Mama and Ruth are sad that you left, but they both know it's for the very best reason—your education in a free world.

Your old teacher, Herr Steuer, as well as the new, Herr Schäfer, hope you will not forget them. They feel very much part of your life, preparing you for a fruitful future.

Dear little Thea, I wonder if you know the great responsibility we all have laid on your shoulders. I hope it's not too heavy a burden.

Your loving Pappa

Remembrances and Reflections

My mood was very mixed—anxious to leave, and yet fearful with the realization I was leaving my family for a future unknown. This wasn't like going to my aunt's for summer vacation or a semester away at school. This was forever and ever.

November 1934
Dear Little Thea,
Your first letter from the U.S. arrived at last. What a trip you had crossing the ocean. We saw that the *President Harding* was not the ocean liner you had hoped for, but you were well taken care of, particularly in the infirmary. Sitting in a deck chair, watching the sun go down as you sailed out of Queenstown sounds very picturesque and exciting. Getting seasick and not being able to get to your cabin is something else. I am glad your cabin mate finally alerted the steward when she returned and found you absent. It is a pity you had to miss all the onboard activities, especially getting to know your shipmates better. Don't be unhappy about it—disappointed, yes, but don't linger on it. Just project ahead to all the other adventures. It must have been quite a shock to awaken on the train in early morning and find that the country is so flat. I am sure there are rolling hills and even high mountains in the U.S. Just as in Europe, you just haven't gone through them yet.

Here, winter is settling in. Christmas preparations are all over town and we are much more aware of Chanukah since you won't be with us, but Mama and Ruth are sending you their traditional goodies—even chocolate, which is now forbidden to Jews. They now make their chocolate cake out of St. John's Bread. For the first time in many years, Mama is not having her traditional "Goose stuffing"—feeding the geese until they are good and fat for Christmas eating. The government has forbidden any Germans to do manual labor for the Jews. Lenchen and her father are allowed to work for us since they live in the house rent-free.

We look forward to your next letter about your new home and the nice family who opened it up to you. Your friends send you greetings and want to know if you've seen any Chicago gangsters yet.

Love, Your Pappa, Mama, and Ruth

Remembrances and Reflections

Christmastime brought a ritual in which some women from the town would come nightly and hand-feed a dozen geese, fattening them for the holidays and making the German version of very good French "Paté de fois gras."

> November 17, 1934
> Dearest Little Daughter,
> Your letter on your arrival in Chicago we share with the few friends who have the courage to come and see us. It is sad that so many whom we thought our friends painfully avoid us, but at least in the store we are still busy, because people are curious. So, you are now with your new sponsors, Dr. and Mrs. Sonnenschein, who sound like wonderful people. I'm sorry they do not speak German, but you will learn English very fast and Uncle Harry Wolf sounds jolly and caring. Their welcome gift, the Shirley Temple doll, sounds beautiful. You must not think you are too old or sophisticated for it. Remember only a year ago, you and Ruth had tea parties with all your dolls. And even made clothes for them to match your outfits. You say you live in a *Wolkenkratzer* [skyscraper] and take an elevator to your apartment. It all sounds very elegant with their Spanish antiques and family mementoes. Be careful that you don't break anything, rushing around as you do. You must not feel humiliated being in a grade with younger children. It is, I am sure, only until you learn enough English to get along in your grade. Look what you have already learned: That Bret Harte (the name of your school) is an American western hero writer much like our own Karl May, and that the American number one sport is baseball, according to the Kominsky children, who are teaching you all about it.
>
> Please greet the Sonnenscheins and their friend, Mr. Wolf, for us. Also write Elsie (she is rather lazy when it comes to writing) and Aunt Lydia. I know the latter will come to see you as soon as she is able to leave her job. Write soon.
>
> Your affectionate family and Pappa

Remembrances and Reflections

Although I was to be in a foster home, I had my Aunt Lydia, Mother's sister, and her family living in Chicago. Also, her mother-in-law and sister-in-law, whom I did not remember from Europe. They immigrated before 1927. My half-sister Elsie lived in California at that time.

> December 1934
> Dearest Little Daughter,
> What a beautiful time you must have had at your first Thanksgiving, quite a bit different than the Jewish Succoth and the German *Erntedankfest*

[Thanksgiving]. River Forest sounds very beautiful, particularly how you described it with beautiful red leaves and blue skies. Not at all like November in Europe with rainy gray skies. Mama was fascinated by the food that was served. Turkey, which is not as fat as goose and much bigger. Corn, yes you are right, we don't eat that in Europe. It is only for the livestock because it is so rough here. Olives in black—I suppose they came from Italy and Greece. Ah, celery. Here again I only know we do not eat stalks; they are bitter and flat. But you remember Mama's celery root salads, which you so enjoyed. Cranberries sound much like lingonberries we eat with Swedish pancakes. Pumpkin pie is something we should make with our fruit, as we have no recipe except for stews. You see how much you have learned again. We are all well and wait for your letter. We light our Chanukah candles and think of you—

Your Pappa

Remembrances and Reflections

Thanksgiving was in a beautiful home in River Forest, with relatives of Dr. and Mrs. Sonnenschein. About thirty people had gathered to welcome me. The food: sweet potato and marshmallow, cranberry sauce, celery, mincemeat pie, and pumpkin pie were all new and strange. The only thing familiar was the chicken soup. The old grandmother was very disappointed that I could understand only a few words of her Yiddish, which she thought was like German. The children were older, not at all interested in the little girl from overseas.

December 15, 1934
Dearest Little Thea:
Thank you for your birthday greeting to me and also for the one to Ruth. Those were beautiful cards you made. The turkey is very colorful and everybody around the table looks so happy. We hope the package you sent does not get lost, as so many packages from overseas do. It is impossible to send foodstuff, as it disappears in the first post office.

We now are obligated to have a patriotic, once-a-week *Eintopf Gericht* [one-pot meal]. If you don't want to cook it yourself, you can bring your pot to a feeding station, where along with the meal you get a propaganda film about the heroes of the Third Reich. We had a special celebration with the apple cake and whip cream, which Mama managed to exchange for something from our garden.

Every week there is a new order to make it harder for Jews to make a living. Except for a few, people want to pay their debts to me, even some who have not paid for years. We all have colds, but my one Schnapps at night is good medicine and there is always Mama's excellent chamomile tea.

Write soon again; we love you very much—Your devoted Pappa

Remembrances and Reflections

Although every week brought new restrictions, Pappa was still on the city council and the local Nazis were not too anxious to enforce them and force him off.

> December 1934
> Dearest Little Daughter,
> This is the last of 1934, but what will 1935 bring? I dare not think of it, but take joy in knowing that you are so safe. It sounds like you had a wonderful Christmas celebration with a theater party and many gifts. Your American chocolate bars arrived and Ruth will not eat them, especially the ones called "Baby Ruth." She shows them around proudly, a candy named after her. She and Mama made gingerbread with lots of sugar and spices, and potato pancakes. Mama's and my scarf are beautiful and warm, we certainly can use them in this cold weather. Gerda will come to visit before she goes to the U.S. or to Brazil to continue her medical studies.
> "What will the New Year bring?" everybody asks the same question. At least more Jews are asking this themselves and we have more parents worried about their children. Optimistically, some still feel nothing will happen to them.
> I know you are sometimes lonely and long to be with other children, but I think of the great museum across the park from where you live and the fun you seem to have there. You say that there is a real coal mine and you spend a lot of time in it. Ice-skating on the midway and eating roasted chestnuts sounds like a wonderful adventure. Surely you do this with many friends. I know when you catch up with your proper grade you will have lots of classmates your own age. The new semester is not far away and you have something to anticipate.
> We will drink a hearty *Glühwein* [a traditional New Year's Eve drink of spiced, hot wine] to the New Year quietly and wish for the well-being of all our dear ones.
>
> With love, your devoted Pappa, Mama, and Ruth

Remembrances and Reflections

My other half-sister, Gerda, who was studying medicine in Leipzig, was terminated from the institute. What was even more devastating, so was her marriage to a prominent German doctor.

> January 1935
> My Dear Child,
> Now we can write the year 1935 and you are in your new home for almost two months. The note from Dr. and Mrs. Sonnenschein put us much at ease. They sound so happy to have you bring youth and joy into their

home. Their families also sound delighted that you are with them, since they never had children of their own.

Since you left, there have been quite a few changes. People come to the store because they are curious about what has happened to you. Apparently, the government knows very little about the transports. At least, it has not tried to stop them. People now think I may not have been so crazy, after all, putting an ocean between us.

We've visited the Stiefel family in Grünstadt. Their son Manfred is eager to leave. I hope he has success in Stuttgart, as Visas are more and more difficult to get. I told him to contact Family Neuberger, who were so kind to you when you had to go to the consulate. Although the people there were not very sympathetic, you had that wonderful family encouraging you with their hospitality. Always remember people are basically kind and trustworthy. The proof is where you are now and what is being done for you.

Your schoolmates, especially Elfriede, send greetings. I am sorry they were all punished for coming to the railroad station to see you off. I hope you pressed at least one of those roses they brought you, but I suppose wearing their Nazi youth uniform for their farewell to you was not such a good idea. I wonder who reported them.

Since Mama wants to write a few lines and so does Gerda and Ruth, I must close. I also have a meeting with Mr. Heilman, who wants to help us where he can. His sons are fine boys, who are not afraid to speak out.

Please greet the Sonnenscheins for us and do well at school. I know it is difficult when you don't know the language, but soon you will be in your real grade. Again, write a letter to your little sister. She is very lonesome for you and so eager to know about your new life. It is only too bad she was not old enough to go with you. Did you know the wonderful museum you go to in the afternoon was part of the Columbia Exposition in 1898? [Then called the Rosenwald Museum, it is now the Museum of Science and Industry.] Not many children know that and you are able to go there and enjoy it.

Until next time—your loving Pappa

Remembrances and Reflections

Some of my former classmates, who came to see me off, were questioned by the District Commissioner as to why they "farewelled" a little Jewish girl with a bouquet of roses and tears. Who were the teachers and the clergy who came along, what was said, and did they all go to our house afterward?

January 29, 1935
Dear Thea,
Your letter came in record time on Thursday. Usually it arrives Saturday or Monday. So I want to answer it right away. Healthwise, we are in good

shape though winter is taking its toll. Since we don't socialize very much, we are spared the usual colds and coughs. I am still taking the train to Frankenthal because of my eyes and hopefully will receive my glasses shortly. I am thankful I have a Jewish optometrist in Dr. Rahlston, as the others are not allowed to treat Jews. Interesting enough, the Jewish doctors can still treat Germans with certain stipulations, but most are reluctant to do so as they can be accused of "professional misdemeanor" by anybody at any time. We are curious what is happening at school. Have you joined your real grade? You must not worry about your accent and that some of the children call you "kraut." It is better than being called a "dirty Jew."

Gerda is still with us before she leaves for South America. She still has hopes of coming to the U.S.A. She had such plans for you to come to Leipzig someday and study medicine as she did. But you will make your own way, no matter what you study. Please write Ruth a separate letter. She sees so few children outside of our neighbors these days. Thank God Herr Lehrer Steuer, who is now principal, insists on her staying in school despite some of the Nazi teachers' objections.

About Elsie, she writes after a long silence. She is moving from Los Angeles to Chicago to get a job near you. However, she is very vague about it. Aunt Lydia and the Lowensteins wrote that they visited you and that you are so well taken care of that we should not worry. You do not need to feel guilty that they must work so hard and you don't. Uncle Ernest has a good job as a building engineer and Aunt Lydia runs the housekeeping office in the same hotel, so they are very content. Your cousins do not expect you to give them anything of your allowance or your gifts. The boys, in particular, so don't worry so much.

We send you our love as always—your Pappa

Remembrances and Reflections

Father had developed cataracts. Fortunately, there was a prominent Jewish eye doctor in Frankenthal, otherwise he would not have been treated. By that time, no Aryan doctor was allowed to have Jewish patients.

February 4, 1935
Dear little Thea,
Your letter arrived as usual with much awaited hope and anxiety. Ruth delivered all your greetings and messages to the proper recipients, who were delighted to receive them. As usual, our state of health is good to report and can only hope the same from you and that you have plenty of opportunity to enjoy the great outdoors. I cannot imagine what "frozen rock-hopping" must be like on the Chicago lakefront. We were in Frankenthal again where Dr. Rahlston pronounced my eyes in good con-

dition. We have developed a beautiful friendship in these trying times when your former friends disillusion and desert you. But we are still lucky—Mr. Heilman and Dr. Ludwig, the Mayor, could not be more loyal, as are many of my clients. We now get many calls from parents who would like their children out of harm's way—the last being the Stiefels and Kleinbergers (Elfriede). We are getting visits from many relatives, as that is the best way to keep each other's courage up.

We're deep into winter and it sets the mood for the many anti-Jewish regulations that come out day by day. There are still people who think they will be exempted from some of the harsher laws because they know someone important. I think that is a false assumption. When it comes to the final reckoning, it will all be the same, whether you contributed to society, whether you're one-quarter Jewish, or who you know in government. *Quatsch* [Nonsense].

Hope your winter is going well with school uppermost in the picture. I can only imagine your day-to-day joy without fear.

Always with love—your Pappa

Remembrances and Reflections

The Nuremburg Laws regarding Jews were being codified since Hitler was granted and assumed dictatorship. After the Reichstag fire, more and more daily and weekly laws were issued, so many that a bewildered public could not cope with them unless a uniformed SA or SS drove the lesson home with public demonstrations.

Eisenberg, February 18, 1935
Dear Little Thea,
Though I didn't write in Mama's letter last week, you know my thoughts were with you. Mr. Heilman thought it would be a good idea to visit all our relatives and so Cousin Max picked me up Monday morning and we took the "Grand Tour." Beginning with the relatives in Trier. We went on to Wawern and on to Heusweile. On Sunday we visited the relatives in Homburg/Saar. All are concerned what the Saar annexation will mean to them. You can imagine how eager they were to hear news of you and they all want to be remembered. I arrived home last night and even as tired as I was, I was overjoyed to find two letters from you. There are so many questions from everyone. I don't know where to begin. You must send us a day-by-day account of your activities, no matter how trivial they may seem.

There have been new administrative directives pertaining to non-Jews who work for Jews and members in the National Socialist Party who buy from Jews. For example, a Jew may no longer address a Christian, even a friend of long standing, by his first name. In the second instance, it is considered immoral to buy anything from Jews, unless they are the only handlers of the product.

More and more children are leaving, which is good. They all want to contact you, but they may not be going to Chicago. While I was gone, there was the usual "harassment" at the store. Having an "Aryan" manager certainly has its advantages.

Yes, the children are leaving, but at the same time, life goes on and more are being born. The Micher family has great joy in a son, born ten days ago and so we shall all celebrate this event. We have so few celebrations, we make the most of those we do have. For today we all send our love. Ruth asks you not to forget to write the relatives and send pictures.

With devoted kisses—Your Pappa

Remembrances and Reflections

Whenever Pappa was made aware by his friends that a pogrom was in the offing, he conveniently left to visit our numerous relatives. The Aryan manager whom he refers to was, I believe, a Mrs. Kemp, an indomitable lady who, being over forty years of age, could still work for a Jewish concern.

February 26, 1935
My Dear Little Daughter,
Though we received no letter this week, we assume that everything is all right with you. The heavy storms raging on the ocean, no doubt, contribute to the delay in the mail. Although there have been outbreaks of Grippe and other winter illnesses, we seem to be bypassed since we have so few social contacts. So something good can be said of our isolation. Tante Lydia and Grandmother Löwenstein said that Elsie is trying to get a job in Chicago to be near you. Ruth asks daily about the package you offered to send. She looks so forward to it.

The end of the week I am traveling to Heusweiler again to help your Uncle Herman in his business. As you must have heard, Saar is now part of Germany again, and they expect the same problems that trouble the Jews in Germany. We congratulate you that you were put in your proper grade, which means you must be making great progress in your English. Your playmates in your building sound very nice. Imagine, riding an elevator up and down instead of a bicycle. You speak of the father owning a baseball team in Chicago. Is that a business like owning a store? I cannot imagine making money doing that.

Ruth has several school days off in celebrating the Saar annexation. Naturally all the children (expect she) are expected to participate in all-day demonstrations for this event. She is very lonely; please write her more. She gets thinner all the time and does not sleep well. She wanted to knit you a BDM jacket [the Bund Deutscher Mädchen Official sweater for German girls in black, red, and green], but we thought it would not be a good idea and persuaded her to make something with daisies on it. Please, please, write all your news. Although you are disappointed at not having your own room, it sounds lovely where you are, especially the corner for all your books and toys. Gerda is still with us and as you can imagine is sad indeed. We hope the change to South America will be good for her.

With devoted love and kisses—your Pappa

Remembrances and Reflections

The Cominskis, who lived in the same building, were the owners of the Chicago White Socks team, and Pappa was concerned if indeed a living could be made by playing baseball: racing cars, boxing, skiing, and soccer, yes, but baseball?

March 3, 1935
Dear little Thea,
Today, your letter from the 20th arrived and we can always tell when we have mail from you. The postman makes us the first customers on his route, even before he brings money to anybody.

At this time, I am also writing Aunt Lydia, Grandmother, and Elsie. I have held up all my correspondence until your package arrived. It finally came on Wednesday. What a joy! Naturally, the one who had the greatest pleasure was Ruth, since she was the main recipient of all the things you sent. As always, it's good to hear from you. I know it is not always easy and convenient for such a busy young lady to write. But you are a dutiful daughter who knows how much we wait for your letters.

With the celebration for the annexation of the Saar, all stores are closed and there are torchlight parades every night. We are fortunate to be Jewish, as we don't have to march or answer to the party why we didn't march. We have a lot of rain and a flu epidemic. Again we are saved; with so little social contact, we are spared illnesses that affect everyone else, but then we don't have to be in on every misery.

Fastnacht [Shrove Tuesday] is upon us. At least it gives us some relief from the politics and the endless harassment. Mama made her famous stuffed pancakes, but there are no sharp, critically funny speeches as there have been in the past, and even the famous ones like Köln, Mainz, and Frankfurt seem to have lost their bite. Everyone is so afraid to offer an opinion critical of the government.

Gerda would love to have a letter in English so she can practice it with you. She is still waiting to hear from South America about her immigration. Mama says to tell you that Ruth is much happier to go to bed now that she has the beautiful Betty Boop pajamas you sent.

Write soon again. Much Love—Pappa and your family

Remembrances and Reflections

The Mardi Gras is a time for merriment as well as the biting satirical "Buttenreden," a political roast in most of the large cities all over Germany. It was now strictly forbidden, dampening the spirit of the festivities.

March 12, 1935
Dear little Thea,
It seems like nobody can answer your letters but me. Dear Mama is too busy with the household, Gerda at the moment is at the interview in Hamburg, and little Ruth is afraid her handwriting is not good enough for you. *Alles Ausreden* [all excuses], oh well.

I just returned from Heusweiler, where again I helped Uncle Herman with the business. There was an open-market day and business was very brisk. Don't forget Uncle Herman has a lot of business with French goods and the Germans prefer them over their own.

But enough about business. Your greetings to teachers and school-mates must wait until school opens again. It has been closed because of serious Grippe and influenza outbreaks. The weather isn't helping any, cold and miserable.

You still can go skating on your midway with your friends. You mention a friend of Dr. Joe's who is the son-in-law of Thomas Mann. Do you know his name? You know Dr. Mann is one of our most famous German writers. So you see, not all people who leave Germany are Jews. Many of the artists and musicians leave of their own free will. You can be very proud to be in their company. Please send us a new picture. You have grown, but you say you're still one of the smallest and have to walk in front in gym class. Never mind. Stand tall and know you're doing us all proud.

Lovingly—Your Papa

Remembrances and Reflections

Thomas Mann was one of the most famous German writers. His family chose to go into exile in the United States. I believe it was a Prof. Borghese who married one of the Manns' daughters and who was teaching at the University of Chicago.

March 18, 1935
Dear Little One,
As always, you letter arrived on time. You are so good about writing the letters, which we await with great joy. Here, we are still in the grips of winter with influenza all around us. School is still closed and Ruth is bored. I'm taking her with me on my customer trip tomorrow, which should be a nice change for her. Your Aunt Delphine is here and this keeps Mama busy and sociable.

I'm glad to hear you're making such good progress in English. Never mind the children laughing at your accent. There is a famous story about an Italian professor (it might even be Dr. Sonnenschein's friend, Prof. Borghese) who was interviewed by the newspapers about his accomplishments. One of the reporters remarked: "Gee Professor, you speak pretty broken English." The Professor smiled and said, "Yes, and I speak 16 other languages, equally broken." It is what you have to say that is important, and that you can communicate it to others.

In the last months, no children left for the U.S. and parents are getting anxious. We were so lucky to enter the program when we did.

Greetings from all the relatives. I know you cannot write to all of them, but do remember them once in a while. Your classmates are still curious about what you're doing and the life you live in the United States.

Your loving Pappa

Remembrances and Reflections

Dr. Joseph B. Sonnenschein had many friends among the faculty of the University of Chicago. He was Clinical Director for the Board of Health in Chicago, functioning under Dr. Herman Bundesen.

April 5, 1935
Dear Little Daughter,
We finally received your letters from 20 and 25 March and were delighted that you are so busy. Although you didn't understand it all, it must have been very interesting to go to an American Court of Justice. Dr. Sonnenschein was what is called a witness, who must swear under oath to tell only the truth. The fact that you did not understand the case is not important. What is important is you saw the American jury system at work. You are very lucky to meet his friend, the judge, and that they took you to lunch at their club. That is something very American and although I belonged to a *Brüderschaft* [a brotherhood or men's club] with the city council, I am no longer a member there, as I had to give up my position on the council. As Dr. Ludwig stated, "I was regrettably replaced."

The misunderstanding with Elsie and Aunt Lydia, you must not mind it too much. They feel left out of your life, but you cannot live theirs and they cannot live yours. Gerda is in a job with a doctor in Bremen and uncertain about her future, whether in Brazil or the United States.

Mama is already hard at spring cleaning. That never changes; the house must be immaculate from top to bottom. Since she no longer gets out as much socially, she is really throwing herself into the well-being of all of us.

Meanwhile, all our love to you.

Your devoted Pappa

Remembrances and Reflections

It is amazing how my mother changed from a fairly easygoing social butterfly to a dedicated housewife. With the lack of help, the huge house still had to be kept in tip-top order. She still had the ever-loyal Lenchen, who, with her father, lived rent-free in the attic rooms and was still allowed to work for her.

Chapter 6

BECOMING AN AMERICAN

T*here is no sharply defined wall between the materials in this chapter and those in chapter 5. These excerpts extend and deepen our understanding of the acculturation process by which transplanted European children, separated from their parents, adapted to a new life with different challenges. Their stories testify to the remarkable resilience of children.*

The interchange of letters (most of them translated from German) among members of Phyllis Finkel Mattson's dispersed family illustrates the tug in two directions: the sensitive child living in an ongoing present filled with new experiences and a natural assimilation into American culture, and that same child simultaneously connected to her parents' dilemma. Mattson's own narrative frames the letters, allowing an adult retrospective understanding to commingle with that of the young girl.

Following Mattson's story, we have excerpted additional material from the letters of Ruth Schlamme Schnitzer and the memories of Bill Graham. Like Mattson, they are acute reporters on the world of school, and in Graham's case, the world of work as well. While Schnitzer remains outgoing and life affirming in her letters home—perhaps to cheer those from whom she is separated—Graham remembers a period of youth with harsher edges. There is, quite obviously, no uniform truth and certainly no uniform set of facts—beyond the broadest outlines—that are revealed by these tantalizing documents. Nonetheless, it is clear that each child, in his or her own way, develops the necessary coping mechanisms and finds an American voice.

The passage from Arnold Isaak's "Memories" shows him to be no exception. Isaak, who seems to have been particularly well informed (through his mother's letters) about the plight of his family, juxtaposes their story with that of his life in the Mittelpunkt household and at school. Like Mattson, he seems to have hovered between two worlds. Even more striking, perhaps, is the story of his mother's escape to Argentina—with Isaak's brothers—and her strong suggestion that he remain in the United States to take advantage of his American opportunities rather than join them. His discovery of his father's tragic fate at Auschwitz adds another dimension to a complex story of a young mind discovering—building—an identity, while its roots in the past remain severed or obliterated, leaving only memory and the courage of self-making.

FROM "WAR ORPHAN IN THE PROMISED LAND: LETTERS OF A WAR-TORN FAMILY"

By Phyllis Finkel Mattson [2001]

The First Six Months: April 6 to November 8, 1940

April 24, 1940 *[translated from German; sent to Kitchener Refugee Camp in England]*
Dearest Papa!
I'm a *very* naughty child, I haven't written for so long, but I was always busy. I've been in school one week, and I must always do homework and then I must write to Mama, and when I begin to write to you, Auntie says it is bedtime.

I've been with Auntie since Wednesday, for ten days before I was in a children's home. It is good with Auntie and I get along with her children. Her girl is 15 years tomorrow and is called Cecylia. Her brother is 13 and his name is Moe. They are very nice. Yesterday it has been 31 days since I left Mama. I left on March 20. Now, I hope both of you will come soon. I had a good trip, I was seasick for 3 days. I am very good in arithmetic and penmanship.

I was to the movies twice. I saw *The Invisible Man Returns, The Swiss Family Robinson,* and *Remember the Night.* Today I will go again to the movies. The movies here have no intermissions. After Pesach I will go to Hebrew school. When I know a little bit more English, I'll get piano lessons. The children in school are very sweet to me. What is status of your coming here? A sister of a girl that I traveled with was in London and had registered Aug. 5, and she is already in Baltimore. Mama had big quarrels with Gusti's daughter, who is awfully lazy and always complains. She cries all the time and is an awful hypochondriac. When I left Vienna in the middle of the day, there was rain and by evening one could ice-skate. Hopefully, we will see each other soon, Amen. Now Auntie wants to write. How are you? Now many, many kisses. I must now be Phyllis and I don't like it. From your loving Lizzi
P.S. Please be so dear and write Mutti often. Please save this letter and others and bring them with you.

Phyllis Finkel Mattson, age 10.
Archives of One Thousand
Children®, Inc.

What should have been a momentous and memorable meeting with my new family that day on the ferryboat dock is lost in my memory. Since I mention that I spent ten days in a children's home, a social worker from the home would have been at my arrival as well as my aunt's family, but I don't remember any of it. What I do remember is my first meeting with Mr. Bonapart, standing on a terrace of a big building, as a group of us children, probably all new admissions, were introduced by a lady, probably the social worker. He was tall, had thin brown hair and a Hitler-like mustache, which bothered me. He looked us all over and had things to say, most of which I didn't understand because of my lack of English. By his frown, lack of smile, tone of voice, and his pointing finger, I understood that my clothes (my precious maroon velvet dress that I wore for important occasions) as well as my name, Felicitas, were not OK—and that somehow I wasn't OK. He pointed at me and said Phyllis, my new name, I guessed. I remember saying to myself that I would somehow become acceptable to and approved of by all—[a] decision that was to be my driving force for most of my life.

Officially the Pacific Hebrew Orphan Asylum, commonly called Homewood Terrace or "The Home," remained my legal guardian until my father came. These arrangements had probably been worked out with the immigration officials and the German-Jewish Children's Aid, but I didn't know any of this. At the orphanage, I was probably given medical examinations and psychological tests, along with some new clothes. I don't know what took ten days to process me. Perhaps they had to do a home study of my aunt's home, which makes no sense, but then bureaucracy often doesn't.

Auntie was Aunt Laura (which was also my mother's name), who had given me support papers. She was a woman about fifty-five, and her husband, a little man who always wore a hat, seemed to me to be much older, but wasn't. She had emigrated from Galicia, a province of Poland where my great-grandparents and their children lived and the area where I had spent summers in my earlier years; he had come from Russia, and perhaps spoke little German, so that I had few conversations with him. Aunt Laura's brother was married to my mother's Aunt Yetka. My mother and Aunt Laura had met when my mother was a young girl living in Poland, when Poland was part of Austria, and German was the official language, but Polish the common language.

My new home would be in the lower flat of a wooden, Victorian house on 24th Street on the corner of an alley between Mission and Valencia. The house was small compared to the large stone apartment house in Vienna I had lived in, but in my eyes the interior was deluxe since it had a bathroom with a bathtub and a toilet within the apartment. There was one big bedroom used by my aunt and uncle, and the living and dining rooms also served as bedrooms when the wall beds were lowered. There was even a piano, played beautifully by Cecylia.

I shared a room with her. She was pretty with long black hair, and was very good to me. I will always be grateful to Cecylia for helping me to learn English so fast. She never tired of correcting me on the proper pronunciation and helped to make the subtler distinctions in language clearer to me. We had a lot of trouble with the word "become," since in German it means to receive or get; it took me a long time not to "become" an artichoke or a piece of bread when I simply asked for them. She always corrected the "th" sound, unknown in German and difficult to master.

The Mission district in 1940 was a working-class neighborhood of mostly Irish people. Mission Street itself was a bustling street with many shops and many people. My aunt had a millinery shop on this street, and he had a cap factory a few blocks away.

I started school, Hawthorne Elementary, immediately despite my lack of English. I was placed in the low 5th grade, although by my age I should have been in the high 5th. The school was a stucco two-story building, instead of the massive stone structure that I had known in Vienna. The area around it, used for playtime, was also strange. Actually, the playground activities were altogether new to me, since in Vienna there was no playground, physical education, nor recess. In order to help me learn English, I went to the 1st-grade class twice a day to work on reading. Of course, I could read very well, only not English. However, my deficits in language skills were compensated by my math skills, and I was quite advanced in these compared to my classmates; I already knew fractions, while they were studying long division.

There aren't too many other memories of my school days; I could just as well write school *daze*, since that must have been my experience there. Still, I must have enjoyed school, since I liked learning, even though I was isolated by my lack of language. One day, I heard a girl calling me a Nazi, which hurt me so much that I wrote my mother about it; she told me in a letter to ignore such things. I wanted to learn English quickly so that I would not be mistaken again. Looking at the situation today, I realize that the girl could not have known what she was saying, but it is these insensitive encounters that often hurt the most. My "cousins" told me that they were subject to many anti-Semitic insults at the same school. Remarkably, I do not recall any in school, ever.

Luckily for me, the public library was across the street and that helped me learn English even quicker. Cecylia, an avid reader and excellent student, spent a lot of time at the library, and introduced me to this great institution that I had never known before. To my delight, I found my favorite books there—the *Dr. Doolittle* series—and I began to read those that I had already read in German. Any problems I had with words, Cecylia was always willing to help clarify and explain. Most of all, she talked to me, and in a very short time, I became fluent in the language.

Because of the war in Europe, letters were slow in arriving. It often took more than a month, sometimes two or more. In late May, I received the first letters from my parents.

[Often, the letters are addressed to Mrs. Rabinowitz, who is Aunt Laura. The formality of address has to do, in part, with how distant the relationship is. Enclosed in these letters were letters to Phyllis herself. Her father's first letter, written in German, while a detainee in a British refugee camp, ends as follows:]

> You can't imagine how very, very happy I was to hear that you have already left Germany. Now you have to forget all the ugly and unpleasant things you have experienced, be cheerful and happy again, because the worst you have already behind you. You have to start studying hard again, and though your lovely Muttily [mother] and I can momentarily not be with you, you mustn't neglect your lessons; you have to be even more hardworking. I am convinced that you will be even more diligent. Soon you will have learnt the English language completely, and if it goes pretty fast, we will write each other only in English.

I can imagine that you left Mutti only with a heavy heart, but this is just temporary, soon our lovely Muttily will come to you, and later I will come, too. That will be a happy reunion. I am just afraid that when we come that your English knowledge has so much improved that you will laugh at our English. Isn't that true?

Now my lovely, little frog, write me detailed and often. When you write to Mutti you have to be careful, you know that every careless word could harm Mutti. Write me exactly what you are doing the whole day, what you study, actually everything. Your letters would make me really happy; I have, by the way, no other diversion than the letters from you.

I am all right over here. I just wish to get together with you soon. I already yearn so much for you my little Fratz, but you probably don't long for me a lot! Isn't that true? No, don't sulk my baby, I know that you love your Pappi a little bit, but not like you used to. Am I maybe mistaken? We will see when I come to you.

Now many, many kisses from your "bad" Pappi

[The letter of April 21 from Phyllis's mother makes it clear that she and her husband have been separated by the circumstances of war and persecution. Phyllis has become a kind of go-between for them, as they cannot correspond directly. Many of the letters stress the difficulty of obtaining affidavits strong enough to bring her parents to the United States.]

Have you heard from Papa? I have not heard from him in the last six weeks since your departure. If you get mail from him, please let me know. Gusti [a friend with whom Phyllis's mother lived], poor thing is in hospital again, I am worried about her, as you can imagine. Have you got all your things? I am so delighted that you have it so nice and yet long for my sweet Puppshen [dolly]. I am so alone, but please don't worry about me, be happy and cheerful, your mother is brave. Now, Pupperl, you promised to write every week, do keep your promise! I kiss you from the bottom of my heart,

your Mutz

[This later letter—of May 11—adds encouragement.]

I was so glad to hear that you were able to get shoes. I hope you wear your supports. I am glad that you are going to school; do be a good student, my darling, you have a lot to catch up on and you must work hard. Don't worry if others make fun of you because you can't speak English yet. People who like you will point out your mistakes to you, the other kind don't matter. Can you make yourself understood by Cecylia and Moe? I should so like to have a picture of them all. Have you had any mail from Papa?

[One letter from her mother ends as follows and leads to Phyllis's intriguing comments about cultural styles and assumptions.]

P.S. Do return the regards, always remember Gusti, also Dr. Murm., and Fr. Pisk.

It is German custom to include remembrances from other people at the end of letters, and I chuckle now when she reminds me to mention other people in my letters. I suppose it is nice to be remembered, but I found it a chore and it took up much space on our letters. When she asks if my aunt has a maid, that also makes me smile—so many Europeans thought all Americans had maids. In fact, maids were much more common in Vienna, although we didn't have one, nor did my aunt.

I don't remember how my mother's letters of frustration and disappointment affected me, but it was the harbinger of many more during the next year in my mother's desperate effort to join me in the United States. Now I also think of the trouble my aunt and others had to go to in trying to help her. Filing papers, going to consulates, expenses, writing to others—these all were big sacrifices for working people.

June 4, 1940 *[in English, with Cecylia's help, sent to Kitchener Camp in Kent, England]*
Dear Daddy,
Please excuse me that I couldn't write you. Last Sunday we went to the fair. It was very nice out there. I had a wonderful time. We saw Billy Rose's Aquacade. I liked [it] very much. Today we will go again (Cecylia and I). Really it is beautiful at the fair. Tomorrow I will mail the letter; I will continue tomorrow. I am glad that we have only 10 days school. Last Wed. I had a letter from Mama. We will eat now lunch.
    Hello Daddy: Yesterday I couldn't write you because it was too late. That way I wrote today. I am a very good pupil in Hebrew. In one week I will go to the third grade. That's fine! Isn't it? I hope that we will go soon all together, Mama, you, and I.
    Now much . . . much 100,000,000 kisses, your loving Lizzi

[In the same letter, this note from Aunt Laura to Phyllis's father.]

Dear Mr. Finkel,
The dear Lizzi is already a total American. She learns well and speaks good English already. How are you? I am sorry I can't give you a good report about the dear Laura. I feel bad that I can't get a sufficient affidavit, but I don't lose hope. L[aura] Rabinowitz

The World's Fair on Treasure Island was *the* big event of 1940 in San Francisco. I experienced another sense of wonderment—to think that there would actually be a World's Fair in San Francisco, and that *I* would be able to go to it. As it happened, I went to the Fair many times, always filling me with awe and delight. Luckily, Cecylia and her friends were willing to take me along. Looking back, I wonder if Cecylia did not resent having that funny little girl tagging along with her all the time, but if she did, I was never made conscious of it. We took a streetcar to the Ferry Building, then one of those wonderful ferryboats for 10 cents to go to Treasure Island. Week by week we explored new facets of that wonderland. The brilliant lights of the main promenade, the exotic atmosphere of the whole island of palm trees and vegetation, the throngs of people, the amusements for children, all were a wonderful part of the experience. Especially memorable was Billy Rose's Aquacade, as I watched wide-eyed the thrilling performance of Esther Williams diving into a pool through a ring of fire.

We also went to the movies every Saturday afternoon, mostly to the El Capitan Theater that was on Mission and 22nd. I loved going to the movies, but I was surprised that we saw pictures other than Shirley Temple, nearly the only type of film I was allowed to see in Vienna. Some of the films were especially terrifying, such as *Dr. Cyclops*, the story of a one-eyed monster who reduced people to ant-size, which gave me nightmares.

Everything was new and strange to me, but what struck me most was the freedom from fear. For instance, I actually saw girls and women wearing a Star of David around their necks. At first, I cringed with fear for them, worried that someone might attack them, but eventually, I realized with relief, that to be Jewish was not a crime in America. Wearing such an ornament in Hitler's Austria was asking for trouble. Also, it was possible to walk on the grass, something that is clearly forbidden in Austria (and many other parts of Europe) still today. Another thing that was a comfort for me was that men didn't urinate in the streets, and I lost the fear of being molested by lurking men, which gave me freedom on the streets.

The free public library was the biggest miracle of all. I could peruse the shelves to decide what to read, and then borrow books for a week or two without cost. Between those wonderful visits to the Fair, the movies, and the library, my English improved rapidly, while the German faded from my memory, much to my mother's chagrin.

I spent many hours at my Aunt's millinery shop. Hats were an important item of clothing in those days, worn by adults when leaving the house. Her store was close to 24th Street on Mission, close to our house, so I am guessing that I was asked to go there if Cecylia had other things to do. I loved the time at the shop. I liked trying on all those wonderful hats, and I liked the ladies who came in to buy them, but I especially liked "Johnny," the other saleslady in the shop. "Johnny" was a big fat mamma, but fashionably dressed, her blond hair carefully coifed. She was abundant in every way, sweet to the customers and especially wonderful to me because she worked at breaking the language barrier with patience. Johnny was not a young woman—perhaps in her 50s, and she had a boyfriend who was also pleasant to me when he came to the store. Johnny would often bring me little favors, but most of all she just talked to me in a way that felt good, and I knew she liked me. I especially liked Saturday nights, a big shopping night because the customers would often come in with their husbands, and Johnny would become more solicitous: "This color becomes you, Madam," or "the shape is wonderful for your face," speaking softly as she adjusted the hat slightly. It was exciting.

My uncle's cap factory, which also sold men's hats, was on Mission and 16th Street, a very busy intersection. Sometimes I was sent there on errands for some item my aunt needed for her store. I had little interaction with him; perhaps he didn't speak German. On the other hand, my boy cousin, Moe, age thirteen, was a thorn in my side. Unlike his wonderful sister who took such good care of me, Moe constantly teased me and bullied me, as he annoyed his sister as well. She knew how to cope with his constant harassment, but it was very upsetting to me since I had never shared a household with siblings before. Actually, I have never learned the give and take that comes of sibling relationships, and still found it surprising when my children sparred with each other.

I was sent to Camp in July, an extraordinary experience for any child, but especially one from a city in a foreign country. I had only been in San Francisco three months at the time, and my English was yet to be perfected. The orphanage had arranged to have me go to a Girl Scout Camp in the Sierras near Fresno. I had a wonderful time, and a picture I have of myself there shows a peace on my face that I see in the mirror after I've spent a few days in the mountains. I do wonder how well I was able to talk with my fellow campers; I expect that I was really an oddity.

July 28, 1940
Dear Daddy,
On Sunday luckily I came to this camp. It is here very beautiful and very hot, sunny, and everything is green. Friday I went to a waterfall, and

yesterday, Saturday, I went horseback riding. How are you? Next Sunday I will write again. Many 100,000,000,000,000 kisses. Your loving Phyllis

July 18, 1940 *[sent from Mooragh Internment Camp, Ramsey, Isle of Man]*
Dear Mrs. Rabinowitz,
I just received three letters from you and my little one, thank you for that. As you can see from my address, I am now in an internment camp and with me all the other members of the previous camps have been interned. We are all right here; we are treated well, only that we are cut off [from] the rest of the world with a barbed-wire fence and we are not allowed to leave the camp. This is very unpleasant, but we still have one hope and that is as soon as somebody gets the visa and is able to emigrate, he will be dismissed out of the camp. If my papers were all right, I also would have the chance to get the visa; unfortunately this is not the case, therefore I have to wait; maybe my wife arrives there soon and can get me an affidavit. I thank you very, very much for your good care of my child; I will never forget your help. In anticipation of the good news that my wife is already with you, I give you and your family my best regards.

My lovely, little darling,
Today I had another day of joy. Your three letters from 4/29, 5/6, and 5/12 have been forwarded and today I have received them at the same time. Also the picture came and I was enormously happy. Soon your Mutti will be with you; how happy I would be, you can imagine. I write Mutti very often but I haven't heard from her for eight weeks. I am really proud of you that you make great progress in school; I knew that everybody would like you. Over here it is very beautiful; I live directly by the sea. In the next letter I will describe you everything in detail, for today I have to close because we are only allowed to write 24 lines.
Many, many kisses from your loving Papa

I doubt that at the time I understood what an internment camp was, nor do I recall Aunt Laura explaining it to me. The internees were not allowed to write in pen, only pencil. Anyway, he couldn't say any more about it, and thereafter, for many years, the envelope would have a "CENSORED" stamp on it. His internment would have been the most unexpected turn of events—to leave Austria to avoid internment in Hitler's camps, only to be interned in Britain instead. Both parents thought that the other one would be able to come to the United States because Anny was sending them affidavits. They were not able to communicate effectively with each other, and I became the messenger, but I don't think I did a very good job because I have many of my mother's letters that should have been sent to my father, and his to her.

Aug. 7, 1940 *[in English, sent to Ramsey]*
Dearest Daddy,
Sunday I arrived here, from Camp. I like it very much there. We had
swimming, boating, and horseback riding. I almost forgot that your birthday is coming soon. I wish you a very happy birthday and hope that we
will be together soon. Last Sunday, the 4th of August, made one year
since I have seen you. But I hope I am going to see you soon. I know that
God will help us, and everybody who needs help. He has always helped
and God will help us now. So don't despair! Friday is my Birthday and
I will be 11 years old. I'm a big girl now. I have grown about 3 inches.
The time goes so fast. I received a letter from you and one from Mama
last Wednesday. Thank you very much! How are you? I am fine, Love
and 1,000,000,000,000 kisses, your Phyllis
P.S. Cecyle correct me. If she wouldn't, the letter would be terrible.

August 15, 1940 *[sent to Ramsey, translated from German]*
Dear Daddy!
I received a letter from Mutti! It made me very happy since I didn't have
mail for 1 1/2 weeks. Today is Thursday and [last] Friday was my birthday. It was very nice. I received 2 pairs of socks, a jacket, a sweater, a
dog pin, hair things, and candy. Auntie made me a birthday party and
a cake with my name on it. Sunday I went to a downtown show, today
I went swimming. Isn't that fine? I know how to swim like you. I learned
in Camp. Yesterday I was at the fair. It was very beautiful. We saw many
things. How are you? Are you healthy? I am. Many kisses 100,000,000,000
(Phyllis)

In addition to the party, my aunt and family took me to a fancy dinner at Monaco's, a theater restaurant, in the North Beach District. The
Italian menu had many courses and then entertainment on a small
stage—a magician, a lady singer in a beautiful dress, more music. The
birthday cake was also new to me, and I was delighted to see my name
written on it. I was well feted on the occasion of my 11th birthday,
much more than I would have had in Vienna.

*[What follows is a letter, translated from German, to Aunt Laura from
Phyllis's mother, also named Laura.]*

Vienna, Aug. 17, 1940
Dearest Aunt!
I thank you for your mail. I am not worried when I seldom receive mail
from my child. I am convinced that she is in good motherly care and I
feel that she is happy and satisfied in your home; she is longing a little
bit, but that is understandable. Is she well behaved and aware of her
duties? Please write me about it. If God wills, I will be able to take your

place in a few months. Please don't be impatient; I know that it is hard for you to take care of another child besides your regular duties, but believe me I am not longing for anything more than to show you and my good friends my gratitude.

I greet and kiss you, Your Laura

August 20, 1940 *[written in English, sent to Ramsey]*
Dear Daddy!
It has been a long time since I have received mail from you. How are you? I hope you are fine! I went swimming today! I had a lot fun. I'll go back to school in one week. How is everything? I hope you'll get a visa soon. Have you mail from mother? I was Sunday to a nice movie! My back is brown as an Indian's! Love, Happy Birthday, 10,000,000 Kisses, Phyllis

School resumed in the fall, but my memories of the following two months have vanished. Letters from my mother should have warned me that changes were coming, but I blocked those out until I had the letters translated so many years later. One letter would have told me that my aunt was unhappy with me, but I do not remember feeling it at the time. I stopped getting letters from my father, and my mother's letters became progressively more anxious, worrying about me and because Gusti, the lady with whom she had lived, died, and my mother had to move.

Vienna, September 8, 1940 *[translated from German]*
I had a lot to do at her home and now that is over, too. I have to leave the apartment and right now I do not know where to go, now it is very hard, but something will happen eventually. . . . I hope you are good, well behaved, and tidy and do not make additional work for the dear aunt. Have in mind what sacrifices [she] makes; therefore be grateful and do what she asks . . . with joy and pleasure, this is then only a small part of what you owe her. . . . Mutti

The letters from September may not have arrived before I left my aunt's home. I don't remember what was going on in September and October. I do not recall any disagreements with my aunt, although there was strife between Moe and me; his teasing was quite unpleasant, though I do not remember any reason for it. I just remember one day in November the social worker from the orphanage came and told me that I would be leaving my aunt's place to go to a foster home. I can't recall my feelings at the time, blocked out, as in shock. I was told that I should not try to get in touch with my aunt or her family. It was not a happy moment and so I forgot the events that led up to it.

These seven months had been hard on my whole family. My father had been interned by the British—made into a prisoner of war—and shipped off to Australia, thus losing his chance to come to America to take care of me. My mother had her visa applications denied, while her situation in Vienna became more precarious in addition to moving. And I, happily enjoying my new home, was forced to move without understanding why. When would we all move together?

[Phyllis next lives in a foster home. In her full memoir, she has written separate chapters about her time in foster homes. Her attempt, in later years, to reconnect with her Austrian past is presented in chapter 7.]

LETTERS

By Ruth Schlamme Schnitzer [1937]

My dear ones,

Before I tell you about the concert, I want to shmooze a bit and I want to thank you for your letter No. 37. I was very interested in all the news. It appears that soon there won't be anyone left in Wuerzburg. I would advise Anni R. not to come here, because they don't know anything about gymnastics. In school they have games, and after school, children take [tap] dancing lessons. The Americans say that the children get plenty of exercise by swimming, ice-skating, playing tennis, golf, etc., and therefore there is no need for gymnastics. At Monroe High School, which I shall attend, they have just opened a fabulous swimming pool, and the children take swimming instead of gymnastics.

Amelia Earhart is an American pilot, who started yesterday on an airplane trip around the world. Of course, the newspapers are very interested in her and everyone is following her flight.

Yesterday there was a terrible disaster in Texas. The heating system in a brand-new beautiful school was leaking oil, which exploded. The blast tore the roof off the building and 500 children and 100 teachers died. Isn't it dreadful? I hope that the mess with the heaters will not be too bad. We're certainly better off with our heating system.

Have you decided to buy a certain radio or is Mr. St. coming five times a week? I have the "Stillvergnuegte Streichquartett" with me. The other day I started "Joern Uhl" by Frenssen. I wonder when I will master it!

Aunt L. sent you a letter in English today, Mutti. If you can't make it out, send it back and I shall try to translate it. But it would be a disgrace if an intelligent woman like you could not read it!

I was very enthusiastic about the concert. Not only was it a beautiful program and so well played, but I was also charmed by Iturbi! He conducts excellently and without a score! Uncle M. says that Iturbi, on a

Wednesday, for instance, has not looked at the score, and by Thursday he knows every note for every instrument in the orchestra. He also is supposed to be one of the best pianists. Tonight he is playing the Beethoven solo and conducting at the same time, but not in Rochester, as the entire orchestra went to Ithaca. You probably know the Beethoven and Brahms, Mutti, but for me it was all new. I also liked the Debussy. The last work was something entirely different, Ravel. A bit peculiar, but I liked it also. It was always one melody, which was repeated and repeated with different instruments. First there was a flute solo, then a duet, and then more and more until there was an awful noise at the end. After the concert, I spoke with Dr. Weisberger and I gave him the message that he should write to Aunt Paula. However, he said that he needs to write about 30 letters, but he will see what happens. Marlene had invited me, but I canceled. One Saturday I would really like to be at home so that I could read, write, study, and listen to the radio. I'm not expecting any mail since I received number 37 yesterday.

Monday, March 22, 1937
Yesterday was the first day of Spring. There still is some snow on the ground and it is still cold. I can hardly wait until summer. Starting Friday, we will have one week's vacation, including Seder night. That will really be something. Uncle M. does not have any idea of what is expected of him. Well, we'll see what develops!

On Saturday I listened to "Faust" on the radio. Next week the New York Opera is coming here and they will perform "Lohengrin." But it is so expensive that there is no possibility that we will be able to go. Too bad! It will be performed in German.

Just a few minutes ago I received 3 "Illustrierte" [magazines] for which I thank you, dear Opapa. I always enjoy reading them.

Today Aunt L. gave me one of her very pretty blouses. Yesterday I baked Aunt Paula's cake. That was really something! I didn't know how to say "Plaetzle" [cookie] in English, and after they finally understood what I was trying to say, our store didn't have them in stock. So I improvised with the small round "things" that they brought me instead. It wasn't enough, but they all devoured my little, flat, messy cake with great zest. They also sent me the photos, and I selected one to be enlarged. It could be better.

I will close for today. Regards to EVERYONE and a thousand kisses for you from your loving Ruthle

Wednesday, March 24, 1937
It's always so wonderful to come home from school and find mail on top of my dresser. This morning there were 2 magazines from Opapa. After lunch there was your dear letter No. 38. I thank you from all my heart for both. In every letter you're telling me about new people who are coming here. That's great. When the two Kurts get here, we will have a sizeable J.B. ["Jugend Bund," or Jewish youth group] in N.Y. But there

is no girl among them. Mutti, in the end you won't let me go there? According to Otto's sketch, I can easily visualize my room. But I feel a little bit blue. When I think of home and my room, I can't visualize completely how much my room has changed.

We don't have any problems with our radio. Most of the time we listen to N.Y., Buffalo, or Rochester. I understand that B. is a very large city, only 1 1/2 hours from here by car. We will pass through there when we drive to Niagara Falls.

If only Spring would come!

Friday, March 26, 1937
Today is that great holiday in Germany, but not over here. We don't have school, but all the stores are open. I just feel like writing you in English. I never did it before. Yesterday I had a lucky day. Aunt L. brought me some nice elegant black shoes. Very simple, but nice. Aunt Sofie Rubinstein, the sister of aunt L., sent some money for the children to buy gifts for Pesach. So aunt L. bought me new roller skates, and I can't wait till the streets are cleared from that snow. And I'll get another beautiful gift! Skis! From a friend of ours, she doesn't need them, and she'll be glad to give them to me. Isn't that swell!

Saturday evening
Today is just an ordinary day, and all the happiness of the Seder is gone. It really was beautiful, even though all was read in English. But we fulfilled the obligations as well as we could and it was very festive. I am curious to know what you did. My last Seder at Buzi, of course, cannot be compared with the one we had here yesterday. I bought a hyacinth for aunt L. She was delighted, but said, of course, that it wasn't necessary for me to do that. But I told her that I always brought my mother flowers. If only I could do that next year! On Seder night we said—instead of next year in Jerusalem—"next year with my dear ones."

Today I had to go to the movies with the children. Even though we saw a delightful picture, I'm furious right now. 1. We got home too late and we were chastised, 2. We missed the time in which we wanted to dye Easter eggs, and 3. Marlene called and invited me for tomorrow and I have to stay at home because the adults are going to Temple and the maid observes Easter.

We always undertook something at Easter, and it was so lovely and springlike. Last year that was our beautiful trip to Heidelberg, wasn't it? And here the weather remains cold. There is snow and we have to stay home and do our work. Well, it won't hurt me!
I kiss you a 1,000 times, and now I'm going to bed! Your loving Ruthle

Monday, March 29
My dear ones,
Yesterday I had to work and stay at home. In the afternoon I saw a dry spot on Belmont Street. So I took my roller skates and taught myself to skate. At first it was awkward and I couldn't move from the spot or slide

backwards, but after only 10 minutes I made good progress. Of course, I still have to practice a lot. To my dismay, there came Harry Rotsch, bringing a friend with him, who knows Uncle M. Well, Harry is definitely from Wuerzburg. He inquired once more about his parents. The boys stayed through dinner, and I was dead tired when they finally left.

Today after breakfast I went to Falkenheims, and now I'm going to the Leseritzens and bring them a huge pot of tulips for Pesach from Aunt L.

Now I'm so tired that I can hardly stand up anymore. Today was such a wonderful day. I spent the whole afternoon on my feet with Ferne. We walked the long way to town, first to the dentist, then to my doctor who vaccinated me against diphtheria, then to the post office, then to various department stores, and also to the photographer where I picked up my portrait. Unfortunately, they made a color photo and overall it could be better—I look so fat and stupid! I'm curious to see what you have to say about it. Here school will start again on Monday. Otto is better off! But, on the other hand, we don't have school in summer. Good night!

March 31, 1937

Today I'm really enjoying my vacation. We always sleep until 9 o'clock, then I practice, and then I go outside to roller skate. Just now I went bicycling on Helen's bike. Oh, it was again so beautiful in this wonderful spring weather.

I also looked through my letters this morning and decided that the Hamburgers are almost as loyal as you in writing such loving letters. Really, they are so interested, as if I belonged to them! Their sons agree with me that when one is far away one forgets all the bad and evil things and remembers with gratefulness all the beautiful times with our families.

Tomorrow is the first of April. If I don't mention it to anyone here, no one will play tricks on me; maybe I can trick them. Now spring is here and I have another big worry—the weather was one of them. This is my figure. It is absolutely horrible how fat I am getting, and yet everything tastes so good. Sometimes I think I can't take it anymore. Wherever I go I am the fattest, and I always have good intentions to eat less, but most of the time Aunt L. makes me to eat more.

She always says not to worry about it, that I'm not too fat and that later on, when I'm fully grown, I can do something about it. Rubbish! All my clothes are getting too tight and short on me. I get jealous when I look at the photos from 2 years ago when my proportions were exactly right.

Are you eating bread? I don't. I also don't touch the cake that's in the house. I'm doing this for the first time. And since I stay away from bread and cake, I really enjoy the taste of Matzos. Tomorrow I'm going on an outing with the scouts. I feel guilty for cutting this letter short. 1,000 kisses, Ruthle

April 1

My dear ones,

When I came back from the scout outing and I saw the mail, I jumped for joy. . . . I'm happy to know that I may expect a package, but I don't want you to spend so much money on me. Tomorrow I'll send you the pictures. I'm sending one as a Bar Mitzvah gift [for her brother, Otto] and one for Opapa. I bought a book for Otto, which will be mailed direct from the store. We'll see what he can do with it. He must learn English. It is an Indian tale. It is too bad that I cannot see our "new" apartment, but I'm happy for all of you that you were finally able to renovate the old place. Aunt Elsb. still has not found a way to get the package from New York to Rochester. I can hardly wait anymore.

I am very sorry to hear about the death of Paul Rosenheim, but I cannot blame him. It's great that the Germers and Hamburgers are coming to the Bar Mitzvah. I would have loved to see them and to help you at home with this big festivity.

We gave my blue skirt to the cleaner and when we got it back the gloss had come off it. Today Ida is coming; it was my turn to have her over. Yesterday I was together with Ferne from morning till evening. I really like her so much.

Oh, my dear ones, you are so good to me! Today I already received the packages and I'm jumping with joy. I thank you from the bottom of my heart. I laughed about the "Wuerscht" [sausages]—that looks as if I wouldn't get enough to eat here. Only yesterday we had "weissen Pressack." But, of course, we will eat them with gusto. I know that the chocolate and easter eggs and Bissen should be delicious. All my acquaintances will get a taste. They were already enthralled by the first shipment of "German Candy." Dear Ottole, I am especially grateful to you for the lovely gift. It's on top of my dresser, so that I can always see it. In reality I like you better, but it is not bad. I will also enjoy using the lavender, and tomorrow I will make the pudding with vanilla sauce. With the same mail I also received the magazine and will start reading it at once. I already received birthday greetings from Erwin and Traute S. I really would like to know why everyone is in such a hurry about my birthday. Today is only April 2. If I receive everything so early, my birthday will be very quiet and lonely. With Erwin everything seems to be OK and hopefully you spoke to him at the train station.

Evening

It snowed again, but since it's April, it's very possible that the sun will come out again tomorrow. If I can get someone to come with me, I would like to see *Maytime*, with Jeanette MacDonald, which you, dear Mutti, recommended.

Right now I'm making the almond pudding, but I'm having difficulties with the measurements. (How does one say "Mass" in English? Because the word "Masse" has a different meaning.) It looks like the pudding is turning out pretty good! But there is so little in one package. Also, the directions for the milk are silly, because it is already cooked when it comes into the house. Aunt L. loves the chocolate, and she said that they don't make anything like this here.

Now all of us here are keeping our fingers crossed for my Ottole! The letter will probably be public knowledge.

Your loving
Ruthle

April 3, 1937
My dear ones,
Today I went to the movies with Ferne and heard Jeanette MacDonald and I am beside myself because it was so wonderful, not only because both (Nelson Eddy) are superb singers, but also they are so good looking and charming and very fine actors. By seeing these kind of films, one gets to hear different operas.

Monday morning, April 5
Yesterday I had a still more beautiful musical experience. [The] Luries took me along to the Iturbi concert. I can only say that this man is something extra special. He played the Beethoven Concerto No. 3 while conducting the orchestra at the same time. While still playing the piano with one hand, he gave the downbeat with the other hand. When playing with both hands, he directed by moving his head. He knows every note of every part. Not only does he do all this without a score, but he really is almost even a better pianist. He is traveling all over the world. Perhaps you can arrange somehow to hear him. Next season we will have Yehudi here. I'm already looking forward to that.

Yesterday the Luries and I were invited for coffee at the Falkenheims. She had baked some fantastic things. Of course, the American housewives were very impressed.

Today it's back to school and our lovely and lazy vacation comes to an end. I hope that Aunt Elsbeth will send the package soon. Instead of the package, I received a card from R., saying that next week they will go to Schw. and then they will make up the package and send it to me. It's so nice of them to do that! I got used to being in school again.

Wait, I did receive a package—from Erwin in Switzerland—his photo. It was photographed by "Biber" and I don't think it's an outstanding picture. Anyway, I was happy to receive it as a birthday gift. Aunt L. told me that Miss Rose was here and that they talked about Otto. She also asked whether I need a dress or anything else. But for the time being I have enough, but I did order a garter belt. I'm getting nothing but birthday mail! I don't know why everyone is in such a hurry. Also, Otto's card came from Wiesbaden, which confused me very much. I hope to hear more about it soon. Right now you are really living it up!

Klaus wrote me such a nice letter that I decided to do something for Aunt Paula the next time I write. That guy really made something of himself. This afternoon I received the letter from Opapa, for which I shall thank him separately. Again there came another letter from the Hamburgers. Aunt Bronia writes so affectionately. But now, since I know that they and so many other people are reading my letters, I don't feel like writing too much about my private life. You hopefully are interested in everything, but not everything is for publication. I find that my letters are constantly getting shorter due to the fact that I have so much to do. Right now there are 7 pairs of stockings waiting to be darned, and so many people are waiting to hear from me.

On Thursday I must pass a test for Girl Scouts. In school we took up the Crusades. I don't really know what they are in German—*Kreuzfahrer*? We learned that all of them came from Europe and went East in order to keep the Turks from entering the Holy Land. I had never heard of them before.

I wish Otto sometime could have Miss Hammond; she is so nice. On the Saturday after my birthday, I am allowed to have a birthday party. Isn't that great? There will be approximately 10 girls. I could also ask some boys, but I don't feel like it because I don't know any nice ones.

Wednesday, April 7, 1937
Today I can acknowledge your dear letter No. 42. I'm always happy to receive your mail and I was especially pleased to receive a better photo of Otto. I think that my package will arrive just in time for the birthday. Otto is something else! I believe I could not have traveled all by myself to stay with strangers in Wiesbaden. What a silly ass I am—did the same by traveling to America by myself.

Yesterday at school a boy gave me a scrap of dirty old paper he had found in a yard. On it was a German poem, which he asked me to translate for him. Another boy has a grandmother who can speak a bit of German and he asks her for certain German expressions which he then passes on to me. All of them are so interested and also full of ideas. The other day they did a funny play and also a modern version of *Romeo and Juliet*. After one kissed the other, he had red spots in his face from the lipstick. They are always doing stuff like that. They wrote letters to the heads of state of various European countries, and they make cartoons of these people and tell jokes about them.

I don't know whether I told you that there is a little German boy in my school, but I never see him. However, today I spotted him when his mother came to pick him up from school. She is from Cologne, a cousin of Miss Rosenfeld. Her name is Weinberg and she said she had already heard about me.

Now I hope that Spring is definitely at last here. I just did yard work. This consisted of cleaning the back yard. That is a "Hinterhof." It was a big mess. Last summer they had vegetables, but this year we will only plant flowers. They have water hoses and all the garden implements and

Uncle M. is the gardener. We also have a balcony attached to the house, and I can hardly wait till summer gets here. But now I have to get back to my homework.

Greetings and 1,000 kisses for all of you,
your loving Ruthle

Friday, April 9, 1937
My Dear Ones,
I'm sorry I did not have a chance to write to you yesterday. Anyway, nothing special happened. I was at my scout leader's home and talked with her. I also passed most of my test, and on Tuesday (my birthday) I will finish it. I am supposed to tell a story about an animal. I decided to talk about Helen's dog. I also passed the knot tying, as well as the American anthem and everything about the flag. The flag is almost a holy thing here, this "Star Spangled Banner." Just now I received another letter from Mr. K in Italy. He writes such nice letters. I will really have to do my best to answer him soon. Uncle M. bought the Playel Duet, which [is] more difficult that the ones you have, Mutti. We'll start working on them now.

April 10
Two more days till my birthday, and all the mail is here already. Was that a great joy this morning when 5 letters and 2 cards for Ruth Schlamme were among it. The nicest and most dear to me was, of course, your letter which really touched me. I thank you from the bottom of my heart and hope that all your good wishes will be fulfilled. I like the photo very much and am happy to have it. I am so proud of my big brother. Now to the other mail—there was a very nice letter from Norbert and a card from Omama and Aunt Thekla. Also I received a very nice card from Hexle. She writes so affectionately and is always afraid that I will forget her. I had mail from all my Wuerzburg friends, Liesel and Beate, Lore N. and Lore F. and Hede. I was so happy with all those letters. Please, Mutti, can you thank them on my behalf, for the time being. I also was very happy to receive a very nice letter from Herrmanns. I guess that's about it. Just now I found a card from Ursi. She wrote that she is sending me a package and a long letter. The package hasn't come yet, but what do you say to that? She must really dote on me. But now I must go to lunch. I had an excellent violin lesson with duets. Uncle M. still has not developed my pictures, but I don't want to remind him too many times.

Sunday evening
Yesterday Marlene and I went shopping. I did not have to pay for my stockings and garter belt, the bill goes direct to Miss Rose. I spent the evening at Ferne's. She was newly outfitted from head to toe, also paid for by the Committee. This morning we had Sunday School, as always, and this afternoon we went for a terrific auto tour. Of course, Ferne went with us. We laughed and giggled a lot with Uncle M. We enjoyed the

beautiful weather and ice cream and candy. For supper I was at Ferne's. Her aunt played bridge with us. I really finally wanted to learn how to play bridge, but, of course, I didn't understand it too well. Tomorrow I'm going back to school. I wish I wouldn't have to go to the Leseritz's because I'm still expecting mail and a package and I'm afraid I won't have the time to look at it. Well, we shall see. Good night!

Sunday evening, April 12
Well, I really don't know what to do; I'm bursting with joy! And I really don't know how to thank you, especially you, my dear, wonderful Mutti: Now from the beginning, this morning I received a birthday letter from Riesenf.-Westing, with 1 dollar enclosed, in which they notified me that the package is on it's way. Of course, I could hardly wait to get home after school, and sure enough, there was the package. What joy! Riesenf. enclosed some chocolate and Paula W. sent some very sheer stockings. I really like the aprons, the colorful one I wear to school as a dress. The dirndl is darling—only a little bit too long, also the apron dress. Here they are wearing everything shorter. The slips are beautiful! Of course, I really expected them to be lovely (but not quite as beautiful). Well, when I saw the knit dress, I was dumbfounded—such a lovely thing! And I love the color and am taken with the wool and the style. Well, Muttile, how did you manage to accomplish something so beautiful in such a short time? I'm really ashamed that I sent so little to Otto, but then he has so much more, namely you, dear parents! If you would be here, it would be my happiest birthday ever! At least I have your loving gifts.

I'm really not expecting anything from the Luries. I can't believe that I'm already 15. But now I'm happy and full of hope for a reunion with you by the time I'm 16. Miss Leseritz just gave me a gift—candy. I will start the next letter on my birthday, but I won't get home until the evening.

Again many, many thanks and 1,000 heartfelt kisses,

from your loving and grateful Ruthle

Tuesday, April 13
My dear ones,
O.K., now my 15th birthday is over. Actually, I really had a wonderful celebration, but not at home. Your gifts made me especially happy. At breakfast everyone sang "Happy birthday!" (That's like "Hoch soll sie leben!") When I got to school, the whole class sang it, and they got out the flag and told jokes and stories, all for me! When I came home for lunch, there was a letter from you, Mutti, and from you, Papa. Of course, both of them made me very happy. Both of you thought that by the time your mail arrived my happy day would be over. Annemie congratulated me and also Mrs. Wechsler, and I thought that was so nice of both of them. I also received a long letter from Ursi.

After school I went to the scout meeting, and they sang for me again. Ferne gave me a girl scout whistle. Another girl from my class gave me a handkerchief. When I got home, there was a surprise waiting for me. David gave me 3 pair of ankle socks. Isn't that sweet of him? Aunt L. said that at the store he made such a to-do until he picked out the right colors. The saleslady laughed and asked him whether this was for his sweetheart! He certainly likes me very much.

You know, Mutti, the coat from Aunt Lotte goes perfectly with my knit dress! It makes a knockout outfit. Well, if you are still sending me a green suit, I will think that I am the daughter of a millionaire! I will be thrilled to have it and hope it will get here soon. As to sewing, I am completely on my own expertise because neither Aunt L. nor Molly have any idea about sewing. More than likely I will shorten my "dirndl" and apron on Ferne's sewing machine. Now it's no hardship wearing the fashionable shorter lengths because my legs have gotten a bit thinner.

By the way, I recognized the buttons on the dirndl. Well, tonight I will sleep into my 16th year. I heard about the young Steinh., but I never met him. Hede wrote me about that terrible case. I'm not going to give Ferne your condolences because she does not want to be reminded of her sister's death. She is her normal self again and is in good spirits and very nice. Are you going to take a picture of Otto in his long pants? Both of his photos are on top of my dresser, one of them stuck in the mirror. Now it's high time to say good night!

Wednesday, the 14th
Today I received Rita's dear birthday letter, and I thank her so much. I also got a wedding announcement from Trudl P. I don't know where I will find the time to answer all these letters. We have beautiful spring weather. I put on ankle socks and my red crocheted dress with a cardigan on top and went to school and afterwards roller-skating. The older I am getting, the younger I feel. I jump rope with the greatest pleasure and I run around in the street like a 10-year-old. Well, that's the way I feel. No one is criticizing me and I'm so happy that spring is here. Some little plants are already appearing in our garden, and everywhere one can admire the crocus in bloom. Today I played baseball for the first time. It is very difficult because one is supposed to hit the ball with a long stick. I think I can't ever hit that ball.

I still received 2 more gifts: a book from Mrs. Cohen (*An Old Fashioned Girl*) and Molly gave me Cutex for my nails, which is very popular here.

Thursday, the 15th
Today Ursi's little package, containing Swiss chocolate, arrived. Also, today is Aunt Lillie's birthday. I bought her 2 pretty handkerchiefs and gave her some of my chocolate. She was very happy with everything and said she would have liked to buy me something, but that I have everything I need. She doesn't know what to say when people ask her. Miss

Rose also wants to give me something, and I think she is sending me face powder. This has never happened before—I completely ran out of "wishes." Of course, I cannot ask anyone to give me a bicycle. That would be the only unfulfilled wish; otherwise I am happy and healthy.

At noontime a Jewish man from Frankfurt came by, selling sausages. He said he used to come every Tuesday to Wuerzburg, where he bought cattle. I don't know his name. He speaks very little English. Aunt L. bought a salami. She could communicate pretty good with him. We sent him to the Falkenheim's.

Now I still have a lot to do. Goodbye for now.

FROM *BILL GRAHAM PRESENTS MY LIFE INSIDE ROCK AND OUT*

By Bill Graham and Robert Greenfield [1992]

Within a year, I caught up. When I was twelve, they put me in with the twelve-year-olds. The language I got in six months. The accent was gone within a year or less. Because it was a way out. Somehow, when the accent was lost, the kids in the neighborhood accepted me. Then I switched over from P.S. 104 to Macombs Junior High School, P.S. 82, on University Avenue right next to the Park Plaza theater. That was a big break. Within the year, I was a New Yorker.

Al's Candy Store. It was right down the hill from Montgomery Avenue at University and 176th Street. There was a Chinese laundry on the hill and at the corner, there was a drugstore and next to the drugstore, there was the candy store. Everything in America in my mind relates to three things. Back then, the cost of the *Daily News* was two cents, a roll was two cents, and a container of milk was sixteen cents. That's the foundation of the American economy in my mind.

My job in the morning was to get up and go to the store. It was one of the things I didn't mind doing. I go out. And Roy didn't wanna do that. I just loved it. Hey, snowstorm? *Far out.* Rain? *Yeah.* I'll go outside. I'll meet somebody; I'll come back two hours later. "Where are the rolls?" they'd ask. "I met Sam and we got into a little stickball game and. . . ."

Religiously, this was what I was sent to get: four rolls, a container of milk, and the paper. Sometimes, we ran out of butter. I'd get butter. It was rationed, so I'd get the little stickers. Meat, I never bought. Candy store for the paper. Dairy two doors down. Container of milk, rolls, paper. Every day. Like a *clock.* . . .

Mrs. Sheridan had this beautiful clear face. She wore her hair pulled back into a bun and she was totally dedicated to her students. In a movie, she'd have been played by Maggie Smith. When I saw that movie *The Prime of Miss Jean Brodie,* I thought of her. I used to get into trouble *all* the time. For fighting in the schoolyard. Twice I got caught wheeling and dealing in the schoolyard, selling baseball cards and shooting crap. The principal couldn't deal with me. So he sent for Mrs. Sheridan to talk to me. She reminded me of my foster mother because she was there for the *right* reasons. She really wanted to teach and she really cared about the kids. She made every one of us feel like individuals. She was some fine lady. . . .

Early on, I *knew.* I don't know when I found out, but I found out early on that when you take these children in, you get forty-eight dollars a month. Then it was raised. It got up to fifty-four dollars a month. I didn't want somebody to pay for my keep. I wanted the money to come from me—I wanted to earn it—pay my own way. The reason I sold baseball cards and played craps in the schoolyard and went looking for any afterschool and weekend job I could find was to earn money. In terms of paying my foster parents, it was like, "You're good to me, but I'm not yours. I don't want somebody else to pay for what you do for me. I'm gonna do it." It wasn't something that I suddenly thought of one day. It started with the nine weeks of nobody wanting me.

First there was delivering *The Bronx Home News.* Then groceries. There was another kid who delivered for a butcher store next door. Sometimes, he got sick. In time, I delivered both groceries and meat.

A dime tip was standard. Sometimes from a real shithead, I'd get "Thank you" and the door would slam in my face. Sometimes a nickel, but the dime was the standard tip. For years and *years.*

Happiness then was when I got a sixth-floor walk-up. I'd be carrying a box with bottles of apple juice in it, vegetables, potatoes, all kinds of heavy cans, weighing *tons,* or maybe two or three bags. Six flights straight up and I'd be making all those turns on the stairs. I would hit that last step and I'd have all these bags and I'd give them to the lady and it was *serious time.* She'd say, "Hold on, sonny." Then I had to wait. Every grocery boy, everybody who first started earning money this way, the orgasm was in the slap of a quarter as compared to a dime.

When I got hit with a quarter, it was like someone saying *"Right on!"* to all my labors. A wise decision. In other words, somehow you're aware of what I just went through. A *quarter!* Usually, I got them on Undercliff Avenue because on Undercliff Avenue they had *money.* Those were the big buildings where people lived who had gone from taking orders to *giving* orders. The *bosses.* Accountants, or people who owned stores. They could afford to live in those apartments. Whoever made it then lived on Undercliff Avenue or on the sixth floor on Popham Avenue overlooking the river. The sixth floor in an elevator building with a view of the river? And you had groceries *delivered?* You know when I had groceries delivered to my house? *Never.*

Starting I think in 1944, I paid my foster parents every month the forty-eight dollars for my keep. I also bought a U.S. War Bond every month for eighteen dollars and seventy-five cents, which was what a twenty-five-dollar bond cost. *Every month.* To help make ends meet, my [foster] mother also delivered telegrams. I sometimes helped her and Roy do that. Every day I'd cross the street from school, put my books down, and go deliver groceries for the Eagle Market. I had a bike with a box on it. A three-wheel tricycle with an old green wooden box mounted on the front held in place by steel braces. I'd get home, eat, con the homework in any way I could, and then the schoolyard. Back to P.S. 82 from seven-thirty to ten at night. Half-court basketball indoors in the night center. Twelve-basket games and the winning team stayed on the court.

On weekends when I was delivering groceries, I used to cut out and get into a game. Just lock the wheels and go play. By the time I was sixteen, Jack Molinas was playing. Eddie Roman from Taft. Fatso Roth. Ed Warner from Clinton. Floyd Lane. The New York City high school all-star team, they were my heroes.

In the schoolyard, it was always playing for the sport of it, but also playing for *something.* Like softball games there on the weekends. Heavy cement softball games. Fast pitch. *Serious.* Quarter a man. I played, but not great. My favorite game then and now was street touch football. I *love* touch football. Anywhere from two to seven guys on a side.

Stickball was sewer-to-sewer. Hit by yourself and then run bases. Second base was at the next sewer. Car, sewer, car, sewer. Off-the-wall catch, *out.* Catch off any building, *out.* Guys playing stoop ball and "Captain" with a Spaldeen. One block away, that was the heavy marble block. Against the curb. Down between 175th and 174th, that was all marbles.

From the middle of the street to where the coin would be put up, leaning against the curb, it would be a nickel if you hit it. You'd pitch or throw the marble. If you didn't hit it, the other guy kept your marble. So what? If you hit, you got the nickel. For a nickel you could buy thirty or forty marbles. A nickel was a *nickel.*

From the opposite sidewalk, against the other curb, was a quarter. It would be like a hole in one. Guys would throw *missiles* toward this quarter. Five at a time. They would go bing! bing! bing! All of a sudden, one would hit. The real heavies would say, "*A-ha*, he figgered out the curve." But if you're a street marble player, you *know* the curve. A quarter back then meant a hundred or a hundred and fifty marbles. It was a quarter and three. Three tries. And on the second or third one—*BANG!* That was a *major* score. . . .

I never was *bar mitzvahed*. I started going to school and then I had a fight with the rabbi about paying attention. I didn't have any patience. The Hebrew school was right across the street from my house. I was into it, I was reading Hebrew. But I just wasn't studious enough. The family was not religious. My father could not read Hebrew. I never thought twice about it really. Religion wasn't important to me. Other than for the facts of my life. . . .

My Russian name was Volodia. In Germany, I was "Wolfgang." My sisters called me "Wolfy." In France, I became "Guillaume." My friend Sammy Schtuck in the chateau called me "Gui." William is Wolfgang. "Bill" is the slang name. It's just a nothing name. It doesn't say anything at all. It never has.

I never took the last name "Ehrenreich" because I never knew about my real family. The adoption thing came up early on. Then the idea was dropped and not really discussed again. How can you be adopted when you don't even know if you have a real family or not? Early on, there was some talk of it with the Foster Home Bureau. The reason it wasn't discussed again was that I thought that after the war, I'd be reunited with my real family.

The war ended in '45. Just before it did, the Jewish Foster Home Bureau contacted me with the news that HIAS, the Hebrew Immigrant Aid Society, was planning on sending teams of special investigators into the concentration camps and internment centers once the war ended. I went to a large building down in lower Manhattan with all the photographs and papers that I'd kept from my early days. Family pictures and letters. They made copies of everything, which were then sent on to Europe with these investigators. They knew full well that millions had been slaughtered. Then the miracle. They found my sister, Ester. I was fourteen at the time. . . .

At first, Ester wasn't certain what happened to my mother. I was told—through her. I was told through the records of HIAS. They notified me. What I think happened to me early on was that a subconscious wall went up. "I'm out here on my own. I don't have *anybody*." An island that I've lived on all my life. I knew I had to fend for myself and be careful not to let anything too close for fear of losing it again. There went my father, my mother, my sisters. What's the sense of opening that door? What's the sense of getting off the deck? I'd only get knocked down again. Before I do get up again, I'm going to make sure to look around really slowly. First, I'm going to make some moves. At least, that's a theory.

Early on, this coat was formed. I mean, I never remember being truly lost or emotionally sapped by the loss of anyone. That doesn't mean I don't care. Or that someone else loves deeper than I do. Or that I don't know how to grieve. But I do know I've always been prepared for loss. And therefore was never left totally naked.

I often ask people, "How old were you when your father died?" Or "How old were you when your mother died?" "Eight," they might say, *Oh.*

You grew up without a mother through your formative years? You never had a father? I understand something about you that I could never really put into words. It's like we share something others can't comprehend. . . .

The Park Plaza theater had a little round box office in front. It was Art Deco. Loew's Paradise–type deco. One balcony. Loew's Paradise had *two.* There were two movie houses that I used to go to besides the Park Plaza. The Zenith at 170th Street and the Mount Eden. If I went before 10 a.m., it was eleven cents to get in and the first five hundred kids got comic books. It was always two movies and a serial, and I was a big Phantom fan. Some kids' favorite was Dick Tracy or Terry and the Pirates. Mine was *The Phantom.* Like a weekly TV show. I'd go every Saturday morning to keep up with *The Adventures of The Phantom.*

The first movie I ever saw in America was the greatest movie I ever saw. I think I went with my foster mother. *Four Feathers* with Ralph Richardson. An *amazing* film. And *King Kong.* Every year, at least once a year, the Zenith would bring back *King Kong* and *Gunga Din* on the same bill. With *The Phantom,* of course. There was a time when I could have played *all* the parts in *Gunga Din,* including Sam Jaffee as Gunga, Cary Grant, Douglas Fairbanks, Jr., and Victor McLaglen. I always went for dramas or adventures. Never comedies or musicals.

I had great heroes and I was very much influenced by the kinds of roles some actors played and how they played them. Paul Muni. *Big* fan of Paul Muni. Charles Laughton. Best of all by far, John Garfield. *The Fallen Sparrow, Sea Wolf, Body and Soul,* and *Gentleman's Agreement.* Garfield for me was Everyman. He always played the role of the guy that was fucked by the fickle finger of fate. He was never totally a bad guy. Even when he was a bad guy, I knew *why*. I believed society did it to him.

Whether it's the actor or the person watching him, I don't know. What impressed me about Garfield was the way he always expressed just what he thought his rights were. He had street class. Who am I to say how he influenced me? What have any of my heroes done for me? I don't know. But I do know I hated Joan Crawford.

Even when Garfield made a movie called *Destination Tokyo,* with Cary Grant, where he did sort of a number as an actor, "Okay, you want me to play this part? Okay, I'll talk Brooklyn," he still pulled it off. I just believed him. In *Body and Soul,* when he fell for the wrong actress, it just tore me apart. I used to sit there and say to him on the screen, "You dumb fuck, don't you see what she's going to do to you?" In my life, I came to see men totally controlled by women and women totally controlled by men. Just the way that Garfield in that movie got caught.

I was never studious. I was never inquisitive, other than about basic survival things. I worked hard after school and I loved sports. My grades were good because when I had a test, I would cram. For two days, I'd have a photographic memory. Sometimes, I'd write things down on the inside of my hand. Not too often. The worst was in physics and chemistry.

"What's the first color inside a frog's neck?"

Who *knows* what a frog's neck looks like or *should* look like?

"And the pubation period of an owl in Egypt is *what?*"

Whenever something made no sense to me, I gave up. Whenever I thought, "Why should I know this?" I didn't.

I was good at math and geography and history. English too. What I wasn't good at was biology and chemistry. Explaining how internal combustion works so the car moves. Or what batteries are all about. I have no idea. To this day, it is inconceivable to me that when I push a button, the TV goes on.

I made the swimming team in DeWitt Clinton High School. The breaststroke. But I didn't stay with it. I never went to practice enough. Although I really wanted to be part of it, I had set myself up to work. That I *had* to work.

FROM "MEMORIES OF ARNOLD ISAAK"

By Arnold Isaak [1994]

In Frankfurt, just as my father and mother were saying their last goodbyes, my father reached into his pocket and pulled out a shiny

United States ten-cent piece. Its unofficial name is a "dime." My father handed it to me and said: "Here, I can't give you much, but this way you'll never be able to say that you came to America broke."

Those were the last words I ever heard my father say. It was, however, not the last I would hear from my father. . . .

[Isaak narrates the train trip to Hamburg and then the voyage to America with other members of a Children's Transport consisting of about a dozen youngsters. He was the only child who did not know his ultimate destination, as a foster home had not yet been selected for him. After staying in a New York hotel with the other children for several days, he was put on a train to Chicago.]

In Chicago, a representative of the "Children's Transport" met me at the train and took me to my new "home-to-be" on the South Side. The family's name was Mittelpunkt. They had two sons. Both were younger than I was. Their apartment was small. Just two bedrooms and a closed-in porch. The closed-in porch was my bedroom.

The Mittelpunkts were fantastic people. They had no money because Uncle Dave, as I was asked to call him, had lost his store during the Great Depression, and was now working as the manager of a grocery store. The only thing these outstanding people had to give was love and care.

So they gave of themselves. They treated me as their own son from the time I arrived until the time of their death just a few years ago. They were my foster parents and always called me "their son."

I first attended grammar school on the South Side of Chicago. It's strange how you can remember things that happened so many years ago.

Because I had studied English in the Jewish school in Offenbach, and because I seemed to have developed a natural tendency for languages, I was immediately put into the seventh grade. However, on my very first day in school I learned that there were definite differences in languages. We had been assigned a project to write an essay on the Robin (Bird). I wrote a long, two- or three-page dissertation on what I perceived to be the Robin. It was, I thought, a great piece of work. I felt very proud when I handed it in, only to be put in my place with an "F." A Failing Grade.

Well, I just couldn't understand. I went to the teacher with the Encyclopedia and showed her all the features I had written about. The teacher listened to me carefully and smiled. She said: "On the Raven, you get an A+ . . . but on the Robin you get an F." Yes, because of the language problem, I had mistaken the Robin for Raven. Luckily for me, the teacher permitted me to hand in "The Raven" and not the Robin.

Back "home" in Muhlheim, all hell broke loose with Kristallnacht.

My brother Liebmann was in Offenbach that afternoon. All of a sudden, he saw the Brownshirts storming the inside of the main synagogue in Offenbach. He saw them starting to break the windows and to take the Torahs from the Ark. He was frightened, but did not panic. He quickly called our father in Muhlheim and told him what was happening. Luckily, the Nazis got a so-called late start in Muhlheim. As the story has been told to me, my father rushed to the synagogue in Muhlheim with my brother Herbert. They took the two Torahs from the Ark and secretly buried them.

You have to understand that it is against Jewish tradition to let a Torah be dropped to the ground or to be burned. However, it has been a tradition in Jewish history that Torahs and scriptures may be buried for safekeeping. To understand the importance of a Torah, you have to understand its true meaning. The Torah is the law of Judaism. It is always handwritten by scribes on parchment. Each week it is a tradition that a portion of the Torah (the Law) be read from the pulpit. And, it takes a full year to cover the entire Torah's readings.

As had been done for centuries, in times of danger and catastrophe, the Torahs from Muhlheim were buried. Where, I do not know. However, the burial of the Torahs from Muhlheim remind me of the "Dead Sea Scrolls" that were buried hundreds and hundreds of years ago by Jewish groups whose lives were endangered in the desert of the Middle East.

Yes, my father saved the Torahs . . . and an hour later the synagogue was in flames. But, the burning Nazi bastards never found the Torahs.

About two weeks after I arrived in Chicago, I got my first job. I wanted to save money to send to my family in Germany. The job was as an afternoon paperboy at the corner of Stoney Island Avenue and 67th Street. I would go there direct from school and attempt to sell papers to people getting off the streetcar and just, in general, being on the street. I clearly remember that the weather was bitterly cold. The wind whipped around the corner, making it even more frigid. However, we were able to keep a bit more comfortable because we had large 50-gallon drums in which we burned scraps of wood and paper.

My job only lasted about three weeks because the Mittelpunkts wanted me to spend my afternoons studying. They were right. At that stage of my development, school and lots of studying were more important than the fifty cents a week I was being paid as a newsboy.

A week later I got another job—Saturday afternoons only—passing out movie schedules for the Parkside Theater. Again, it only paid half a dollar a week. But, it was enough to keep me in extra candy and an extra movie.

During the summer months I was an assistant counselor at a boys camp. It provided me with time to be outside, do something worthwhile, and stay in physical shape. Of course, I also had my room and board for the entire summer. Less of a strain on the Mittelpunkts.

Each week the letters I received from Muhlheim sounded more ominous. You could read the terror between the lines. When I would ask about family members and other friends from town, the answers were always carefully chosen: "They're away on vacation" . . . "They left for Italy" . . . "They moved to England."

When I once asked about my Uncle Moritz Lehmann, the husband of my father's sister, Bertel, I was told in a letter that he had gone on a business trip.

It is true that he went on a business trip, but never came home. Somewhere on the road, he was picked up by the Gestapo. He just disappeared. However, to give you an idea of the filthy cockroach mentality prevailing at the time, read on. One day about three weeks after his disappearance, my Aunt Bertel got a notice from "the good folks" at the Gestapo. They told her that she could pick up his ashes if she paid them DM 500.00 (five hundred marks). Yes, the filthy bastards had murdered this gentle man and were now trying to get money for his ashes.

On September 1, 1939, the war started. In one of my mother's letters, she stated that she was going to get away with my brothers regardless of the cost. She had seen just too much. Little by little the town of Muhlheim became more and more Juden Frei [free of Jews]. Life became almost unbearable.

At a later time my mother would tell me of the difficulty just putting bread on the table. She had gone to the grocery store near our house and asked to purchase some flour and some other basic foodstuff. Although she had known the shopkeeper for years, this time, and from that time forward, the woman refused to sell her anything.

"You damned Jews aren't ever going to get any more food from me. Go eat your lousy matzos, 'cause you'll never get another morsel from me while my son is on the front fighting the Russians."

Yes, the Hitler frenzy had caught up even with some of the more civil burghers of Muhlheim.

Then, all of a sudden in the middle of December 1939, my weekly letter from my mother stopped coming. It wasn't until about the middle of January 1940 that I received a letter from my mother.

The letter was from Italy.

Somehow, she had gotten to Genoa with my four brothers, on her way to Buenos Aires, where her brother Fritz had been able to arrange the immigration papers for her and my brothers.

Many years later I would hear the story of my mother's and my brothers' Exodus from Hell. How they struggled on the roads, in the middle of the winter, dodging the ravages of war on their way to Genoa, Italy. All alone, without an adult male to assist in the escape, because my father was not able to get out at that time, they kept going South.

Mellita Isaak, the thirty-nine-year-old wife of Leopold Isaak, left Muhlheim on December 29, 1939 with her four children in tow, to fulfill her destiny. She saved all of her children from sure death in the ovens of Auschwitz.

What is even more remarkable about the feat she accomplished is the fact that it was done during the height of war in Europe. Every nation in Europe, except for Switzerland, was joined in the struggle against Hitler and Mussolini. There she was with four boys, ranging from the age of fifteen down to the age of five, wandering strange roads and countries to get to her port of embarkation.

Even today, fifty-five years later, I am amazed at the inner strength she must have had to succeed in bringing her children to safety. Yet, she once told me that we all have more strength than we think, especially where life itself is concerned.

So, sometime in January 1940, my mother and four brothers arrived in Argentina. Although their lives were no longer in danger, their lives were very, very difficult. Liebmann, age fifteen, Herbert, age twelve, and Ludwig, age eleven, went to work and to school. Only my youngest brother, Josef, age six, was able to go to school on a full-time basis. The struggle to survive was still foremost in the air.

Letters from my mother told the story of their very difficult lives. My brothers Liebmann, Herbert, and Ludwig were working full-time jobs and going to school. Seven days a week the long tedious hours of hard work and studies were the norm . . . with virtually no time-out to enjoy their newfound freedom.

In addition to the responsibility of feeding and nurturing four young boys, my mother had the added burden of caring for her father, now in his eighties. He had immigrated to Argentina a couple of years earlier. The family had a small three-bedroom apartment in Buenos Aires. One tiny bedroom was for my mother. The large master bedroom was occupied by her father, and the third bedroom was shared by my four brothers. They slept two to a twin bed.

To help put food on the table, my mother would create bakery goods that were sold in and around the Jewish community in Buenos Aires. Sleep was something that was a luxury for my mother, having to care for four boys and a very demanding father. My brothers all started to work as apprentices in what I would call "survival crafts." One studied as a shoemaker. One studied as a goldsmith. One studied another craft. It was not pleasant for my brothers, whose hands and heads were not in line with their crafts. However, in order to comply with my mother's demands, they went along . . . hating what they were doing. The tension between my mother and brothers always ran high. Yet, they also understood the whys and wherefores. They lived. They survived. They flourished.

Of course, the Arnold Factor also started to raise its head. What was the Arnold Factor confronting my mother?

"'How can you leave your son, alone, in the United States while you're here in Buenos Aires?" "What kind of mother are you not to send for your son?"

In an exchange of long letters in the spring of 1940, the so-called Arnold Factor was resolved. Although somewhat painful, it turned out well for all. I cannot remember the specific words. Yet, the concept of the letters was clear and concise.

My mother let me know in no uncertain terms that I could, if I wanted to, come to Buenos Aires to be with her and with my brothers. She also let me know in no uncertain terms that I would have to leave school and go to work. I would have to go to work to support myself and to help support the family. After all, I was the second oldest in the family.

As much as she would like me to be with her, she felt that I would be better off staying in the USA, going to school, and staying in school. First of all, she wanted me to graduate from grammar school in June 1940. She also told me that I would have a better chance in America if I went to high school and to college, and that would only be possible if I stayed in America.

Therefore, my mother and I decided that I would not come to Argentina to live. She promised that she would come to visit me as soon as possible. And, if I still wanted to join the rest of the family, I could always do so after I finished my education. During the exchange of these letters she also let me know that she would not be able to give me the kind of security I had in the United States.

The rest was simply accepted as fact. I would stay in the USA and go to school and not become another mouth to feed in Argentina.

Of course, the situation for Jews kept going downhill in Germany. Letters from my father were sporadic. After the attack on Pearl Harbor, letters from my father were sent through the International Red Cross. Strangely enough, my father's attitude was still quite positive. He actually still thought that he would not become a target. How he could still feel that way is something I will never be able to understand.

In the summer of 1942, I again worked at a boys' camp as a counselor. It was also the time I would receive my last letter from my father.

The letter had been forwarded from the International Red Cross. It was a devastating letter. My father had been badly hurt in another accident at a labor camp. He was writing from a hospital, and his handwriting was weak. However, it was the contents of his note that I shall never forget. In the letter, he asked that I somehow wire the sum of five thousand marks (DM 5,000.00) to a certain numbered account in Switzerland. The money to be wired in so-called good funds, backed by gold. (Five thousand marks were the equivalent of just US $1,250.00, twelve hundred fifty U.S. dollars.) He stated that if the money were sent within the next few weeks, he would be able to buy his way out of Germany. Imagine, here I was, a boy of sixteen years of age, being asked to send $1,250 U.S. dollars to buy my dad's life from the Nazis. Of course, since 1942 was still the tail end of the Great Depression, and because I was still a boy without the means to get the money, I was not able to buy my father's life. Yes, those bastards in their brown uniforms put a $1,250 price tag on a life.

I still have that letter somewhere. It was the last letter . . . the last plea from my father. $1,250.00 for a life. There were no more letters . . . no more words from Leopold Isaak, my father.

I learned later that sometime after the late fall of 1942 my father's starved and broken body was consumed by flames, with his ashes sucked up through the tall chimneys and scattered by the wind over the countryside of Auschwitz. "Yisgadal. . . . Ve Yisgadash. . . ."

In my last year in high school, where I ranked in the upper eight percent (8.0%) academically, I was also given the honor of being named to the First String State of Illinois Soccer Team, an honor reserved for only eleven students in the entire state. It was the second athletic achievement I had reached; the first had been winning the High School Pole Vaulting Championship of Chicago when I was only in my second year of school. When graduating time came in the summer of 1944, it was time to enter the armed services of the United States.

Chapter 7

FULL CIRCLE

M*any OTC children had the opportunity to return to their hometowns as adults, and several have left their impressions. Some, like Charles Juliusburg, Arnold Isaak, and Benjamin Hirsch, made their visits during service in the armed forces of the United States. How ironic to return to the place from which flight was necessary in the uniform of a country that had led the way to conquest of the Nazi empire. Manfred Steinfeld, as noted in chapter 1, returned to his hometown in uniform as a liberator. Other rescued children came years later, often accompanied by children of their own, in the hopes of some sort of completion or healing, or just out of curiosity. Part of their identity was left behind, and they needed to discover something about who they were and who they are. The impressions are as varied as the individuals themselves and the reasons for going back. Many returnees did not find the reconnection that they sought.*

In certain ways, the OTC second generation bears the pain of their parents' losses, as well as being beneficiaries of the opportunities their parents gained by being sent to America. In many cases, the younger generation received only incomplete information from their parents, who were often silent or guarded in answering questions about their early years in Europe. These children, too, needed to tap into those distant roots and come into closer contact with a unique heritage. A sense of incompleteness, of exile, in the parent led to a similar feeling in the child.

This need has led us to include two narratives that are in the voices of the children's children. The first, an excerpt from Fern Schumer Chapman's Motherland, *is a powerful rendering of a mother and daughter retracing the mother's past. The second such passage is from Rose Marie Phillips Wagman's journal, "Returning to My Roots." Mrs. Wagman is the daughter of Ilse*

Hamburger Phillips, whom she accompanies, and whose voyage diary is found in chapter 3.

To conclude, we once more engage the memories of Phyllis Finkel Mattson, whose trip in an attempt to reestablish connections with relatives is frustrated by unexpected indifference and hostility.

FROM THE MEMOIR "MOVING TO THE FRONT"

By Charles Juliusburg [1992]

The 13th Armored Division continued moving East, toward Germany. We found out, after we arrived there, that we were in Alsace Lorraine. This territory was annexed by France from Germany after World War I, about 1918. In the late 1930s, before Hitler's Germany invaded Poland to start World War II, Hitler's army invaded and occupied Alsace Lorraine and claimed it to be German territory that was unlawfully taken from Germany by the Allies after the First World War. At the time of reoccupation (1938), the western allied powers were ill prepared for war, or for any military confrontation, and Hitler got away with his bluff.

Now, the allied forces were advancing to retake this territory. I have no idea where we were when we finally stopped. We were "somewhere" in France. The civilians spoke French. I was given orders to "find" the six clerks who were assigned to work in the personnel section of our battalion, each of whom had traveled across France with his respective company. I was given a jeep, a jeep driver, and an armed guard, and off we went. None of the roads had "street" signs, none of the houses had house numbers, and our compass just pointed "North," which did not help us a bit. We had no maps. Everyone had occupied an empty barn, or any house that had been vacated by its former occupants. And nobody put a sign in front of the entrances indicating that "here lives Company C, 24th Tank Battalion" or any such nonsense.

It was getting dark, and occasionally we could see a glow of a burning cigarette. We cautiously approached the cigarette and asked the GIs to identify themselves. They did. It occurred to me that this was not the way to do business in a war zone. But what did I know? We "found" 2 or 3 of our companies, before we discovered a barn where some commissioned officers were having a mini drinking party. I knew many of these officers, and most of them knew me. We were told not to take our job so seriously and were invited to join them in a drink or two.

In those days, one or two shots of whiskey on an empty stomach were enough to put us to sleep. On our way back "home," the barn where we were billeted, our jeep traveled on two wheels when negotiating a curve. I don't know how we made it, but we made it. I told of my experience in a whisper to the soldier on the straw next to me. The following morning, all the occupants of "our" barn told us that they heard my whispers in the furthest corner of the barn.

After daybreak, we located the remaining companies and ordered their clerks to join us so we could put together our office and headquarters. Living in a barn, with cattle as our roommates, was totally inadequate, and to me, personally, unacceptable. Although warmer than most other quarters, the odors were overpowering to us city folks. And the occasional encounters with a live mouse or rat was more than I was willing to put up with.

We found a vacant two-story house nearby, and occupied it. We, the personnel section, took the 2nd floor; the rest of the headquarters personnel took the ground floor. The house was unfurnished. It had a fireplace on the 1st floor. We "found" and "liberated" (stole) a potbelly stove and some stove pipes, which we fashioned into our stove's chimney. We broke one of the windowpanes to allow us to put the chimney's other end to the outside.

We slept in our sleeping bags on the cement floor. Cold, uncomfortably hard, but dry, and absolutely free of any strange odors. It was hard on our kidneys, too. On the stairway between the 1st and 2nd floors, we kicked in another glass windowpane, so we would not be forced to go outdoors to urinate. For more serious business, we had dug a latrine trench near our house.

One day, the unmistakable odor of a good, hot meal reached our 2nd-floor office. Upon investigating the source of the odor, we found that the 1st-floor headquarters had built a fire in their fireplace, and were roasting some meat. The guy who was doing the roasting sliced off a piece of meat with his bayonet and placed it into the palm of my hand. (No dishes.) It was one of the most delicious meals I had had in seemingly months and months. I then found out that someone had machine-gunned a wild boar in a nearby forest, and I had just eaten a part of it. The very thought of it made me ill, and I vomited it out. Oh well.

The boys on the 1st floor enjoyed the warmth of their burning fireplace, and kept the fire going day and night. Lo and behold, the inside of the chimney caught on fire, and we, too, on the 2nd floor enjoyed some warmth. There was no fire department to call, so we all were deployed in a bucket brigade formation and hauled water from its source to the roof of our building, and poured it down the chimney until the flames were extinguished. It was serious business and very, very hard physical labor. All of us were exhausted from that experience. We were told that the U.S. government reimbursed the farmer, owner of the property, for the damages.

We continued our trek toward Germany. My next home was a wooden shack. No glass in the windows, not all door frames had doors in them. *But* there was a mattress in one of the rooms. I, the ranking non-com, decided the mattress was for *me*.

We must have been close to the front lines. It was here that I heard, for the first time in my life, artillery being fired in earnest. It was also here where I heard small arms fire after dark. Our guards, and everyone else for that matter, were fully aware of the fact that we were close to action, and in plain English, when someone heard a noise, he fired in the direction of the noise.

It was after dark, and we had no light. We searched all the rooms for a candle. I leaned against a doorjamb, and the whole door, frame and all, fell from my weight. It must have been loose from either earlier aerial bombardment or shell fire. Of course, I fell to the ground with the door and landed on top of it. No laughing matter.

We finally were exhausted enough to try to sleep, despite the noise of the distant artillery fire and the occasional small arms fire. I lay down on my mattress only to find that the noise of the mice, or whatever, inside the mattress was too much for me. We tried to kill the noise with the butts of our carbines, to no avail.

It was here where members of the 13th Armored Division engaged the Germans. Our artillery shelled the enemy. All members of our division (including me) received a battle decoration with one battle star.

FROM "MEMORIES OF ARNOLD ISAAK"

By Arnold Isaak [1994]

Because I had studied preflight training for three years while still in high school, I was able to join the United States Army Air Corps.

In filling out the paperwork during the time of my induction into the Air Corps, I realized that I could claim my mother and three younger brothers (Herbert, Luis, and Josef) as dependents.

By cutting my pay to just $21 a month, the United States Government then paid my dependents (mother and three brothers) about a hundred dollars a month. What a lifesaver that turned out to be. I'm told that the first thing my mother did with the money was to purchase a used Singer sewing machine. She did sewing for the family and for others both to save money on clothes and to earn a few extra Pesos for daily living expenses.

It is my brother, Jose, who often reminds me of those few dollars that kept the family in Argentina alive at a very critical time. However, I never realized how important those few dollars were to them.

After a period of training, I became a member of the United States Strategic Air Forces Technical Intelligence Division and was stationed in and part of the Headquarters Staff in England. From there we would fly into France and Germany to do our work.

While stationed in London, I remembered that one of my cousins, Julius Fleischer, had also left Germany by himself and had gone to England just before the war broke out. So, I thought I would take a chance to see if I could locate him.

After weeks and weeks of detective work—and some luck—I found my cousin. He told me that his sister, too, had gotten out by herself and had gone to Palestine. However, he had no idea as to his parents and as to the rest of the family. In general, our thoughts and ideas were not good. In fact, the feeling we had was hopeless. Of course, we decided to stay in touch.

Julius had been a middle distance runner and almost made the British Olympic Team in 1948. Memories that come back at the oddest times.

Immediately after the fighting stopped in Europe, an opportunity arose for me to go on a special technical intelligence field trip into France and Germany. I had volunteered for the trip in the hope of getting to Muhlheim to look for my father. The team consisted of a jeep driver, an armed guard, an American Scientific Rocket and Aircraft Expert, and myself. I was the Air-Intelligence Translator.

Our objective: Find hidden German Rocket Scientists and any and all documents related to German Aircraft design, experiments, and tests.

One of our goals was the Luftwaffe base at Hanau. So, once we were done in Frankfurt, we headed East to Hanau. Of course, Muhlheim is on the way. So, I had our driver stop in the town of my birth. We didn't go directly to the center of the town. I had the driver pull off the road and head for the old Judenfriedhof, the Jewish Cemetery. I had wanted to stop and place a remembrance stone on the graves of my grandmother and my grandfather. As we pulled up to the gate, I could see that the Nazis had done their work here, as well. The front gate was knocked down. All the stones had been knocked over. Many were broken. Weeds had overgrown the graves. It was tragic. Tears came to my eyes and I went into a rage.

I had the driver of our jeep take us to the City Hall of Muhlheim. The entrance to the Mayor's office was being guarded by two Air Corps MPs. Of course, they stopped me. Once I explained who I was and why I wanted to see the Mayor, they let me inside. I asked for the Mayor. He wasn't around. So, I asked for someone who might be in charge. I can't remember his name, nor can I remember his official status. But I do remember clearly what happened next.

Shouting, I said: "Do you know who I am? Does the name Isaak mean anything to you?

"Do you remember Leopold Isaak, or the five sons of Leopold Isaak? Well, I am one of the sons . . . and I've just come from the old Juden-friedhof."

The man, in his late sixties or early seventies, looked at me, squinting through his thick glasses, in what I felt was disbelief.

"Ja, Ja! Aber dein vater ist doch nicht mer da." Yes, Yes! But your father is no longer here.

In the rage I had from seeing the destruction of the cemetery, I had momentarily forgotten that my number one concern was to get information on my father. However, at this moment, my thoughts were still centered on the cemetery. My anger just exploded.

Even though my next actions were understandable, I am not particularly proud of what I did, because I actually threatened a man's life.

I unsnapped my pistol and drew the "45" from its holster. I pulled the slide back and put a bullet into the chamber, and with the same motion flicked the safety to "off." I stuck the "45" under the old man's chin, stretching his head toward the ceiling. I shouted that he had just forty-eight hours to get the cemetery cleaned up.

"Please, please don't shoot. It wasn't me. I'll get it done. Ja, Ja."

I could feel the fear the old man experienced. It bothered me, too, that I could have pulled the trigger and killed a man who was no threat to my life. I moved away from him to the front of the desk. The old man just stared at me, shaking. He finally sat down, not taking his eyes off mine. We were staring at each other for what seemed like an endless interlude. I took a few deep breaths, put the safety to "on" and pushed the "45" back into the holster.

I sat on the edge of the desk, opposite the old man, exhausted. The shouting had brought a couple of the old man's coworkers to the door to see what was going on. He just waived them away, silently.

"What can you tell me about my father?"

"He was one of the last. They came for him and took him away."

"When?"

"I don't know. I can't remember. It was a few years ago."

"What about the Lehmanns?"

"I don't know. I just don't know."

The old man couldn't tell me any more about my father, nor my uncle and aunt. Nor could he tell me anything about the Rollmanns or the Stiefels—two families whose names I had remembered, and with whom I had shared memories. So I left, reminding the old man that I would be back to check out the cemetery.

I wanted to show the rest of our team where I had lived. We drove over to Trachtstrasse 24. Our house was easily recognizable, because the word "JUDE" was still barely visible on the bricks. That's because the Nazis had painted the word on our house with tar, and the tar could never be fully removed.

We stopped the jeep and I got out. Several people stuck their heads out of the windows across the street and down the street. All of them quickly closed the shutters and disappeared. That is, all except the Klauers, next door. They recognized me as an Isaak, and told me that my father was taken away a couple of years ago. They weren't sure if it was 1942 or 1943. However, they said it must have been in the early fall, because my father had filled his pockets with all the pears he could pluck off the pear trees.

They had no idea where he was taken. Nor had they any idea of what happened to the Lehmanns.

We drove through town looking for Jewish survivors. Nothing.

I asked our driver to please stop at the Catholic church. It was here that the Sisters had given me first aid after one of the terrible beatings I had sustained at the hands of the local Hitler Jugend. Only one of the Sisters seemed to remember me . . . thanking God that I was still alive. The driver and the guard stopped in the back of the small church, kneeled down, and crossed themselves in a quick prayer. All three of us left some Army Script (Occupational Money) in the poor box and got back into the jeep.

At that point, I remembered something very interesting. I asked the driver to pull around and head for a meadow not far from where I used to live.

I turned to the three other men in the jeep and asked: "Does the name Hannah Reitsch mean anything to you?"

"Of course," was the answer from the aircraft expert with us, "she was one of Hitler's best test pilots. In fact, if I'm not wrong, she did a lot of the tests on the ME-262." (The ME-262 was the first pure-jet fighter plane to see combat near the end of the war.)

"Well, guys! Believe it or not, I remember that she flew in here one time in a fancy white glider and landed right out there. It was a great propaganda move on the part of the Luftwaffe to get kids interested in flying. While she supervised, kids were being taught the basics of takeoffs and landings in very old unsophisticated gliders. I can't remember the year it happened, but it sure got kids interested in flying."

It seems odd now. However, seeing that beautiful white glider coming down in the meadow got me interested in building model airplanes and in aerodynamics. That's how I ended up in the U.S. Air Corps.

A few days later, after we had been to the air base in Hanau, I stopped again at the Judenfriedhof in Muhlheim. The front gate had been repaired and there was a large lock on the gate. We pulled the jeep close to the wall and I looked over the red bricks and found the old man had, indeed, kept his word. The headstones had been re-erected and the graves were outlined in small, whitewashed stones. The cemetery seemed peaceful, and I was at peace with myself.

I jumped down from the jeep and just walked around this small plot of land that had been the last resting place for the Jewish Community of Muhlheim since 1893. The silence was eerie. Not a word was said when I got back in the jeep. The Aircraft Expert, with whom I shared the back seat, just put his hand on my shoulder.

We headed for the highway and I left Muhlheim knowing for sure that the bastards had shipped my father off to the ovens sometime in the Fall of 1942. I would not return to the place of my birth for another twenty-one years. The only thing there, for me, in Muhlheim, was the cemetery and the gravestones of my ancestors.

In December 1945, our Intelligence Unit was transferred back to the United States from London. After a forty-five-day "rest and recuperation" furlough, I was stationed at Wright Field in Dayton, Ohio. There, we set up a specific unit having to do with the entire German aircraft industry. In early June of 1946, I received a letter from my mother stating that she was not feeling well. Taking that as my cue, I was able to obtain a three-week furlough in the hopes that I could get down to Buenos Aires to see my family.

FROM *HEARING A DIFFERENT DRUMMER*

By Benjamin Hirsch [2000]

[1954]

The next weekend I applied for a pass to go to Frankfurt, and since I had no chance to screw up yet, I was not turned down. The anticipation was great. I had called Dr. Klibansky when I first arrived in Germany, and told him that I would make an appointment with him as soon as I was settled and able to get a weekend pass. I made the

Benjamin Hirsch in front of photos of the Holocaust Memorial he designed for the William Bremen Jewish Heritage Museum, Atlanta, Georgia. Photographers LeAnn Shaw and Michael Dubrow. August 2003 edition. Courtesy of the *Atlanta Buckhead* magazine.

appointment and informed him that there would be matters I wished to discuss with him, other than the power of attorney for the house. I was anxious to meet this man who had known my father intimately, as his attorney and close friend.

Arriving at the Banhoff train station in Frankfurt was a strange experience. I expected to have explicit memories of the place where I had last seen my mother, a little over sixteen years before, but I didn't. I did feel a chill and I had this feeling of having been there before, but even though I had vivid memories of that day on December 5, 1938, I could not superimpose those memories onto that bustling train station in 1954.

I was told that it wasn't particularly safe for an American G.I. to stay in a German hotel, and that there was a serviceman's hotel in Frankfurt that was run by the army. This hotel became my base of operation for all the trips I later took to Frankfurt.

My appointment with Herr Klibansky was at 10 in the morning. I left the hotel at 9:00 a.m. just to make sure that I wouldn't be late, in case I got lost. I arrived so early that I walked around the block a couple of times before going in. I was still about twenty minutes early and was told that Herr Mueller, Klibansky's partner, who was to be at the meeting, had not arrived yet. After a few minutes, Herr Klibansky ushered me into his office and proceeded telling me of his close relationship with my father. He was a very large man, corpulent would describe him better, with a mustache and a pair of red suspenders that held his pants up just below his protruding belly. It was special hearing him speak of my father, although he didn't hold back on his criticism of my father for failing to heed the warnings, and not taking advantage of opportunities to escape Germany. When I asked him why he stayed, he said that his was a totally different situation. I wanted to like him, but I suddenly became very suspicious of him, and nervous to the point that I wished I had the choice of not giving power of attorney to sell our house to this self-righteous son of a bitch. I particularly did not enjoy seeing him lean his rotund body back in his chair while passing judgment on my father for not leaving, when he supposedly had a chance. I wondered about how genuine his friendship with my dad was, and I couldn't help but wonder how he had stayed alive and was able to maintain his corpulent body, although almost ten years had passed since the end of the war.

He asked me how I managed to get sent to Germany for duty, while the United States armed forces were involved militarily in Korea. I sketchily told him of the circumstances that brought me to Germany, and of my efforts toward that end, and then I told him why it had been so important for me to come at this time.

Herr Klibansky was a very blunt man, and just as he wasn't shy about criticizing my dead father to my face, he had no compunction about telling me that I was on a wild goose chase. He added that if I had contacted him from the States, with regard to Werner and Roselene, he could have saved me a lot of time and anxiety. He had known my Uncle Philipp well, and could verify that Philipp had watched from afar, behind several rows of electrified barbed-wire fences, as his sister, my mother, with her two youngest children walked naked into "the showers" for delousing. Uncle Philipp, in his position as chief chemist while interred in Auschwitz, came upon a list that included a Mathilde Hirsch née Auerbach, and two children, Werner Hirsch and Roselene Hirsch. Recognizing their names, he ran out, to be as close as possible, to verify that this was in fact his sister, niece, and nephew.

I stared at him in disbelief. I was beginning to understand why ancient Greeks used to kill the messenger of bad tidings. I had asked him to give me leads to help me find Werner and Roselene; instead he confirmed, with an air of certainty, that the reports of their death, that I had refused to believe, were true beyond a shadow of a doubt, as far as he was concerned. I was too numb to let my bad feelings for him surface.

As he spoke, Herr Klibansky began to realize that what he was telling me so matter-of-factly was having a traumatic effect on me.

He assured me that, according to my uncle, Philipp Auerbach, my mother, sister, and brother had no inkling of their pending fate, that he had seen them from afar as they were waiting in line to enter and he felt sure that they thought they were to be deloused in the showers, not gassed. It was small comfort, but it was at least something to grab on to, at a time when I needed to hear anything positive to keep me from total despair.

Herr Mueller's entrance was almost a welcome intrusion, but I wasn't quite ready to get down to business. They proceeded to prepare the required paperwork for me to sign over the Power of Attorney while I was slowly returning back to earth. By the time they finished the paperwork, I was better able to focus on the business I was there for, but I was a bit reluctant when they gave me the papers to sign, because I had only been instructed to give the Power of Attorney to Klibansky. I was being asked to give it to Klibansky and/or Mueller. Herr Klibansky explained that he planned to go in for surgery in the very near future, and that Mueller should be able to take action in his absence, in case a buyer showed up while he was incapacitated.

Mueller spoke excellent English and was amiable enough. I just had a queasy feeling about turning over the Power of Attorney of what once was our family home, to a German national who was not Jewish. By this time, I didn't fully trust Klibansky, and I was totally uncomfortable with Mueller. Klibansky, sensing my inner turmoil, assured me that he was the one who would be in charge and that adding Mueller to the document was only to facilitate matters. I reluctantly signed the papers, and then wrote to my siblings to keep them abreast of what I had done in their behalf; then I went back to the base feeling that I had accomplished step one of what they had asked me to do, even though I was not particularly in favor of selling the house. I sat on the train back to Fürth limp as a dishrag. My expectations of finding Werner and Roselene alive had been dashed so abruptly that I had been unable to prepare myself for the letdown. In retrospect, I can't imagine any scenario that would have prepared me for such a devastating letdown. I actually was glad to be going back to the mundane army existence. Regimentation and mindless busywork was just what the doctor ordered to keep my mind off of the confirmation that my younger siblings were indeed dead.

I returned to the base very depressed. I, for the first time, realized that finding Werner and Roselene was a pipe dream at best; I just didn't expect the search to end so quickly. I resolved to refocus my energies and make the best of my stay in Germany by pursuing other goals and activities with my spare time. I enrolled in an advanced calculus correspondence course under the auspices of the army, even though I had all the calculus credits required by Georgia Tech for an architectural degree. Some of the material was review of what I had taken at Tech, but there was plenty more to sink my teeth into. I actually found myself waiting with anticipation for each lesson to arrive.

The U.S.O. in Fürth gave all sorts of classes. I availed myself of the art class, which turned out to be an opportunity to draw or paint in virtually any medium, with very little, if any, instruction. This was good for me because all I really wanted to do was try my hand at oil painting again and I had in mind certain portraits I wanted to do from photographs. The first painting was from a photograph of my parents' engagement. Since the photograph was in sepia tones, I had to fly by the seat of my pants to guess what colors to use. The portrait took less time than either I or the instructor had anticipated. The colors were dark and somber, which made the whites of their eyes stand out on the canvas. It was far from a masterpiece and barely respectable for a first try at portrait painting, but as soon as it dried, I wrapped and sent it to my sister Sarah in Atlanta.

My second effort at portrait painting was more ambitious than I had imagined. Sarah had sent me a picture of her two oldest children, Thyle and Neal. It had been done by a professional photographer, in color, and seemed easy enough to paint from. The problem for me was that they both were smiling with their mouths open, and try as I may, I could not get the hang of painting open-mouthed smiles. They were probably 3 1/2 and 1 1/2 years old in the picture, and as I got more frustrated at failed attempts of getting the mouths acceptable, I surmised that they would be teenagers by the time the portrait was finished. As it was, I never finished it. By the time I received orders to report to Schweinfurt, I decided to wrap up the unfinished portrait, which only lacked finished mouths, and sent it to my sister.

My tour in Germany was going to last less than a year, which was plenty of time, so I thought, for me to find and visit the O.S.E. children's homes in France, in which I had stayed while hiding from the Nazis. That became my next quest. Unfortunately, it would also end up leaving me totally frustrated. This time, my frustration was with the absence of resources available to me, as one who didn't speak the language, while I was making efforts to revisit places of my youth. On my next trip to Frankfurt, I visited several travel agents, and though my German was sufficient to get by in most situations, I might as well have been speaking Chinese for all those folks cared. Throughout my stay in Germany, I also visited travel agents in Nuremburg, Fürth, Wurzburg, and Munich. They all said the same thing, "There are no such places as Montmorency, Chateaux de Margelies, or Chateaux de Morrell in France." As far as they were concerned, my past was a figment of my imagination. I was positive they were wrong, but I could not find a source of better information in the limited time available on my occasional passes from the military base. To the army's credit, all of the mindless crap they threw at us when we were recruits in basic training trained this soldier to cope with being stonewalled and with the general frustration of dealing with the bureaucratic nature of Germans, whether at civilian or governmental levels.

The first Friday evening that I wasn't on some kind of duty, I went with Chaplain Goodblatt to services, which I had been told were being held at a municipal building in Nuremberg. When I got there, I remember being impressed with the aura of history in this apparent courthouse building. I was surprised to see that there were over thirty worshipers in the room that was being used for the Jewish Chapel, one of the largest congregations I had seen at a regular Friday night service related to an army base. Some of the congregants were American civilians and there were even one or two German civilians. The Chaplain handed me a tallis (prayer shawl) and a siddur (prayer book), and instructed me to lead the services.

Reluctant as I was to question the direct order of an officer, I looked at Lieutenant Goodblatt with chagrin, and explained that I had not led a service in many months, and that I was just not prepared to lead this august body of worshipers, which included the captain of my engineering company, my commanding officer, who I had not realized was Jewish, in prayer. The Chaplain put his arm around my shoulder and gave me a fatherly look, and said that I should not be nervous, that he had all the confidence in the world that I was up to the task. He later confided to me that there had been no one else to lead the service besides himself, and that he felt that he had to train me so that he could concentrate more on his sermon.

Had this not been the army, I never would have accepted such a dubious "honor," without prior notice. I followed orders and led the service, though I was unsure of which melodies to use and was quite rusty on the Hebrew recitations. I hesitated several times during the service, looking toward the Chaplain for guidance on which parts to repeat out loud and which tune to use. Each time he just waved his hand for me to go on and decide for myself. I began to realize that I was on my own, and just continued on as best I knew how. When the service was over, I was embarrassed. I felt that I had botched up the service by being ill prepared, but the congregants were very kind, and told me that I had done a wonderful job. I knew better, but it was nice to hear a good word even though I felt I had screwed up. I made a promise to myself to practice before the next Friday night, to let the congregants know that their confidence in me was not misplaced.

On our way back to the base, the Chaplain asked me if I had been aware of the significance of the building in which our services were held that evening. I remarked that I had admired the classical architecture of the structure, and commented that it appeared to be an important civic building, but other than that, I had no idea of what he was getting at. He knew that I was a survivor of the Holocaust, and of my recent disappointing meeting in Frankfurt with Herr Klibansky. "There was a reason that I pushed you to *daven* from the *omed* [lead the services] tonight," he said with a look on his face that indicated that he knew something that I didn't know. "Tonight, you just led *Kabolos Shabbos* [ushering in of the Sabbath] services at the Palace of Justice, where the Nuremberg Trials were held six years ago." He looked at me to see my reaction. I was speechless. Not another word was spoken until we arrived at the base. We exchanged greetings of "Good Shabbos" as he went his way and I went mine. I didn't sleep much that night, reflecting on the irony of the situation. I couldn't help but wonder, if my mother could see what I was doing, how she would react to the situation. . . .

My pass was waiting for me the following morning. I decided not to mention the guard mount incident to Rambo, being fairly sure that he was a party to the shenanigans. Over a week had passed since my last trip to Frankfurt, and I was looking forward to closing the sale of the house and celebrating. I checked into the hotel and took the elevator to my room. My Russian friend was at his post and was surprised that I was not aware that my attorney refused to complete the necessary documents to close the sale of the house. I assured him that I didn't know what he was talking about, and asked him to start from the beginning.

He had gone to see Herr Mueller, as I had suggested, and gave him all the background information necessary for the closing documents. Since he was going to pay cash, everything should have been very simple. After interviewing the prospective buyer, however, Herr Mueller informed him that he would not be able to buy the house. When my Russian friend asked why, Herr Mueller only responded that it just was not possible. My friend was disappointed, but assumed that I had changed my mind and that was the end of the matter.

I was confused and angry. I would have at least expected to be notified by my attorney if there was a problem with the sale. I called Herr Mueller and asked to see him right away. He could not understand my agitated state, and proceeded to explain what seemed perfectly obvious to him, or anyone who was concerned with upholding the integrity of class distinction in the Reich. It was very simple, the would-be buyer was a peasant, not even German, and he should not be allowed to become a landowner.

By this time, my blood was beginning to boil. How in the hell did Klibansky hook up with this bigot, and how could he entrust the power of attorney for my parents' house to this German, whose bigotry could qualify him for the Nazi party? I asked to speak to Klibansky and was told that he was very ill and may not survive his illness. I tried to control myself. I told Herr Mueller that while I may understand his strong respect for class distinction, that I was the client, and that only I could make the decision of whether or not to sell the house to a given buyer. "You cannot sell a German house to a Russian peasant," he protested. It was his only response.

I slammed my fist on his desk and put my face within an inch of his. "Yes I can, and I will," I screamed back at him. "And you will prepare the necessary papers, or I will find another attorney!"

He defiantly looked me in the eye and said "Ich farshtei nicht." Literally translated, the phrase he spoke means "I understand nothing," meaning "I don't understand." That was the first time he had said anything to me in German, and his previous statement turned out to be the last time he said anything to me in English. This pitiful excuse for a human being, who was fluent in English, insisted now that he could only deal with me in German. I turned and left in frustration, not knowing what to do.

I took a long walk to cool off and headed back to the hotel. My Russian friend seemed to be more inured to the German class system that somehow survived the war. I refused to accept the situation and promised that I would seek legal assistance through the U.S. Army. He appreciated my outrage at this discrimination against him and said that he would welcome any intercession, but it was apparent that he was resigned to the fact that he would not be allowed to purchase my family's house.

As soon as I returned to the base, I started looking into the legal status of Herr Mueller's refusal to sell our house to my buyer. I met with attorneys in the 7th Army HQ, only to find out that the situation was hopeless. Even though we were the owners of the house, we could not, as absentee owners, force our German attorney to sell the house to someone he did not feel was fit to buy it. Incredulous as it was, he told me that my hands were tied as long as Mueller would not willingly return the power of attorney to me.

I got up to leave and turned back for a parting shot. "Didn't we fight this war to put an end to the German bigotry and hate that almost destroyed Europe? Didn't we win this war? Don't we have any way of protecting American citizens' rights to deal with their property, particularly if that property is all that is left of the possessions of their parents who were murdered by Germans?"

It probably wasn't fair to put this guilt trip on him. He shrugged his shoulders and made a gesture of helplessness. "I wish there was something I could do to help you, soldier. I know it's not right, but it's the policy of the United States Army, we are not allowed to interfere in local legal matters."

If I wasn't so angry, I probably would have cried. I saluted the lieutenant, made an about-face, and left with whatever dignity I had left.

FROM *MOTHERLAND*

By Fern Schumer Chapman [2000]

[In 1990, Edith Schumer Westerfeld, one of the OTC children, returned to the hometown from which her parents had sent her forth some fifty years earlier. She was accompanied by her daughter, Fern Schumer Chapman (pregnant at the time), who arranged the trip and prepared the account of Edith's reunion with past scenes and people. This excerpt, chapter 9 in the book, tells of the "confession" of Hans Hermann, the town historian, who is the women's guide through most of Edith's homecoming visit.]

It's a bright, sunny Thursday morning and Hans has invited us to his house so we can see his garden. After a late start, we drive a few blocks from the hotel to a quaint, humble neighborhood of one- and two-bedroom homes, nothing older than twenty years or so. Hans's house stands out, surrounded as it is by the last colorful geraniums, impatiens, mums, and roses of the season. This impressive carpet of blooms is broken only by the occasional landscape ornament.

Fern Schumer Chapman (right) and her mother, Edith Schumer Westerfeld, 1995. Photo courtesy of Fern Schumer Chapman.

After we've admired his flowers, Hans asks us to come inside. We enter a dark, narrow hallway in his small house. He briefly introduces us to his wife, Alice, an attractive woman in her sixties. Dressed unpretentiously in slacks and a golf shirt, her gray hair casual in a shoulder-length bob, she stands in the kitchen doorway and greets us with great warmth in broken English.

"Velcome, velcome home," she says, smiling. I think she means, Welcome to *our* home. "Good you here."

Hans leads us into the living room, but Alice doesn't follow. Instead, as if on cue, she excuses herself, and a moment later, I hear her clanging pots.

The modest living room feels like an extension of Hans's second-floor museum. Artifacts that didn't fit there fill this room's floor-to-ceiling shelves in a jumbled, helter-skelter fashion. Worn glass bottles, musty books, skulls, arrowheads, even old hats clutter the dark room, making it feel smaller than it is.

In contrast, tidy and spare are the burning memorial candles arranged on a bureau next to the pictures of Hans's dead son. The sweet smell of the candles' incense suffuses the room.

"I have something for you today," he says solemnly, rubbing the back of his neck as if it aches. "Please sit down." He points to a crowded seating area. Barely able to squeeze my knees between the coffee table and the couch, off-balance from my belly, I stumble and rattle the cups on the table. I flop backward onto the overstuffed couch, blushing with embarrassment. Hans, tense and preoccupied this morning, doesn't notice; my mother's back is to me as she looks at the pictures on the bureau. I'm just relieved to be seated.

I look at the coffee table and realize that everything is all prepared, as if Hans had premeditated the setting. A coffeepot, a water pitcher, fine cups and fancy glasses, plates, spoons, cloth napkins, and pastries in a wire basket are neatly arranged on a tray in the center of the coffee table. Next to the coffeepot on the tray is a carefully folded copy of the *Darmstadter Echo*. When I see the paper's banner, my stomach takes a precipitous, anxious dive.

Hans sets himself stiffly on the edge of a slipcovered armchair opposite the couch and then exhales a tense, shallow sigh. My mother, banging her knees just like me, settles down on the couch next to me.

"I want to translate an article for you that appeared in today's paper," he says in a rehearsed, taut voice. "It's very important to me that we read it together . . . out loud."

He pours us each a cup of coffee, offers cream and sugar, then picks up the paper. "I will read it in German and then translate it for you into English," he says. He pours himself a tall glass of ice water and then snaps open the paper. My mother and I exchange a nervous, quick glance, unsettled by the careful arrangement of this scene.

"*Unvergessliche Begegnung mit Stockstädter Jüdin*" is the headline of the story, meaning "Unforgettable Meeting with a Jew of Stockstadt."

"Here's what the story says: *Jahrhundert in Stockstadt gelebt hatten, nur noch zwei; die Familien Westerfeld und Kahn.* . . . At the turn of the century, two Jewish families lived in Stockstadt—the Kahns and the Westerfelds," he begins, his voice a note higher than usual. "In 1891, Siegmund Westerfeld was born in his family home in Stockstadt. During the 1920s, he opened his own business in that house, selling meat and seeds for the farmers to the market. Today, at the same point a different business flourishes. It is a kiosk selling liquor and magazines.

"Still, whenever town historian Hans Hermann walks past the new business, he always thinks about the old business that Westerfeld ran there. Hermann remembers that his father bought food for the pigs at the Westerfeld house. He remembers seeing the local farmers bringing cows to the house so that Westerfeld could bring them to market. He remembers seeing Siegmund unloading wagons full of produce into the shop. He even remembers small things. For example, he says that on the left side of the shop Westerfeld put sacks of feed. On the right, shelves were stocked with preserved goods. In the house, the Westerfelds had one of the first telephones in the town."

Hans pauses, licks his lips, and then continues. "In 1935, 55 men from Stockstadt started to threaten the Westerfelds and their customers. It got so bad that Siegmund was beaten up in the middle of the street. Nobody did anything to resist the Nazis or help the Westerfelds. The t-t-townspeople," he stutters, "the townspeople all . . . all looked the other way." Hans's voice trails off at the end of this sentence.

He stops again, collects himself. Hans seems compelled to do this reading, but I wonder whether he'll be able to get through it. His voice shakes and the newspaper crackles in his trembling hands. He can hardly hold it still so that he can read. I hear the words he said to me at his son's grave: *I know what you want to know, but it is very delicate. I will tell you the truth when I'm ready.*

He doesn't really seem ready now; but then Hans finds his voice again. "Westerfeld went to the Lord Mayor and the Assembly to complain, but he got no sympathy. When he left the Town Hall, the farmers beat him up again and threw him down the two-story staircase. Many farmers owed Westerfeld a lot of money since Westerfeld often extended credit to them. The farmers didn't come to Westerfeld's aid because they didn't want to pay off their debts.

"The terror against the two families became worse and worse." Hans is translating more slowly now; he comes to a stop and takes several sips of water. Then he perseveres. "Moses Kahn, the grandfather of the other Jewish family in town, sensed what was happening. He took Siegmund Westerfeld aside and told him that the Kahns were going to start a new life in America. Kahn wanted Westerfeld to persuade the family to leave, too. Westerfeld said he couldn't do that because his mother, Sara, would rather die than leave. She insisted that she was born a German and would always remain a German. Westerfeld wouldn't go without his mother.

"But the Westerfelds decided to send their daughters, who were then twelve and fifteen, to America. In 1937, the Jewish Children's Bureau helped place Betty in a home near Chicago. A year later, Edith went to live with an aunt and uncle, also in Chicago. Before leaving, the girls pleaded with their parents to join them in America, but the Westerfelds said they were too old to start over. They didn't believe that the Germans would do them any harm.

"On November 9, 1938, there was to be the pogrom called Kristallnacht. In Stockstadt, everything was calm. But in the bright daylight of November 10, a troop of black-shirted fascists from Darmstadt stormed the house of the Westerfelds.

"Siegmund, Sara, and Frieda—" Now Hans breaks down; tears roll down his face. He fights to regain his composure, but he can't collect himself. Several moments pass. He straightens the paper, swallows to regain his voice, and finally continues reading.

"Siegmund, Sara, and Frieda sat on the street curb with their hands in their faces and cried as the Nazis destroyed their home. For a half hour, the Nazis raided the Westerfeld home and threw things out of the windows—dishes, clothes, lamps, silver, clocks, linens, toys, mirrors, pictures, candelabras, even furniture like chairs, dressers, and beds. Half the village stood in a large semicircle in front of the house, in the space where the children once played. The townspeople just stood there watching." Again Hans pauses, takes several deep breaths, then presses forward.

"Some stood in shock with their mouths open. They knew they couldn't do anything. They feared for their own lives. But others stood there smiling.

"'I was sixteen years old then and remember that I was disgusted,' explains Hermann. 'But I didn't know how to react. I didn't know if I should react. I was torn.'

"After this day, when the Westerfelds lost the last things they owned, they could no longer live in Stockstadt. The townspeople boycotted the Westerfeld business; they had no opportunity to earn money. So the Westerfelds were left with no choice but to sell their home and move to Darmstadt. There, Siegmund worked for a while in a Jewish furniture store where he had had a job during college.

"A few years later, in 1942, Hermann was a volunteer to the Marines. He was naïve and proud of his uniform. One day, he was strutting through the streets of Darmstadt in his uniform when he came upon Frieda. By this time, Siegmund was already in concentration camp and she was living in an apartment for Jews that SS soldiers guarded.

"Hermann noticed Frieda first and saw that she had grown old and gray since the last time he saw her, though she was only forty-two years old. She was wearing a nice navy dress frayed from wear. It had a yellow star on the front and back. When Frieda recognized Hermann, she reached for him, hugged him, and started to cry. This was extremely dangerous, since a decree in October of 1941 made 'friendly relations of any kind with Jews punishable by imprisonment.'

"She cried to Hermann that they had taken Siegmund to a concentration camp near Berlin called Sachsenhausen. She was desperate.

"'Please help me,' she begged. 'Please, please. You can do something. You must. I was your neighbor, your friend. I watched you grow up.' But Hermann says he was overcome with angst and fear."

Hans stops cold, paralyzed by emotion. He drops the paper in his lap, places his hands over his eyes in grief and shame. The entire room is charged. His story mesmerizes me, but I can hardly bear to watch him, to listen to another moment of his torment. Part of me wants to ask him to stop.

"All right, Hans," my mother says softly, swallowing hard and waving her hand to say that he doesn't have to go on. "It was a long time ago. Forget it."

He wipes his eyes with his sleeve. "I can't," he says. After a long pause, he says again, "I can't. I can't forget."

The uncomfortable silence grows longer and longer, at last prodding Hans to begin reading again.

"He was frightened to be in this situation. He knew he couldn't help her.

"'I . . . I put my hands up,'" Hans slowly chokes through the words, "'and . . . and . . . and turned away without saying a word.'"

He stops for several seconds, stares at the page, never looking up at my mother. "This event with Frieda," he continues, "has haunted him for his whole life. She was in such bad circumstances and he didn't help her in her moment of need. He never saw her again.

"Siegmund died of hunger in concentration camp in 1941. For several years, Hermann says, the Town Hall kept a sign posted on its bulletin board announcing Siegmund's death. He went every week to check the board to see if there was news about Frieda, but there never was. No one knows for sure what became of her. Many think she died in a concentration camp in Poland. Hermann remained a volunteer through the end of the war.

"Just a few days ago, the past came alive again for Hermann. An American woman, Edith Schumer, came to Stockstadt and claimed she was a Westerfeld. The Town Hall officials immediately called Hermann because he is the keeper of the records and they thought he might like to talk to her about her life and early German experience.

"Hans felt he needed to spend the week with Edith and her daughter to share the past and the history of the family. But, during the week, a lot of hurts came up again. He felt he owed them more than his time; he owed them some explanation. So he asked the *Darmstadter Echo* to write a story on his experience. He wanted the newspaper to tell his story so that he could admit his role in the past.

"'I wanted Edith Westerfeld, her daughter, and all of Stockstadt to know what really happened,'" Hans says with finality. *"Wir sind mit ihr verbunden—wir haben nichts gemacht."* "We became bound to her because we did nothing."

By now, so many emotions flood me that I sob just for some sort of release. As I dig in my purse for a tissue, I notice that the hairs on my arms stand on end. Then I look at my mother, and to Hans. All of us are weeping and sniffling and we catch each other's gaze. But none of us touch or hug. No one can talk; we're each alone with our grief.

Then my mother—oddly, the most composed of the three of us asks him directly: "Are you asking for my forgiveness?"

"No." He clears his throat and adds, "No, I don't think so. I just . . . I just wanted you to know.

"I guess," he says after some thought, "your forgiveness doesn't really matter." His emotions well up, blocking in his throat. "Because I'll never forgive myself. Even if I want to, I can't."

His sleeve blots another batch of tears. "I've learned to live with it, I suppose, just as you have. But it's always with me.

"Every night of my life, before I go to sleep, I see an image of your mother in that dress with the yellow star," he says quietly. "Or I see me, swaggering in that uniform. Or I feel myself put up my hands, almost instinctively, automatically, without any thought. I feel myself turn away from her. Over and over again."

Again, he takes a deep breath. "I suppose that is my punishment," he says, matter-of-factly, as if he had come to terms with it a long time ago.

"I am forever condemned by my memory."

FROM "RETURING TO MY ROOTS"

By Rose Marie Phillips Wagman [1997]

July 16, 1997

After a little deli lunch (bread, salami, salad, sweets) we walked to the house where mother lived until she came to America (1936). My grandfather (Hans Hamburger) and his father before him (Isaac Hamburger) were master butchers. The shop was on the first floor and the living quarters on the 2nd and 3rd level. The house (which also has a business now downstairs) is in beautiful condition. In fact this little town has done a great job of preserving many very old buildings. The oldest structure dates to the 12th century—a tower that stood at the entrance to Bad Kissengen [BK].

After our lunch we walked to Peter Maessen's bar/restaurant. He is 55 yrs. old and has been studying BK's past for most of his life. He has compiled a sort of roster of residents of BK since 1848—names, addresses, and type of business. We enjoyed looking up all the Hamburg-

Ilse Hamburger Phillips (second from left) and daughters Rose Marie
Wagman (left) and Susan Good (right) with the Mayor of Ilse's hometown,
Bad Kissingen, 1997. Courtesy of *The Dumas Clarion*, Dumas, Arkansas.

ers here since that time. We will find out more in the archives later this
week. We do know that all of the Hamburgers—Wolf, Isaac, and Hans
were master butchers. Mother's great aunts had a boardinghouse. Peter took us out in the street and showed us where Sally Hamburger
(another butcher) had lived and where Henry Kissinger came every
summer during his youth—to visit his uncle. Henry Kissinger's mother
and my grandmother were cousins. Peter is such an interesting man.
I'm sure we will go to his place again while we're here. . . .

July 17, 1997

We took a short walk into the forest where mother used to play. Kept
looking for Hansel and Gretel! We weren't really hungry for lunch, but
stopped in the outdoor restaurant by the forest—had yummy sweets
(plum kuchen) and cappachine (really good).

While waiting on the little boat to pick us up, we wrote a total of
14 postcards (the 3 of us). Returned to our hotel just in time to meet
with mother's school friends—Anne Marie, Ilfrieda, another Ilfrieda,
and Marga (whose family had a bakery at the end of mother's street).
They were all so happy to see mother. Mother was the youngest of all
of them and her German improved as she became engaged in intense
conversation about their past. We had a delicious dessert party with

the ladies in the Kurgarten Café. Anne Marie brought adorable school photos of May Day celebrations, etc. Mother was a tiny child—the smallest in her group.

They all remembered what good food they had in the Hamburger household. Anne Marie came from a large, poor family with 5 children. She reminded mother that she had eaten lunch with them every school day for a year and what a great cook Aunt Jenny had been. I talked to mother about why Aunt Jenny had been the boss of their house. She explained that Mamaw ran the butcher shop while Poppa was out at the slaughterhouse, taking orders at the big hotels, delivering, etc. Aunt Jenny did all the cooking, instructed the maids to clean, do laundry, etc. I guess it was a great arrangement for all. . . .

July 18, 1997

We had to wait around awhile as the mayor of BK was not quite ready for us. During this time we sent Lour and Ron faxes to let them know we were fine.

Around noon we walked next door to the Town Hall. It is such a beautiful place, formerly home of a baron and baroness—bought by the town from the baroness after the death of her husband (when she was short of cash). It has been restored beautifully. This is the office of the mayor—called the *Oberburgermeister* here in Germany. Christian Zall (mayor) greeted us warmly. He is quite a ladies' man—56 years old and very nice-looking. He spoke very good English. We had such a nice visit in his private office. . . . he presented her with a silver commemorative medallion of BK and an adorable children's book written (and illustrated beautifully) about a BK legend. Later on, we saw the statue (also near the Town Hall) of the beekeeper of the legend. . . .

We walked back to the hotel in the rain. Just had time to change into dry clothes when mother's school friend, Renata, arrived. We met her in the lobby for coffee and huge, ice-cold strawberries with yogurt. Soon we were joined again by Hilla and another of Mother's school friends, Bernhardt Neiland. . . .

We had quite a few lively conversations going on around the table. Bernhardt's father was a tailor. He brought with him the measurement book from the 1930s with Frau Hamburger's measurements. This was my grandmother—Rose.

Hilla brought with her a scrapbook she had made of her family when she was only 15 years old. It was totally unbelievable—one of the most beautiful and special objects I have ever seen up close. . . . Their home was confiscated by the Americans stationed in BK— and not returned to them until 1957! From a Jewish viewpoint, we forget that the German people suffered a lot from the war, too. We just never think about it. . . .

Bernhardt, Susan, mother, and I drove to the old Jewish cemetery. It needed some loving care. Since Mr. Betch (now more than 80) is unable to see about the cemetery, it has gone into disrepair. We did manage to find a lot of Hamburger family graves. Margot Hamburger (mother's twin who died at the age of 2 months) is on the 14th row from the back of the cemetery on the end. Her tombstone is very small but still in good condition. Mother's grandparents, Regina and Isaac Hamburger, are buried on the second row from the back—4th headstone. Their marker is in excellent condition—a large flower basket of stone on top. We also saw plots for Rose, Fanny, Lena, Laura, Tina, and other Hamburgers.

We took Bernhardt home, returned to the hotel to change again, then out for dinner at Peter Maessen's restaurant. Oops, I goofed—first mother, Susan, and I went to the synagogue. It was restored or rebuilt where mother used to go to Hebrew School. Hilla told us it was dedicated 2 years ago. Of course it is Orthodox. We went in and wished the men Good Shabbas—never have I been in such an unfriendly place. They were waiting for a minyan [the quorum required for Jewish communal worship]—Don't know if they ever had a service. We left, as we were definitely not welcome there. There is a nice marker on the building next door showing where the Temple used to be. It was burned and totally destroyed on Kristallnacht. . . .

July 19, 1997

On the way out of BK we went back downtown—Mother wanted to see her house once more (#9 Grabengasse). I insisted on ringing the bell. (Mother really didn't want me to.) An elderly, white-haired lady called to us from the third-floor window. We think her name was Mrs. Metz. Mother talked to her in German, told her we were from America and that this was once her house. Her only response to our request to see the house was "Nein"—very rude and somewhat upsetting—definitely a disappointment. . . .

We had a lucky day today. We found Sugenheim—a little village that does not even appear on a map—without getting lost even once. The purpose of the trip was to find some remnant or reminder of the Walter family (mother's maternal grandparents). Mother had not been in Sugenheim since maybe 1932, so we really weren't expecting to find too much there. Susan parked the car in the middle of town . . . and I jumped out to see the World War I monument. Immediately, I found the name Heinrich Walter (1884–1916) killed in World War I. This was mother's Uncle Heinrich, whom she never met. My grandmother had two brothers who both went to war—one never returned and one was severely wounded—lost an eye and a hand. He wore a prosthesis and a glove to hide it. (This was Uncle Albert.) As we were visiting on the sidewalk across from the monument, we noticed some people at their front door. They had come to the door to greet their visitors from Berlin. We approached them in hopes that they spoke English and could help us find the Jewish cemetery. This was really a lucky moment for us, as Mrs. Springer and her son Berndt were able to show us the house where my great-grandparents (Babette and Abraham Walter) lived and had a butcher shop, the location of the synagogue, and where other Jewish families had lived. They then proceeded to get in their own car and lead us about two miles out of town to a very large, very old Jewish cemetery and burial house. Unfortunately, we were not able to enter. It seems that all the Jewish cemeteries have been locked for their protection. A key must be obtained from the mayor's office. Of course this could not be done on a Saturday. . . . Mrs. Springer apologized a multitude of times for Hitler, etc., etc. She told us nothing had happened to the Jews in Sugenheim. Most either died or left before it was too late. She did tell us that an official was sent to remove all the prayer books from the synagogue and burn them—Actually, I think the local mayor was forced to do this. . . .

FROM "WAR ORPHAN IN THE PROMISED LAND: LETTERS OF A WAR-TORN FAMILY"

By Phyllis Finkel Mattson [2001]

Searching for My Family

My father and I didn't talk about our life in Europe, so I forgot all about the family left in Europe as I went about my Americanization. In 1947, we received a letter from Uncle Dzuniu. Judging by the letter, my father had been able to contact Dzuniu, my mother's younger brother. By that time, my father also knew through inquiry to the Vienna Jewish Community Center that my mother had died in May 1942, but he did not tell me.

Vienna, June 26, 1947 *[Translated from German]*
My Dearest!
I am looking for you already since 1945 and I have found you with trouble and sweat. You can't imagine my surprise when I received a sign of life from you; unfortunately I am the only one left of your family. The

good [wife] and child and my good mother have been destroyed in one day. Heshiu was the first in our family who has been killed; Stella was shot [when] she started to run; Hella and Bella were killed a few days later. You can't imagine this if you haven't seen it; my mother was chased to death barefoot; over here all people were shot at the cemetery. I can't explain it if I had a full month. I can't write now how I saved myself because I'm very nervous; I will explain next time. . . . The family from Lawoczne are all in Vienna. . . .

I am living in Vienna and I am, thank God, all right. Now I am looking for a possibility to emigrate, I don't know where to yet. I will inform you about everything. Now I ask you to tell me everything about Sigfried [Phyllis's father's nickname] and Lizzi. I hope that I'll meet you all in life.

Dzuniu

My father translated for me, leaving out the gory details, saying only that there had been a "massacre." He didn't even mention that the Lawoczne family was in Vienna. I only recently found the above letter and had it translated. In 1947, I had appreciated that Dzuniu made the effort to find us in the United States through a Red Cross search, thus linking us to our family. In addition, he later sent us $100, a goodly sum then, which we appreciated even as we wondered how he had so much money when people were sending CARE packages to their relatives in Europe. The money was used to purchase me a very good sewing machine. My father continued to correspond with him, although infrequently. My father did not relish writing letters; perhaps the years of writing to me had made him weary, or perhaps he had some reticence to communicate more intimately with his deceased wife's family. Surely, he had to feel some discomfort in having survived, but I never heard him say such words. Shortly before his death in 1971, my father returned to Europe for the first time and was wonderfully received by Dzuniu and the rest of the family, making him wish that he would have gone before.

In 1955, I was twenty-five, still single, and had been working as a social worker in Wisconsin after I had earned a Master's degree from the University of Wisconsin. I had saved some money and decided to go to Europe. It was to be a survey of European cities, including two weeks in Vienna to see Uncle Dzuniu. Very few people were traveling to Europe at the time, especially young women traveling alone. I was very proud of what I had accomplished by my own efforts in the United States, and that I had been able to save $600, enough money to go to Europe for two months. My father was pleased that I wanted to go to Europe to see Dzuniu, so I don't know why he hadn't told me of the relatives living in Vienna. Thus, I expected to find only my uncle and his new wife and child, Heini, then five, but almost the whole family from Lawoczne was there—the Schleifers, Golda and Bernard, Yetty Rothman, and her daughter Susie, now married. I was astounded, but pleased, to meet these close family members whose very existence I had entirely forgotten.

The biggest problem of our meeting was language: I spoke broken German, but German wasn't their first language either. Some knew a little English, but it was much effort for them, so like my early visits to the farm, I wasn't able to communicate with them. Even Uncle Dzuniu had little to say to me, language being but one problem, his depression another. At that time, his business was not going well, he and his wife barely talked to each other, and when I asked him about my mother, he began to cry, but would tell me nothing, although he must have known what happened to her. Thus I was very disappointed by my first experience in Vienna—strangers on the train had been more communicative than my family.

Later I would be told this story: When the Germans invaded Poland in 1941, Dzuniu lost his family by the Nazis or more likely by Poles. As he described in his letter, apparently he had been out of town, and when he returned he discovered everyone had been killed. He joined the underground resistance in Hungary and was captured several times, but escaped. He married again and moved to Israel after the war, but then moved to Vienna, and later to Frankfurt. Later, he became quite wealthy as a hotel owner and real estate dealer, but never happy. He died in 1979. His son, Heini, who lives in Frankfurt, Germany, with his Italian wife and two wonderful girls, speaks the best English and for a while was often in touch with me. He is the only relative that came to visit me in California, once in 1978 and again in 1996, and I visited him in Frankfurt several times, but this relationship has ceased as well, not by my doing. He doesn't answer phones and doesn't respond to my letters.

In 1955, even as I was visiting in Vienna, the Schleifers and Rothmans would be emigrating to the United States within a week; their children, Eva and Arthur, were already in New Jersey. By 1972, my next visit, most of them had returned to Vienna. I made several more trips to Vienna over the years, hoping to reconnect with this family, but it never happened. Although they were all cordial and hospitable to me in Vienna, they never wrote or communicated with me after I left. I was a stranger in their midst, one that they didn't particularly approve of. Sharing life in Lawoczne and in refuge in Hungary, Vienna, and New Jersey, they had remained close, although I didn't see much love between them. I had been an outsider from the beginning by living in Vienna, seeing them only in summers and without a common language, not part of this circle. They were not interested in my life or my experiences in the United States, nor my father's story. Aunt Yetty even asked: "Don't you wish you could live in Vienna again?" A ludicrous notion—I was so glad that I didn't live in Vienna, I couldn't even imagine it because I found Vienna dreadful in its superficiality and I loved America so. They never asked and weren't interested in how I had survived without a family in America. Nor did I impress them with my accomplishments in California; perhaps they expected to me to bring gifts or display wealth. Perhaps in their minds, a person who could travel must be rich. When I got to know them, I didn't like them because they seemed superficial and snobbish to me. The war, creating very different experiences and lifestyles that we do not share, is much to blame for our estrangement. I am sad not to have found my family.

Still, I needed my relatives to tell me about my youth, to refresh some memories, and to tell me about the rest of the family, so I kept going back. In 1972, I brought my children and husband. Although they were polite, they were sorry that I had not married a Jew, but did not shun him as they shunned Heini's Italian, but converted, wife. They were nice enough to my husband; Cousin Heini, Dzuniu's son, then twenty-two, even wanted to do some business with him, a real sign of acceptance. In 1974, divorced by then, I brought my children. Without knowing any of the details or reasons for divorce, they disapproved of my action, although several of them were also divorced.

In 1979, I stayed with Eva and her mother. Golda was a tiny woman who lived into her nineties, always busy doing housework, never sitting down, not even for meals. She was a wonderful cook and was very interested in me, but we had trouble speaking to each other—her language was Polish, Yiddish, and some broken German like mine. She was the only one who treated me with love. When her husband, Bernard, had died in New Jersey, Eva, by then married and divorced, decided to return to Vienna, although Golda did not want to go. She had liked America. In Vienna, Eva worked as a seamstress and a dealer in antique jewelry. She was beautiful, with dark auburn hair, twinkling brown eyes made-up to highlight them, beautifully dressed, even at home, and very clever. She disdained my plainness and treated me like a poor relative from America! I had hoped that by staying with her, closeness would follow because of our age and English ability.

She did not like to speak about the old prewar times, nor of her experiences during the war, but occasionally some stories were revealed. For instance, Shoniu, the oldest Rothman son, had been conscripted by the Russians into military service in 1939, and later was in prison in Siberia for many years. When he was released, he returned to Poland and placed ads in many city newspapers looking for his sister and mother and luckily found them in Vienna. They quickly got him out of Poland and he ultimately went to New York, returning frequently to Vienna to see his mother and sister. Shoniu is now in his eighties, ten years older than I, healthy, virile, and enjoying his life in New York. His memory of those times seems to be excellent, but it is not something he cares to speak of. However, recently, he told me that the Rothman family comprised 150 members and they, on the whole, were well-to-do. There were servants, no doubt, to help with running the homestead, but as I was [a] small child visiting them, I cannot recall what we would today call wealth or a life of luxury, nor did I experience being a part of a large family.

Another story was of escape from Poland. The Schleifer parents and their children, Eva and Arthur, and Yetty and Susie Rothman had escaped from Lawoczne by walking through the forests many nights as the Germans were coming to Poland in 1941. They fled to Hungary, but how they survived there after fleeing, how and when and even why they came to Vienna, nor why they returned to Vienna after being in the United States for several years I never found out. I persisted with my questions because I wanted to hear more, but they quickly wearied of talking, and Eva wouldn't allow me to use the recorder.

I had begged Eva to take me to see the farm and Stryj, then part of Russia, but she had no desire to revisit her past. However, after the dissolution of the Soviet Empire in 1991, I pressed harder and she finally agreed to arrange a trip in 1992. Arthur, her brother, who was living with her in Vienna, would be our driver. It was a short, four-day trip, much of the time spent on the way. We were able to visit Stryj, former home of my grandmother Hannah. Arthur, who had lived with her while he was in high school, was able to find her house and the candy store she and Heshu had owned. It was located by a small walking mall that he had remembered as a grand boulevard where families had promenaded with their children. I recognized the back stairs of the house, and was thrilled with the idea of putting a picture to my dim memories. The outhouse area had been replaced by a big apartment house. We tried to go to Lawozcne, but there was only a gravel road, and the little Citroen couldn't negotiate the rough road. I was very disappointed not to be able to visit the homestead, but it probably would have been replaced anyway! However, I did see the little stream that I had remembered as a big river.

In Lviv we went to a museum of Ukranian house types, and in these houses my cousins remembered their past. There was a big, hive-shaped clay oven in the house with built-in ledges surrounding it. Arthur recalled sleeping on such a ledge getting warmth from its sides. Eva recalled that the local farmers' houses had dirt floors, whereas her house had had a wooden floor. Implements hanging on the wall reminded them of how they were used for everyday chores. At last, I got some details! In the end, they said they were glad that they had gone on this journey of remembrance, and were pleased to recall at least some parts of their past with some fondness. They told me little about me as a young summer visitor, but that didn't surprise me; my visits were only a small part of their early lives. However, I was impressed with their remembrance of languages—Slavic, Polish, Ukranian, and even some Russian. They had not used these tongues for decades.

I was disappointed that we didn't get to Lawoczne, but satisfied just seeing the houses in the countryside, now more modern and sporting TV antennas, the old wooden churches, complex to the eye with their many cupolas, the women still wearing babushkas and boots and herding their one cow as it grazed on the road. Young girls wore high heels and modern clothes. Large horse-drawn carts still carried the hay, and water came from central wells. There wasn't much car traffic, but we were stopped periodically by police for speeding—which we weren't. A five-dollar bill held with the driver's license covered the "fine," the simplest way to get by. Our biggest anxiety was finding gas stations that had gas to sell.

I loved seeing the lovely landscapes—the forested mountains still providing timber, and the gentle fields now filled with their distinctive haystacks. The scene did not look like 1992, but more like the dim memories I had clung to. My cousins blamed the Russians for keeping the area so primitive, but for me its simplicity made the journey to my past complete, even if the people from this landscape are not part of my present world.

AFTERWORD

"How was it possible for you to get out of there?" That is the question that has been posed to me over the years by a good many acquaintances when they found out that I immigrated to the United States from Hitler's Third Reich. I had to explain, as this collection of memoirs so amply demonstrates, that the problem was not one of getting out. For many years, perhaps until late 1940, the Nazis encouraged Jews to leave their domain. The problem that all of us faced was to find a country that would let us in.

I was indeed one of those fortunate enough to be allowed entry into the United States. I have gone through life knowing that if it were not for the fact that this country provided me with a haven, I would not have made it past my twentieth birthday.

"But why did you come alone as a teenager? Why did your parents not join you?" These questions, too, have been posed to me. The answer is that it was U.S. law, specifically the Immigration Acts of 1921 and 1924, that allowed me to enter the United States but did not make it possible for my parents to accompany me or follow me at a time when the door to leave the Nazi state was still open.

It was in the wake of World War I that the U.S. Congress became increasingly inclined to restrict immigration into the United States. President Wilson had vetoed such legislation, but Presidents Harding and Coolidge agreed to sign laws imposing severe immigration restrictions. One of these restrictions involved the imposition of what became known as the national-origins quota system.

The Immigration Act of 1924 called for a study to be undertaken of the makeup of the population of the United States in 1890 in terms of the countries from which citizens' ancestors originated. The issuance of 150,000 immigrant visas annually was authorized, but subject to quotas assigned to each country in proportion to its contribution to the 1890 population as determined by that study. On the basis of the determinations set forth in the document that emerged from the study, the largest quota by far was assigned to Great Britain, followed by Germany and Ireland. The 1890 date had been chosen deliberately, so as not to count the large number of immigrants from southern and eastern Europe who had arrived in the United States in the period from 1890 until the outbreak of World War I. Visa applicants qualified for a quota on the basis of their place of birth, not their citizenship.

The numbers of post–World War I applicants for quota immigrant visas from Britain, Germany, and Ireland were smaller than the quotas assigned to these countries. The result was that at the end of each year, these available but unused numbers were forfeited. By contrast, many of the smaller quotas were heavily oversubscribed. Visa applicants from the latter group of countries were told that they had been placed on waiting lists, with a chance that their names might be reached in one, two, or three years after their applications had been filed. To qualify for an immigrant visa, one had to qualify for a national-origins quota that was open or, if it was closed, to have one's name reached on the waiting list.

Qualifying on the basis of one's place of birth was only one of the new requirements. Another one was that the applicant had to demonstrate that he or she would not become a public charge. Unless the immigrant had sufficient funds to demonstrate that he or she could be expected to support him- or herself fully, an "affidavit of support" had to be produced in which a citizen of the United States promised to see to it that the immigrant would not become a public charge. The signer of the affidavit had to present evidence of assets and income that would assure the consul that the promise of support could be fulfilled.

That is the background against which many of the stories in this collection can be fully understood. The reason why I could qualify for an immigrant visa that allowed me to enter the United States in 1938, whereas my parents could not qualify, was that I was born in Austria, whereas my parents had been born in Poland.

Many of the accounts in this compilation tell the stories of children who came to the United States under the sponsorship of charitable organizations and were placed in foster homes. But there were also many of us whose immigration to the United States was handled within the family and who upon arrival in the United States stayed with close relatives. I was one of them.

As I have already noted, my parents were natives of Poland and I was a native of Austria. Our family was not the only one in this situation. A good many young Jewish couples from various parts of the Austro-Hungarian Empire had settled in Vienna after World War I, when the empire had collapsed and some of its parts became Czechoslovakia, Hungary, Poland, Romania, or Yugoslavia. And there were also Jewish emigrants from East Central Europe who had settled in Germany.

How did the provisions of the Immigration Act of 1924 affect a family such as ours, and others who were similarly situated? I recall the details of our case to this very day. On March 11, 1938, after my parents and I had heard the radio announcement of the German ultimatum and the expected Nazi takeover of Austria, we knew we had to leave the country. My father made it clear that he wanted us to immigrate to the United States, where he had close relatives. He promptly wrote to his uncle to request an affidavit of support.

The uncle, whose business had been ruined in the Great Depression, was unable to provide a credible affidavit but obtained it promptly from a first cousin of my father, who was sufficiently well-off. On April 6, only twenty-five days after the Nazi takeover, my father submitted our application and affidavit of support to the U.S. consul in Vienna. In due course, the processing of the case was begun. Before long my father was notified that it might take perhaps as long as three years before our family could qualify for a visa.

As I recall, the annual quota for natives of Poland was slightly over six thousand. There were tens of thousands of Jews in Nazi Germany and Austria who were natives of Poland. Considering also that there were millions of Jewish residents in Poland as well as ethnic Poles who applied for visas, our being on a waiting list with only about eighteen thousand persons ahead of us was possibly due to the fact that, thanks to my great-uncle's prompt response to my father's request, we had proceeded so quickly after the events of March 11, 1938.

Perhaps it was the consulate that told my father that even if he and my mother could not qualify for a visa immediately, I could. Perhaps he got that information from another source. At any rate, by the summer of 1938 it was understood that my application for a U.S. immigrant visa was to be separated from that of my parents and a new affidavit would be issued for me. I was to immigrate to the United States alone, with my parents following me once their names were reached on the waiting list.

As I recall it, the German quota was about twenty-three thousand and the Austrian quota about four thousand. I might not have qualified for a visa as quickly as I did if I had depended on the Austrian quota. However, one of the fortunate developments for me was that the United States recognized the incorporation of Austria into Germany for national-origins quota purposes. The two quotas were combined into a single quota of twenty-seven thousand for Germany, including Austria. While Jews living in Austria knew on the evening of March 11, 1938 that they had to leave the country without delay, many German Jews did not feel that same urgency until Kristallnacht, November 9–10, 1938. German Jews signed up for immigration to the United States after November 1938, but were more relaxed about it prior to that time. That is why in the summer of 1938 the combined German-Austrian quota was not oversubscribed and why I was able to obtain a U.S. immigrant visa within months after my application had been filed.

The question that can appropriately be asked was whether the law could not have been amended to deal with the urgent problem created by Nazi persecution so as to allow more Jews from Nazi Germany and Austria to enter the United States. This could indeed have been done. It was not done first of all because during the Great Depression, with millions of Americans out of work, there was fear that new arrivals would add to the difficulties of the job market. But there was another reason, a reason that many Americans of the late twentieth century and early twenty-first century will find difficult to fathom: anti-Semitism was a serious problem in the United States in the 1930s. Efforts by some members of Congress to ease immigration restrictions were promptly countered by bills that would restrict immigration further. Quite a number of the congressional sponsors of anti-immigration bills were unashamed anti-Semites.

What is particularly sad to say is that the restrictions on immigration encountered by so many Jews who sought to enter the United States in the 1930s was the intended consequence of the Immigration Acts of 1921 and 1924. As Howard Sachar puts it in his authoritative *A History of the Jews in America* (1992), although many Americans were frightened by Italians and Slavs, "[o]f all the white immigrant groups seeking access to [the United States], the Jews remained the least welcome." It was the fear of the country being flooded by Italians, Slavs, and particularly Jews that caused the Immigration Acts of 1921 and 1924 to be enacted.

It is worthy of note that after World War II the attitude in the United States toward Jews and toward immigration changed drastically. The civil rights movement, under which the country began to live up to the promise of the Declaration of Independence in the treatment of

African Americans, also affected Jews. Discrimination against Jews in education, employment, and places of public accommodation, still in evidence in the late 1940s, faded in the 1950s, and practically disappeared in the 1960s.

The national-origins quota system was repealed in 1965. Furthermore, special laws were passed shortly after the end of World War II that allowed so-called displaced persons, including many Jews, to enter the United States outside the national-origins quota system. In the 1980s, substantial numbers of Soviet Jews entered the United States under the Refugee Act. They were the remnants of the East European Jewish communities, who for centuries had been the center of Jewish life worldwide, communities that were totally destroyed by the Holocaust.

Most of the six million would not have immigrated to the United States even if the country's doors had been open, as no one really anticipated the program of mass murder that was initiated in 1941. Yet, most of those whose life stories are told in this collection would not have come alone but with their parents if the parents could have qualified for immigrant visas. My parents, like those of others whose reminiscences appear here, perished in one of the death camps.

So we came alone and we had to make it on our own. We are grateful to this country for having saved our lives and for having given us opportunities that we would not have had even if the Nazis had not

Dr. Herbert Freudenberger, Ph.D., receiving a Lifetime Achievement Award from the American Psychological Foundation in 1999 recognizing his work as a practitioner and researcher, which included pioneering research on the subject of "burnout," a condition he defined in his 1974 book, *Burnout: The High Cost of High Achievement*. He came unaccompanied to the United States in 1940. Photo courtesy of the American Psychological Foundation, Division 42 of the American Psychological Association and photographer Alan Entin.

taken over the European continent. I believe that we, in turn, have given back, that we have made contributions to the communities in which we live and to our country.

Perhaps the most poignant moment of my life came when I walked into the hall in the Palace of Nations in Geneva, where the United Nations Human Rights Commission was holding a meeting. As I took a seat behind the nameplate "United States of America," I thought back to a conversation I had had with my father fifty years earlier. I was in elementary school then and was absolutely fascinated by geography. I had somehow gotten the notion that persons who like geography should become diplomats. I had, therefore, made up my mind that when I grew up I would become a diplomat. In fact, as we would walk past the Consular Academy, located just a few blocks from where we lived (which, by the way, is now the U.S. Embassy in Vienna), I would announce to my parents that someday I would go to school there.

I became so insistent about becoming a diplomat that my father finally decided to take me aside for a serious conversation. "We are Jews," he reminded me. "Jews cannot get jobs as diplomats." I was crushed.

This conversation, the sad and resigned observation of my father, flooded back into my consciousness as I sat in that hall in Geneva where the United Nations Human Rights Commission was about to meet. My spine tingled as I looked at the nameplate in front of me. It showed that this one-time refugee kid, who had arrived in the United

U.S. Ambassador Richard Schifter (Ret.) in American Army jeep, World War II. Archives of One Thousand Children®, Inc.

States all alone, was here to represent the "United States of America." When it was my turn to address the meeting, the Chair recognized me by intoning the words "United States of America." When the roll was called on a vote and the clerk called out "United States of America," it was my turn to answer "yes" or "no." As I sat there I wished, I wished so very much, that my parents could have been there to see their son, the diplomat, representing the United States of America.

Richard Schifter
Former U.S. Representative to the Geneva-based U.N. Human Rights Commission, Deputy U.S. Representative in the U.N. Security Council, Special Assistant to the President on the staff of the National Security Council, Assistant Secretary of State for Human Rights and Humanitarian Affairs, and Special Adviser to the Secretary of State. Current Chair of the International Relations Commission of the American Jewish Committee, and Chair of the Board of Directors of the Center for Democracy and Reconciliation in Southeastern Europe.

FINAL THOUGHTS

The Nazis and their supporters sought the death of an entire generation of Jewish children. They saw this objective as the key to their monstrous goal: the total and permanent destruction of the Jewish people. One million five hundred thousand children, Jewish and non-Jewish, died at the hands of the Nazis. Sadly, both before and after the nightmare known as the Holocaust, genocide directed at children destroyed millions of children and their families worldwide. In their memory, and for those today still facing the threat of genocide, we dedicate this prayer. It was written for New Year's Eve, 1934, by Hans J., one of the One Thousand Children cared for by Gabrielle Kaufmann. Newly arrived in America, he was to become a teacher and poet. His words, the words of a child at the dawn of the coming Holocaust, remind us of the work still to be done.

> Dear God,
> In this New Year,
> Enter into all people's hearts,
> Join all countries in peace,
> Bless each good person and mankind's holy righteousness,
> Bless goodwill,
> But vanquish evil.
> Take away the hate from people's hearts,
> And dear God take away all pain.
> Continue giving strength to the weak,
> And have patience with us.
> These are my wishes for the New Year.

About the Editors

PHILIP K. JASON is Professor Emeritus of English, United States Naval Academy and Director of the Naples Center Writing Program at Florida Gulf Coast University. He is the author of numerous books, including the *Encyclopedia of American War Literature* (2001).

IRIS POSNER is the President and co-founder of One Thousand Children®, Inc. (OTC).